PRIDE
AGAINST
PREJUDICE

CONSERVATION OF HUMAN RESOURCES SERIES: 9

OTHER VOLUMES IN THE
Conservation of Human Resources Series

PRIDE
AGAINST
PREJUDICE

WORK IN THE LIVES OF OLDER BLACKS AND YOUNG PUERTO RICANS

Dean W. Morse

Foreword by
ELI GINZBERG

LandMark Studies
ALLANHELD, OSMUN   Montclair

811858

ALLANHELD, OSMUN & CO. PUBLISHERS, INC.

Published in the United States of America in 1980
by Allanheld, Osmun & Co. Publishers, Inc.
19 Brunswick Road, Montclair, N.J. 07042

The material in this publication was prepared under contract number 21-36-73-51
from the Employment and Training Administration, U.S. Department of Labor,
under the authority of Title III, Part B of the Comprehensive Employment and
Training Act of 1973. Researchers undertaking such projects under government
sponsorship are encouraged to express freely their professional judgment.
Therefore, points of view and opinions stated in this document do not necessarily
represent the official position or policy of the Department of Labor.
Reproduction by the U.S. government in whole or in part is permitted for any
purpose.

Library of Congress Cataloging in Publication Data

Main entry under title:

Pride against prejudice.

    (Conservation of human resources ; 9)
    1. Minorities—Employment—New York (City)
2. Afro-Americans—Employment—New York (City)
3. Puerto Ricans in New York (City)—Employment.
4. Minorities—New York (City)—Interviews.
5. Afro-Americans—New York (City)—Interviews.
6. Puerto Ricans in New York (City)—Interviews.
I. Morse, Dean. II. Series.
HD8081.A5P74   331.6   78-65534
ISBN 0-916672-67-0

Printed in the United States of America

To
William Ashby
and
Cecil Cox

CONTENTS

respondents into analytic tables that can be treated statistically. Professor Morse recognized the irreplaceable value of letting the respondents tell their own stories in their own words, without the interposition of scholarly apparatus. By following this route, Professor Morse has assured the reader of not only an intellectual but also an emotional experience. He has opened windows to understanding the life experiences of members of minority groups about whom most American middle class citizens are woefully ignorant, to their own and society's detriment.

When he opted for this less conventional route of inquiry and formulation, Professor Morse found encouragement in the long-term research orientation of the Conservation of Human Resources Project, Columbia University, which from the outset had found merit in explicating case materials of the unemployed, labor leaders, executives, middle-class black youth, members of the military and their children in assembling building blocks for its human resources approach. The principal model on which he drew was *The American Worker in the Twentieth Century* by Eli Ginzberg and Hyman Berman, Free Press, 1964.

The juxtaposition of the life histories of older blacks and younger Puerto Ricans within the same volume requires the reader to be sensitive to historically discrete time periods. In the case of the older blacks he must remain aware of the fact that the childhood, youth, and early adulthood of most of the respondents were shaped by conditions early in the century. Many of the black men served in World War I. Oppressive racism and discrimination continue to exist, however, and they continue to weigh heavily not only on the ghetto population but on all black persons, even those who have succeeded in acquiring a good education, a good job, and a good income. It would be a travesty not to differentiate the disabilities with which the present generation is still struggling from conditions facing blacks just prior and subsequent to World War I when segregation was still in full force. One of the collateral benefits of a close reading of Part One is an appreciation of the overwhelming burden of racism during this earlier period; its slow erosion during the prosperous 1920s and the Great Depression of the 1930s; and its more rapid erosion as a consequence of World War II and the subsequent large-scale migrations. This has finally begun to alter the life chances of many, though by no means all, blacks.

If the timing of the full emancipation of black men and women and their effective integration into American society remains unclear—Martin Luther King suggested that it was unlikely to occur until early in the twenty-first century—much is also problematic about the future of the young Puerto Ricans whose life stories are presented in Part Two. In the first instance their future will be much affected by the rate at which they will be able to secure sound educations and good jobs in New York City and the Northeast, where most of them live and work. The downbeat nature of the region's and the city's economy during the 1970s has had a serious retarding effect on the upward mobility of the Puerto Rican community.

But even if the economic outlook should brighten—the data for 1977-78 are encouraging if not unequivocal—the futures of the young Puerto Ricans whose early lives are set forth in Part Two will also be linked to developments in the Commonwealth of Puerto Rico at every level, economic, political, and social. The shape of these developments is still largely concealed by the multiple flows of people, income, and ideas between the island and the mainland.

No one can read the stories of these young Puerto Ricans without being moved by the problems that they confront and their determination to resolve them. Yet only part of the solution lies with them; much will be provided by the sensitivity and responsiveness of the white majority's helping hand.

A reader of these histories faces a difficult task. He can easily be overwhelmed by the cumulative evidence that a society steeped in prejudice and insensitive to the needs of people for employment generates much human loss and social waste. But that is only one part of the larger story that emerges. The second bears on the relatively greater or lesser success that seriously disadvantaged individuals have had in surmounting the barriers in their environment and carving out more or less satisfactory niches for themselves. The positive note is sounded not once but repeatedly. Each reader must therefore decide for himself the relative importance of environment and personality in shaping and reshaping the lives of these members of two minority groups that are at best on the periphery of our society and economy. The reflective reader faces still another challenge in assessing the speed with which the more detrimental environmental forces are giving way and the success that members of the black and Puerto Rican minorities are likely to achieve under more supportive circumstances.

This book will not provide definitive solutions to these complex problems, but the careful reader will be in a much better position to find the answers once he is enriched by the experiences contained in these life histories.

Eli Ginzberg

ACKNOWLEDGMENTS

An opportunity to talk with a number of people, young and old, who collectively had been the center of my earlier investigation into peripheral workers, was offered me by the director of the Conservation of Human Resources Project of Columbia University. The stories of these people constitute the great bulk of the pages which follow. Without their willingness, and in many cases eagerness, to tell their stories, this volume could never have come into existence. My thanks and appreciation go first to them.

At the same time, there were a number of individuals who played an integral part in amassing these stories. They found people who would talk with us. Through their sympathy, tact, and empathy, they created the sense of trust the tellers of these accounts had to feel if they were to share their experiences. Finally, they encouraged the people with whom they talked to tell their stories because they were able to communicate a belief that such accounts form an essential part of a society's true and complete historical sense. These co-workers, Sanjeanette Harris, William Beedle, Thomas Bell, Charlotte Crump, Ramon Ocasio, Maria Ayala, and Joseph Ceccarelli, each in his or her own way, made a unique contribution to our work. I am very grateful for their participation and assistance.

To Cecil Cox goes a special note of acknowledgment and thanks. Mr. Cox, because of his extensive contact with older blacks in Newark, made many of our interviews possible. His warmth and understanding, his generosity of spirit, and his dedication to his community were a continual source of inspiration.

PART I

Older Blacks

INTRODUCTION

When a person is asked to speak about his life and experiences, he is apt to assume that the listener knows he is recounting a unique set of events; no one else can tell just the same story. He assumes also that the listener is generally familiar with the context within which the account takes place. The more important or strategic the elements of this context, the more the teller assumes that these elements need not be spelled out. The more engrossing the story, the less he is inclined to dilute its dramatic impact with explanatory background material. Even when the listener is white and the teller is black in 20th century America, the black usually takes it for granted that the white listener knows the shaping circumstances which have cradled the individual experience of the black. And he is apt to think, if the white professes some degree of ignorance, that he is either a fool or a liar. The white, he feels, ought to damn well know and has good reason to pretend that he doesn't know.

In most of the accounts in this book there is little general explanation of the course of events. Major historical occurrences are sometimes mentioned and their impact is often described, but usually in a quite specific sense. The listener is supposed to know what the event was and why it was important. And of course older people think that the younger generations should know in general what happened to the generation that preceded them. It is usually a shock to a World War II veteran to learn that his children may have only a vague idea of what that momentous period was (or even when or where it took place).

The stories told by older blacks that follow cover a period roughly since the turn of the century. During this time blacks were transformed from by far the most rural major ethnic group in America to the most urban. Their occupations shifted from overwhelmingly agricultural to primarily

3

industrial. They moved from a southern society which, although no longer based overtly upon slavery, retained much of the paternalism and perhaps even authoritarian violence and caste character of the ante-bellum South. They came into a northern urban industrial matrix which proclaimed an ideology of individualism and Social Darwinism.

At the same time they were, from the point of view of most northern whites, almost "invisible." Where they lived, what kind of work they did, what they did when they were not working—these components of their life simply did not concern the white society except in those specific areas of the northern cities where the blacks tended to congregate. And when the blacks of the northern industrial cities did impinge upon the consciousness of the whites, they were part of the curiosa, the exotica of urban life. In the heyday of radio, one of the main sources of knowledge about their life was the extremely popular series Amos and Andy, which portrayed the black as a feckless figure of fun, a lineal descendant of the black portrayed in 19th century minstrel shows, transported to the urban slum.

During these critical 75 years, however, while the black communities of the South were being transformed and a major part of the black population was being transferred to a profoundly different northern environment, several events and processes impinged with particular and peculiar force upon the life experiences of blacks. Perhaps the most pervasive and persistent force shaping the life experience of blacks born early in this century was the gradual transformation of southern agriculture, which was in part caused by a crisis in cotton cultivation. Organized to a large extent on the basis of sharecropping, a system which usually, though not always, led to the black cultivator being continually in debt and therefore tied to his source of credit, southern agriculture kept many southern blacks near the margin of existence; at the same time it did not provide an adequate basis for absorption of any natural increase in the size of the black population. Somewhat like the feudal system in this respect, southern sharecropping in the first decades of the 20th century ensured that the younger generation was not only repelled by the harsh and uncertain existence of their parents but in part actually expelled for lack of access to land.*

The sons of black tenant farmers in 1900, particularly the excess sons, naturally turned to other occupations and other areas. Some were absorbed in the dirtier, more dangerous and more strenuous jobs available in a South which was slowly developing nonagricultural activities. Saw mill jobs,

---

*The acreage of land in cotton cultivation in 1940 was 4 percent less than in 1900. It is true that there was a very rapid increase in the acreage under cultivation during the period just prior to World War I until the end of the 1920s in response to large increases in the price of cotton, but at the same time man-hours per acre before and during harvest decreased very rapidly. Between 1900 and 1920 man-hours per acre before harvest fell by more than 10 percent and harvest hour requirements fell by 30 percent. Although the production of cotton did increase by about 25 percent between these two years, the man-hours required for its production hardly increased at all. Between 1910 and 1930 the actual number of southern black farms of all types actually fell from 890,141 to 881,687.

railroad, highway and menial construction work, and a myriad of casual jobs were available, almost always at the lowest levels of service and laborer occupations. Operative jobs in factories, however, were for the most part closed to the southern black.

In addition to the economic pressures to which the black in the South was subject, the beginning of the 20th century represented perhaps the peak of violence directed at the black, particularly the black man. And it was the black who had filtered into the southern towns and cities who was most subject to this violence. The decade of the 1890s represented the high-water mark of lynching, but the early decades of the 20th century continued the pattern, if at a somewhat reduced level. Jim Crow laws and practices were comprehensive, and the slightest infringement of them was almost certain to bring some kind of retribution upon the offending black. Corrupt judicial practices and the institution of the chain gang reinforced the system of Jim Crow, and in addition the chain gang was a source of cheap labor for both county and state governments and for a few extractive industries.

This was the setting, then, for the impact of an historical event which is part of many of the stories that follow the First World War. Although migration of blacks out of the South had taken place on a fairly large scale in the two decades before 1914, particularly in the border states of Virginia and North Carolina, migration from the states of the Deep South increased substantially during the decade of World War I and the post-war decade. Southern blacks were drawn into the urban industrial labor forces of the North during the war, but they were also drawn into the military itself. Within the black community, particularly in the North, there was great pride in black military units and great concern about the treatment of black units, both overseas and in the South. The East St. Louis riots in July 1917 (one of the most violent of the anti-black riots in the nation's history, along with the riot in Houston on August 23, 1917, as a result of which 13 black soldiers were hung after court-martial) heightened the increasing sense of injury and injustice that gripped much of the northern black communities.

World War I, however, had a more profound effect on the blacks. Cutting off the very large streams of immigration from southern and eastern Europe at the very time that the demand for industrial and service labor was increasing rapidly in the North, the war set in motion powerful forces to attract blacks into the industrial centers of the country. Earlier migration from the South had in fact provided the channels along which migration could easily flow. More or less sizable clusters of blacks with ties of kinship and friendship to families in the South already had settled in northern cities. Just as in the case of the earlier immigration from Europe where agents from America, working with transportation companies, land companies and northern industrial firms, had recruited immigrants, so agents from the North went into the South to send black workers "by the box car" to northern industrial areas

With the passage in 1921 and 1924 of new immigration laws whose purpose was to pare to the bone immigration from southern and eastern Europe, the stage was set for the continuation of the heavy migration of blacks to the North during the generally prosperous decade of the 1920s.

Since this was also the period of rapid suburbanization of the middle class, spurred by the automobile and higher incomes, a large amount of housing was freed in the older parts of the large industrial cities of the North. The blacks, confined largely to the lowest paid occupations, gravitated into the oldest housing in the central cities. But this housing was for the most part still relatively sound and, more important, an immense improvement upon the kind of housing the southern rural black had always known. Unpainted and deteriorating the city house might be, but it had running water, it had plastered walls and wallpaper, it usually had toilet facilities. It was attractive enough so those blacks with steady and better paying jobs wanted to own one. During these years it was possible for many of the newly arrived blacks, along with those who were already there, to feel that they were becoming part of a neighborhood or community. Indeed, this was the heyday of Harlem as a center of black aspiration and community organization. Newspapers, theater, church organizations—all seemed to be on the threshold of growth and increasing influence in the larger urban life.

By 1930 almost one million blacks lived in the Middle Atlantic region. Their numbers had increased by almost 75 percent since 1920. More than half had been born in the South, the overwhelming majority of these in the states of the South Atlantic region. These blacks in the Middle Atlantic states constituted about a twelfth of the blacks in the country. A large proportion of them lived in New York City and most of these New Yorkers lived in Harlem. Although for the most part they undoubtedly had higher incomes than blacks in the South, they did not occupy much higher rungs on the occupational ladder. Less than 5 percent of all black male workers in the entire country were white-collar workers in 1910. It is true that the percentage of black males in the northern cities who had white collar jobs was slightly higher, but it probably did not much exceed 5 percent of the black males and perhaps 7 percent of black females. Perhaps one out of twelve northern black men were skilled workers, but for the most part in the less-prestigious skilled trades. About one out of six black men in the North worked as a semi-skilled operative. The remainder were either laborers or service workers, generally holding the most menial of such jobs.

Some black men did find employment in large heavy industrial plants as laborers and semi-skilled operatives. They also were employed by small firms in many of the service industries and miscellaneous manufacturing industries where large amounts of relatively unskilled operative work was characteristic.

The occupations, industries and firms to which the black male was attached made him particularly vulnerable to the devastating effects of the Great Depression of the 1930s. Moreover, unlike many of the white semiskilled workers who had come to industrial centers from a rural background and could often return to a marginal existence on the farm, it was harder for the black man to return to his southern agricultural past. The market for cotton was destroyed by the Depression, and there was even less for him to do in the South than in the North. In addition, bad as was the lot of the northern black man economically, he faced an intolerable social situation in the South, even more intolerable for a black man who returned to the South after years spent in northern cities.

Generally the black stayed in the North during the Great Depression and somehow or other managed to survive. *How* he managed to survive will probably never adequately be told. Without the economic contribution of black women, it would certainly have been impossible. Without a complex system of sharing good and bad fortune, typified by rent parties, it would have been impossible. The cost, however, in suffering, in disruption of the orderly functioning of institutions, of the orderly progression of family life, was incalculable. But however bad economic conditions in the great industrial centers were, the forces impelling the blacks to leave the South were still strong enough to produce a continued, although drastically diminished, flow of blacks out of the South to the North and West.

It is one of the bitter aspects of the black experience in America that, at the very period when economic and social forces had initially combined to make it possible for millions to gain at least a foothold in northern industrial centers, a depression whose depth and length was unprecedented in American experience interrupted the process of settlement and consolidation that might otherwise have taken place. No other immigrant group in American history had to suffer as prolonged or severe a depression at the most critical moment of settlement. Only at the end of the 1930s did blacks begin to regain some of what they had lost in that decade. With the onset of World War II, however, much of the expeience of World War I was repeated, but on an even greater scale. The urbanization of the American black was to be substantially completed in the two decades following the beginning of World War II. In 1950 a slightly higher percentage of whites than blacks was classified as urban (64.3 percent as compared with 61.7 percent; Statistical Abstract, 1973, p. 18) but even by that year the proportion of the black population living in central cities was conspicuously higher. Two out of every five blacks in America were living in central cities in 1950. Two decades later four out of five blacks were classified as urban and almost three out of five lived in central cities. A higher proportion of whites lived in what was classified as the urban fringe, roughly equivalent to the suburbs.

The movement of whites out of cities should have increased the supply of housing available to blacks and other minority groups in the central cities.

But during the two decades 1930 to 1950, the combined effects of the Great Depression and World War II had a devastating effect upon the quality and quantity of central city housing.*

With the concurrent decay of a large part of the inner city's capital infrastructure and commercial and industrial facilities, it became apparent that the major cities of the country, in particular those in the older sections of the country, faced the possibility of economic collapse of the central business districts. The response was the movement called "urban renewal," along with programs such as "model cities." This is not the place to assess these programs, but the impact of urban renewal upon the older black communities was all too often catastrophic.

Joseph Lyford's *Airtight Cage* voices the despair and disillusion of one part of the West Side of New York City that was subjected to urban renewal. It may be fortunate that Harlem itself was simply too large to attack as a whole, and perhaps also too sophisticated to allow itself to be torn apart piecemeal by ambitious plans for highways, plazas, and large institutional construction. But the central ward of Newark is a *locus classicus* of the efforts of the urban renewalists. To this day vast stretches remain devastated. One of the consequences of this upheaval was a weakening of much of the coherence and independence of the older black community. Helpless in the face of large-scale social engineering and planning, baffled by the bureaucratic structures that carried out the plans, older black homeowners could only try individually or in small groups to salvage what remained of their blocks and their neighborhoods.

Another irony of the situation of the older blacks in the central cities of the North is that the civil rights movement weakened their authority in the community. The most prominent leaders of the movement were largely southern. The battles took place primarily on southern soil. The troops were for the most part children and young adults. In the struggle older blacks were perceived by many of their children as weak or irrelevant to the struggle. Their achievements were frequently derided, their standards of behavior, religion, and values ridiculed, and the epithet "Uncle Tom" was thrown at them.

Similar tribulations, it is true, had often been undergone by other groups who had migrated to the city. The children of nineteenth century immigrants often mocked the ways of their parents, cast aside religious beliefs and customs, and moved away when opportunity presented itself. Nevertheless the older generation usually had a neighborhood that was relatively intact and institutions, particularly religious institutions, which gave both physical and spiritual succor. The help they received as they grew

---

*Since 1930 there has been almost no privately built housing, except for luxury apartments, in the central cities, and during this same period, housing maintenance expenditures were cut to the bone. In addition, serious over-crowding particularly in the central cities led to a more than ordinarily rapid deterioration of housing, much of it of poor quality to begin with.

old was primarily personal, whether from family, church or local political association. The contemporary older black, born in the first decades of the twentieth century, growing old in the great cities of the North, usually has had to turn to social welfare agencies in time of need. As a group, older blacks have not been able to accumulate the resources—savings, homes, private pensions—which materially assist a large number of older whites. By and large, the blacks are, it should be kept in mind, the first of their people who have had to face the last years of their life in an urban context.

A large proportion of these people came north in the first decades of the twentieth century, urged on by pride, motivated by a desire to make something of their lives, endeavoring to escape the humiliations that faced a black man or woman in the South of their youth. It is that sense of pride and self-worth that is reflected in the stories of their struggles and achievements, in their suffering and survival, even in those instances when the world may have regarded them as failures.

BLACK MEN

James Edwards

I was born in Virginia, but I came up here to Newark when I was four years old. And I've been here ever since. All my schooling has been here, right up the hill here. I've lived in this neighborhood all my life, right around here. I went about two grades in high school and then vanished. My buddies and my brother, wherever they went, I had to go too. But you see, my people, they wished me to go to college. And they would foot the bill. But you know, I just couldn't take that. No, no, they meant well, but I just couldn't sponge on them like that, so I just quit school and got myself a job. I'll tell you about that later but first I want to say something about how it was when we were young folks.

It seems like to me that the boys back in those days were more healthy somehow than the boys are today. They were stronger and I think it was because they ate better and simpler. Their mothers took care of them and watched them and what they ate. You ate right. That was the foundation. You had your breakfast in the morning and it was good solid food. Like we ate plenty of cabbage. And boys, then, I think they were more athletically inclined than they are today. They would fight among themselves. Now we would go down to F.'s gym and we would get into the ring, four of us, and have what they used to call a battle royal. We would slug it out. Whatever team stayed in there was the winner.

Back in those days when I was a boy, there was no such thing as a colored gang and a white gang. It was one gang. That could be Irish, Italian, English, everybody. It was just one gang. We were all mixed together, colored and white, and if you hit me, you had to hit them. There used to be a doctor, right here on B. Avenue and the fork there. His brother, Anthony, him and I, we went all through school together. And he used to come in my house and eat because my mother used to bake them big apple pies, you know, square pies, and drop cakes, sweet potato pie, and his mother used to come around and say, "Mrs. Edwards, why don't you take my boy?"

That's how people got along then. Oh, them were the golden days. We were all together. I would eat in your house and you would eat in my house. There was no discrimination. No. We didn't know what that meant. We lived in a little house, right on C. Street by Broadway, and there were three little houses there. We lived in the middle house and on one side was a German lady and an Italian on the other. And when my mother went somewhere, she said to one of these women, "You look after my kids." When she came back, that woman had better not tell her anything that you had done, brother, because if you had done something bad, you would really get something that you weren't looking for. That's the way it was. Oh, they were strict, but as I said, if you run short of say, sugar, you run next door and get a cup of sugar and then you would pay it back later. Them were the golden days.

But it's not like that today. We don't trust each other. Blacks don't trust blacks, whites don't trust blacks, blacks don't trust whites. We are living in a new world altogether. As I said, I quit school before I finished high school. That's when I got my first job with the Long Piano Company, helping to load and move their pianos. And I worked for them I don't know exactly how long, but the reason I left them was that a corset manufacturer, the Warren Company, a big business, they shipped all over the world, well, they bought a new truck. The truckman that bought it, name of Connors, he furnished the trucks for the Warren Company. He used to go to New York to the docks over there. So the first truck that was up there, it was run by a man by the name of Johnny Connors, but Johnny was afraid that the job wouldn't hold up so he wouldn't take the new truck. They wanted him to come to take this brand new truck. Now that was back in 1916.

I said to him, "Well, if you don't want to take it, I'll take it." I said to myself that it should be a good job, a brand new truck. So I took it and I worked for Warren until I was drafted into the army. I have my draft notice right up there on the wall to this day. Yessir, I was drafted into the army right off of that truck there. And the funny part of that was that before I went into the army, I come back and I went to see Johnny Connors, and I said, "Now look, Johnny, you know that it is tough for a colored guy to get a good job. You take it." And he took it on my advice and it should have been his in the beginning, see. But he was afraid it wouldn't hold up. When he saw how well I was doing—I was getting $25 a week, imagine that, before the first World War, when my brothers and my father were only getting $12 a week. I just mention this to show how much I was getting compared with what others like me were getting. The old man was only getting $12 and I was getting $25. That's why I told Johnny to take it. I said, "It's only seldom that a colored guy can get a good job like that." And when

I left to join the army, Mr. Warren told me like this, he said, "No matter who's here," he said, "you come back again on the truck." But when I got back, I wouldn't do it, you see, because I had told Johnny to leave his job, so that when I came back, he was much older than me, I was a young man so I could do better than him.

So now I'm off to the army. Today, with kids burning their draft cards and refusing to go in the army and so forth, well, if it were up to me to say, I don't think they should be getting a draft card, because the kids today, they are too young, compared to us. You see that picture of me up there. I was a husky, healthy young fellow and I could take care of myself. These kids today, they are nothing but babies. They haven't seen any life and I think it is a pity to slaughter them like they're doing now. How can these kids take care of themselves? Back in them days, I could take care of ten of them by myself. I was so strong and healthy. Most of the boys, I mean my friends, were in the army. They were picked men and they done a job too. I mean, we had a crack outfit. I am not going to brag on us here, but when we got ready to disband, our captain called us together, his name was Captain Carey, from Boston, Mass., and he said, "Boys, I have been in the army 25 years and if I ever had to go again, and they didn't give me a colored outfit, I wouldn't go." And I've never forgot those words.

Now did you see that picture and hear about that boy from Vietnam, the one they can't bury in the white cemetery? Now, you see, things like that, if a kid now loses his life for his country, what is he fighting for if something like that can happen? And Frank Lloyd's boy, the same way. He told his colonel once, when this colonel was giving the same kind of stuff to him, Frank's boy said to him, "Well, what am I over here for?" He said, "I'm supposed to be fighting for my country. And the country must have the duty to protect me and give me my rights."

But the way things are nowadays, they got the thing backward. My grandfather, my great-grandfather, and maybe the father before him and my father, they all been helping America to grow, isn't that right, and they done it for nothing. They didn't get no pay, you know that.

Well, what's wrong with us? What's wrong with us? I've never been arrested in my life. Never, and I have some of the best friends, white and colored. I mean to say, if they would give the colored people a half-way break, I think that you would have some of the best citizens you ever had. There was this colonel from Austin, Texas, and he told the Senate down in Washington, he was a colonel but he was in politics before, he said, "I would rather trust my life with a colored man than anybody I know." That's what he told them. I mean, we never harmed nobody. But the way we been treated here, it seems like we ought to be worth more than we are, you know. But with all this, they didn't break my spirit, they still didn't do it. Well, in the First World War, I was in the 355th Artillery. It was formed here, but we got men from all over, because our outfit was kind of a picked outfit, because it was the first colored artillery in the history of this country.

They didn't think that the colored boys had brains enough for artillery, you know. It's a little different from shooting a rifle. But they made good all right, they made good.

We were attached to the 92nd Division. All the colored outfits were attached to the 92nd Division. And I talked with Pershing himself, General Black Jack himself. The 15th Infantry, they were also part of the 92nd Division. That was a solid colored division. And we were the first group that went over to France. The 15th, and the 7th Illinois, and the 9th Chicago, if I remember right. And they were the ones that broke that Hindenberg Line. When the Germans were within 11 miles of Paris, they put them into action, and our boys started the Germans going back and that led to the end of the war. The 9th, 15th and the 7th from Illinois, boy, them three, that was a crack outfit. But I'll tell you a story about how it was before we went into action.

It took us 13 days to go over, dodging the submarines, you know, and no port anywhere could take our ship, which was the sister ship to the Leviathan that we took over from the Germans. We got off onto a small boat out in the ocean there and went in and got off the small one. Well, before we made camp, we marched about six hours, and then we made camp. Well, about nine o'clock that night, a division moved in right side of us. It was the Acorn Division from Georgia. I'll never forget it; when our colonel found out who they were, he got on the phone and told them, "Move out of here." They just stayed there long enough to get on the march again. Our colonel knew that there would have been a war right there between the two divisions. And he moved them out, because, you see, them boys there, you know how they were against a colored man. And them boys was dead tired too, but they didn't let them stay there, no, no. But how can you fight a war when you got the same men from the same country so far divided amongst each other? It just don't make any sense.

I'll tell you another thing that happened in France. As I said, this captain of ours, Carey, he was one of the finest men that ever lived. Some of the boys from the outfit got downtown one night and they broke into this saloon or whatever they call it in France. And they cleaned it out. So then, in a case like that, they called the company together and they put us in company formation. So this man and wife who owned the saloon, they were supposed to walk up and down and pick out the men that done it. So they walked down that line, and every doggone time they stopped right in front of me. And boy, I was about to explode because I didn't even drink, never did drink, didn't even smoke. So the only thing that saved me was the woman, the man's wife, she shook her head every time.

So then when they couldn't prove it, the captain dismissed the company and then he sent for me and he said, "Corporal Edwards, sit down and let me talk to you. Now you know, we have a record of all our men and I always heard that you were one of the nicest men we have in this outfit." I said, "Well, Captain, I don't even drink the stuff. I wouldn't give a cent for the whole saloon." He said, "You have one of the best records, and I was wondering why they were stopping in front of you, I couldn't believe that you were involved."

Captain Carey, he was one of the nicest men, you see. You couldn't have had a better captain. But he was strict, oh yes. It seems like that company, we were just like one when we marched. He was that good. He made us into a unit, you could almost call it a ballet. Did you ever see the June Taylor Dancers? We were something like that. We had a crack outfit, not because I belonged to it, but it was just a good bunch of men and our captain liked us and we liked him. There was a great deal of pride in being a member of that outfit. It was because we had a good captain and he trained us right. Whatever he said was all right with us.

But you know, we never came into contact with the whites. But there was a great deal of pride among the blacks who were together in this outfit. There was quite a bit written about that division. They thought the world was looking at them and they thought they were America all by themselves. Them boys were fighting men. I am not kidding you.

Anyway, the war ended and I came back home. You remember that I wouldn't go back to my job at the Warren Company because that would have meant taking it from Johnny Connors and I wouldn't do a thing like that. So I worked in a couple other jobs, different places you know, but they didn't suit me. So then I went down to the packing house and one of the men there said, "Well, we don't have anything now, but we are going to have a couple of new men come in and they are going up to the Thomas Mill, on Passaic Avenue in Newark. Do you know them?" I said, "Certainly, my father works there. He's been there ever since I can remember." He said, "Well, you better see Mr. White." So I went up there and worked with Thomas until they had that big strike. But before that strike I had paid the deposit on that little truck body you see right there in that picture. That must have been in 1924. All the Thomas men went out on strike and Thomas wouldn't go along with the union. And I wouldn't go back without the union. Then I went on and got this little truck body. I said, "Now this is my time to start in business." And that's when I started, as soon as we went on the strike and they didn't take us back, why, then, I said, I might as well go for myself. And I have been working for myself ever since.

We used to call this business here a profession, you know, and we specialized in piano work. You couldn't just bring a piano to a house. You had to put it just where it belonged and without a scratch. You had to be responsible. That's why I say you could call us almost a profession. But as I said, you have a handicap when you got the wrong skin. But I made progress, considering the handicap. I started from scratch. At the beginning I had just my two hands. It really started when I saw that little truck body down in South Plainfield propped up on some cans.

We knew the business, you see, and that's why I started it. I couldn't help but be a success because we knew it so thoroughly, like knowing how to take a piano apart when it wouldn't fit otherwise into a house. All through my time, there were only a few movers that you could hire to do that type of work, because they just didn't know it. And we used to do a lot of work for vans when they couldn't handle a job and we could. We would do the part that they couldn't handle.

But as I said, when it came down to the really big stuff, we just couldn't get none of that. No matter how good you were, unless you got a small piece from a big company, you didn't get the big stuff.

In my business there were three of us—my brother, my nephew and me. The first truck was that little chassis that I fitted under that truck body and the one in the garage is the twenty-first. Twenty-one trucks since I have been in business! And the last one is right out there in the garage. We started out with just one truck but over a period of time we reached a point where we were sometimes running three or four. But we never ran over three or four at a time, because we didn't have enough work for more than that. We had all kinds of trucks, including tractor trailers. We had three of them. The last one we had we sold to a firm here on J. Avenue. That's the first one he had and he's a big man today.

In the beginning there was Edwards Brothers, just me and my brother. Then we changed the name to a trade name. We called it the "Stages Company." That was the name we selected for the company and later I'll tell you why. That is still the name of the company but we don't operate it any more. We sold it out in June. The firm that bought it didn't want anything but the corporation and the stock, no equipment at all. But we only had two vehicles left. The big one outside, it's practically new, so we have a man who's interested in it. So after we get rid of that, we're out of the moving business altogether. The company that bought us out, they just wanted the rights, the plates we had. The only way you can start a business like that today, you got to buy someone out.

I should tell you that before we started in 1926, I was working for the Torrance Company, delivering mason materials. They had all of this good stuff sewed up. They were suppliers of smaller masons. And if anybody wanted any of that material, they had to buy it from them, you see. We used to go as far as Philadelphia, White Plains, Poughkeepsie, and all the stations in New Jersey. And I was the key man because I knew the roads. Back in them days, you see, they didn't have signs like they have now. You had to know where you were going. And for that reason, I was a key man. That's why they put me on the difficult routes, like Philadelphia, New York, White Plains and so forth. So you see, between what I had learned at the piano company and at the Torrance Company, I was well fitted for the business.

Something that might be of interest, I think, is how we drivers behaved towards each other, in those days before I started the company, I mean how black and white drivers acted with each other. There was no prejudice then between drivers, oh, no, no. The thing was that people were sensible then, I mean to say, the working class. Because you know, if you and I worked at the same place, we were just real buddies, you know. If I could help you, I helped you and you helped me. When I was working for someone else I didn't run into problems of prejudice. Back in them days, the drivers knew that they had to depend on each other, like if a driver broke down, and there was something you could do to help him get started, why you would do it. Oh, they were all buddies then, back in those days. We did have problems at different eating places, you know, but that's a different problem and that was about the only problem.

But with our own company there was a problem. If you had a business where you started to climb up a little bit, that's where the ceiling was. As far as the company itself, everything went fine. One thing I have heard tell is that sometimes blacks resent another black man being the boss, but I wouldn't say that. Not in our line. Because for this reason here, that most of the men we hired didn't know too much about this business of moving, and they had to depend on you, whether you was black or white. We were the man in charge. We had to give the orders. And, because we always paid good, you see, we would always get the top men. And then we always taught the men. Some of the best men in the business now, we gave them the knowledge of the business, so that they could go into business themselves.

And let me tell you this. Among all the working men we have had, in all these years, we have never had a compensation case, even though our work is supposed to be hazardous work, moving pianos, you know. But we have never had a man try to collect a penny in all those years. Never! And we always got a reduction in our insurance. Because we would tell the men that they had to work according to our plan, not their plan. And they did it too. And they were happy and we were happy.

We hired mostly black men. We had a few whites, but not too many of them. The men liked to work for us because we traveled out of town. A man would rather be sitting on a truck riding to Washington, D.C. or Richmond, Virginia, than climbing stairs around here, you know. And naturally he got his regular pay and $5 more every day that he was away from home. He could sleep in the truck or go to a motel, that was his business, so the men liked that and we never had trouble with them.

There is a new law that is going to put a lot of movers out of business, but, you know, I was in favor of that law. Because the ones it's going to put out of business shouldn't even be in the business. And I say that for this reason. The mover is one of the lowest-paid men in any industry, and it's about the hardest work you can do. This way we have a set rate, just five different prices that a customer can have, that means for a truck and three men. And I say that this is a good thing because if a mover can't meet these rates he should get out of the industry. If he can't make $26 an hour he can't even hire men. You know, you have to pay men just the same as in any other business. We don't have much in the way of fringe benefits, but we try to give them enough so that they can get on. Like, we gave them $3.50 an hour and we paid for their meals. We paid the social security and the unemployment. But the income tax, we let them take care of that themselves because we knew that these men weren't making enough money. It was sometimes hard to get good steady work.

When I say that there were ones that shouldn't be in the business, I mean the fellow who didn't know how to price a job or charge people. There were just too many movers for the amount of work, so that's why we got together, in order to save the moving business. We wanted the business to be regulated so that if a man didn't have a truck up to par, he's not a mover. But if an old piece of junk comes up in front of your door, and he's cheap, you might go for it. But there shouldn't be any amateurs in this business. There shouldn't have been any from the beginning. These amateurs are not really movers. You want somebody who is responsible for your stuff. And even today, for example, I was up to see a party in Brookfield and he was going to give a moving job to an amateur, a bedroom suite that he paid $1,400 for. So I told him, "Now, look, did you want me to come up to look at the job to get a price, or what?" He said, "I want to save as much money as I can." I said, "You've got the wrong idea. Don't you try to save money. You get yourself a reliable mover and pay him. Then he's responsible. You mean to tell me that you paid $1,400 for a bedroom suite and then wrestle for a price to move it? It don't make sense."

That's why we wanted to get rid of all those other guys who are not responsible. It's a matter of responsibility. If something happens, you've got to take care of it. Now, how are you going to take care of it without insurance? So you want a mover, you don't want none of these amateurs, or gypsies as we call them.

If there is any business where you need experience, or where you need skill, you need it in the moving business. That's because I've never known two jobs alike. If I move you, I have a problem in this house. Where you move to is a different problem altogether. And you have to be able to solve these two problems. You never run into the same conditions twice. That's why experience is so important. If you're a driver you can get experience gradually. Our biggest problem in the moving business today is something like a large one-piece breakfront, or these big couches. They're making these couches longer than that wall nowadays. It's not the weight, it's the bulkiness. Now a lady called me up here last night. "Well," she said, "what do you do when you can't get these couches into the house?" I said, "Sometimes you can't even hoist them in because they're making these windows so small nowadays." She said, "Then what do you do?" I said, "I tell my people to go right down here to the Peters Upholstering Company. He'll either make it a sensible couch or make it a nice three-quarter couch and give you an arm chair to match it, so you can put them together so you wouldn't notice that it was two pieces.

That's the point I'm trying to make. With these movers that don't know what they're doing, you know, they'll just take the stuff and for all you know leave it in the hall. And then you have to call another mover to get it in. But if they got the right mover in the beginning, they might not have that problem because that's his job to get it in and out, and he's going to do all he can to get that thing in there, see. Now that's why I told you about taking these big pianos apart. And there's just a few men, the ones that are experienced, that know how to do it. People think that this business is not a skilled job. But there's just as much skill in moving as in anything that you know.

As I said, we were what you could call professionals in that line. And then you know, when you have that experience, and you have top men, you have to make some money to pay those men. We used to cart air conditioners for a friend by the name of Bennet, and we carted for him until the Second World War came on. Then all that priority business come, you know, and he couldn't get any machines at all and he almost went out of business. You couldn't even buy tires, and we couldn't even get enough gasoline to run our trucks during the Second World War. And one man down there told me, he said, "Well, why don't you let the big movers, Nassau Movers, have your business?" I said to him, "You must be crazy." He wouldn't have told that to a white man, you see. If a white man had a certain amount of states in his ICC permit that the government allotted him, he's supposed to get enough gasoline to cover these states. But that's what he told me. I got so mad I walked out and didn't say nothing to him. But you know, we ran our trucks. I'm not going to tell you how, but we ran them. We didn't stop running, that's for sure.

Let me tell you another kind of problem I faced. I had a truck that cracked up between Baltimore and Washington on Route 1 in 1936. So the driver called me and I told him, I said, "Get a man to get it off the highway and then you and your helper, you catch a bus on back to Newark." So then I called up the International Truck people down there and I told the salesman that I wanted to see him. But first I said to him, "I don't want to do nothing until the other driver's insurance man gets here, the driver who hit us. I want to know how much insurance I'll get." So he come over from Jersey City and he and I, we went down to look at the truck that had the accident. And the insurance agent said, "Which would you rather have, the truck fixed up or a new truck?" And I said, "New, because every time you break the housing, you never get a truck straightened out right." So I bought a new truck and they sent the chassis from here down to Baltimore, and they mounted the body on the chassis and brought it up to Newark.

Well, at that time, then, I had to get a new license for the truck. So there was a big line in the motor vehicle office. When I got to the window, I put the application in there. The clerk said to me, "Mister, you haven't got your insurance on there." I said, "I don't have any insurance." And there was a big inspector, the head over there, a sergeant, a great big red guy, and he said to me, "You mean to tell me that you're running those trucks all around without having any accident insurance?" I said, "Yes." I said to him, I said, "I can tell you the reason I haven't got any insurance." He said, "Why?" I said, "I haven't got any insurance because I'm a black man. They won't sell us any insurance." I said, "I don't care what you are, doctor, lawyer or whatever you are, if you're black, you can't get no insurance. And that's the truth." That was in 1936. So a white lady was standing in back of me and she said, "Is that the truth?" I said, "That's the truth." I said that I had been in the army, and I served the country and I done a good job, because I have my record back home, and I said that I've never been arrested in my life. I said, "Because I'm a black man, they won't sell no black man no insurance."

The reason they wouldn't give the colored man insurance, I've been told, was that juries were prejudiced against the black man and they gave such big awards against the black man in an accident case. A colored man could be in the right, but if he was right, he was still wrong, because they would give a verdict against him. Now that's the truth. The juries were all white then. Fifteen or twenty years ago they were all white. So the insurance company would take a beating if they insured a colored man. Now you can ask lawyers, doctors, whatever a colored man was, he could even be a millionaire, and he would still have the same problem.

How did we finally get insurance? I'll tell you. Do you see that incorporation paper over there on the wall? That's how we came to be incorporated. There was a lawyer friend of mine, and I had moved him into his house 31 years ago. He told me, he said, "Well, the only way I can help you is we'll incorporate the business so they won't know who the officers are, white or colored." And that's what we did. When we incorporated we got insurance, because they didn't know who we were.

Remember the problem you have if you live on the wrong side of the railroad tracks? Now I told this man there at the license bureau when I got the plates, I told him, "Look up my record, look at my company's record. We've never had an accident. We've had a clean slate." I wouldn't tell him why they wouldn't give us insurance. I wouldn't go that far as to tell him why.

But later the government took over and made them give us insurance. They had to insure you. You couldn't discriminate against a man because of his skin, you know. If he had a good record, or even a bad record, you did to him what you did to people with a different skin. After we got insurance, we paid the same rates as white people, after the government straightened out that mess. The insurance company we were with then, we were with them for 32 years and we never had any problems. We had one of the best records that a trucker ever had. So as I said, that was the problem we had back in those days, but it hasn't been that way lately.

Now I'll tell you something interesting. During the depression, business wasn't too bad because people done more moving then. Oh sure, whenever you saw a lower rent, you took that house. People are buying more today. They aren't renting as much and there's not as much turnover. You take some of our business. We have moved some large, rich customers out of Newark into west Jersey, south Jersey, Long Island, places like that. For example I might have moved your grandfather, your father and now I move you. We moved three generations in one family. Now we are moving a lot of people out of the city because people, you know, they grow a step higher. The middle class is moving out. Of course whites are moving out more, much more. They got better jobs, more money and they can afford to move out there. It stands to reason, you know, with homes today being pretty high priced, which is why a lot of blacks don't move. You got to have a good job to take care of a home today. Another handicap is that it is hard for a black to get mortgage money.

But as I view the thing, people have the wrong idea in trying to move out of the city. I think the city is going to become more of a commercial center. What we are going to have in the center of the city will be big high rises. No more private homes. Because Newark is a city that has been known all over the world for work. I can remember back when I was a youngster. You could hear the old timers say that if you couldn't get a job in Newark don't try to go nowhere else. Newark was always a manufacturing city, a city of jobs.

I'll tell you one important thing, since you ask me whether I have avoided some of the problems that black people face in business. In 1935, that's when the Interstate Commerce Commission came into effect, they started the ICC to govern trains and buses and things like that. So we got into it, you know, and we got our charter and were classified as long-distance movers. So we were fortunate in that way.

But I was telling you about the handicap that I had, even though I was a veteran of the First World War. At the beginning of World War II, I began to get this government work, moving army personnel, particularly around Fort Dix. But it seems that the ones that were in charge of it, they didn't take too much to the colored man. So the only way the colored man could get anything out of Fort Dix was to get it from a white mover. And that's the way I used to get some of that business.

I suppose you could call it sub-contracting if you want. There was a firm on Rankin Street. Him and I were friends and we used to work together. And he didn't even have an ICC permit, but he could get stuff out of the Army camp and I couldn't, although I had an ICC permit and I was a veteran and he wasn't. He was white, sure.

So that's why I said that with our knowledge of the business here, we should have went places, gone a lot further than we did. But still we made out good. We made a living out of it, you know, for forty years. But we never got no more than that stage of business I indicated. We couldn't advance because we couldn't get large contracts, even in the trucking business. Now I used to do work for this Monroe Laboratory. They're in Kingston now. I carted their products and they were growing every year. And then pretty soon, you know, why this white truckman came along and I was out. That was the way it was, so I was under a certain amount of handicap, you know.

When I was a boy, you remember, we didn't know the meaning of discrimination. But that's changed, somehow. People don't realize that most of the colored people you see up here, they migrated from the South, but do you realize there were just as many whites that migrated from the South. And that changed the picture altogether. I read in the paper not long ago where a young white couple nearby were invited to some kind of affair. So when they came, you know, they had a little collation, but then they got down to business. And this meeting was, just what we are talking about, to separate the races. And when this young white couple found that out, they asked for their coats and wraps right away and they went on out. You see, because as I said, all that stuff is planned, you know. It just don't happen.

To tell you the difference, let me give you a little story. When I was first in business, about five years after I started, I had a load for Providence, one stop in Providence, and the next was in Boston and one was in New Hampshire. So I made Providence first and it was late when we dropped off this parcel. So we stopped to get gas and it was dark. And I said to the gasman, "Is there any place we can put up for the night?" And he said to me, "You see that house right up the street there with the green shutters? The lady's name is Mrs. Johnson and she caters to that kind of trade." I said, "Thank you." And we went up to that house there and rang the bell. She came to the door and it was a white woman. So I said to her, "Pardon us, but we stopped down the road to get gas and I asked them if they know a place where we could put up for the night and he directed us here." And she said, "Well, that's my business." And she put us up in there. The sheets were too clean, too white to get into! And the top part of it was, she asked us, "Do you want breakfast in the morning?" and I said, "Yes." So she knocked on the door in the morning and she asked, "What will you have for breakfast?" And I said I was partial to ham and eggs and I said to the other fellow, "What do you want?" and he said, "Same for me." When we got down, there was this ham steak at least a half an inch. And three eggs and hot biscuits. And guess how much we paid for that meal? Sixty-five cents apiece. 'Course, that was quite a while ago, but that was ham steak, not the kind of ham you get around here. And the point that I was going to make was this. The New England states has always been like this, and I think that is the best part of the United States.

But there is a different story about eating which shows the other side. I went down to Washington once, and this was also in my early days of business. A man down there advertised for trucks for hiring out for road work. At that time it was a strain going down to Washington because you had to come back the same day. So we took the Penn down, me and another fellow, Joe, whose father had a trucking company and two other men. I was the only black man. So we went up to my friend's office and signed our contracts and then it was about eleven o'clock and there was a restaurant right underneath and one of the fellows said, "Well, they serve and we deserve a good meal. Let's go down there." And I said, "No, let's go on further." And I saw a place there with a colored guy sitting there and I made the decision to go in but it was a mistake. We went in and the counter man took the order for the other guys and then he come to me and he says, "Well, I'm sorry, buddy, but you'll have to eat in the back." So my friend, Joe, said, "What did he say?" So I said, "Well, that's the way it is. Down here, they don't mix in here." So he said, "Oh, the heck with it. Let's go somewhere else." And I told him, I said, "Well, if you fellows ain't particular I'll take you to a place where I know that we'll get a good meal." So I took them to Johnson's on New York Avenue. It's a colored place that just cooks out of this world. I knew that, that's why I took them there. So they had hot rolls, and ham and eggs and sausages and everything like that there. And one of them said, "I ain't never had a meal like this in my life. That's two meals!" And he said, "I'm glad that guy didn't serve us because I know we would have never got no such meal as this here." And they talked about that all the way back on the train.

So it can be sometimes good and sometimes bad, what takes place between the races. I don't know. It seems like it's just a case of nature. Sometimes I don't think that it will ever be straightened out. But if you ask me whether it can be straightened out through laws, I would say, no, no, no law can ever straighten out anything like this. It has to be done by the individual himself. I don't think that all this civil rights legislation will amount to much, unless there is a change in people. Because if human beings don't want it themselves, it wouldn't last. No, because, you see, it is more a condition of nature than it is of anything else. In other words, there has got to be brotherhood, like they try to preach. If you don't have that, then the rest is all useless. I would like to see it straightened out, but I don't know whether it ever will.

Nowadays, there are no problems about eating places. You can eat just about any place. And the problem of jobs, it seems to me, is not the same as when I was young. To work today, you have to have a skill. But any young person, I don't care whether he's white or black, if he has it up here, if he's educated, he's all right. If a black man has got an education, he don't have to worry any more. The young black people don't feel that they belong in the system, but that's the point you have to tell them about, that they have got to have education. You know, this drudgery work is out now. Manual labor is out. In order to support a family today, you got to make money today. And the conditions of work that face the young, it's not like when we were young, particularly if you came from the South to the North.

In this area all of us older people remember what happened at Butterworth and Judson. It was so dangerous, you know. Nobody wanted to work there. Oh, a lot of them died too. The stuff was poison. It was something like that time, years ago, when they had that radioactive stuff on watches. A lot of people died from that, oh a lot of them. Women, mostly women, up in Orange. But this Butterworth and Judson, that was a dangerous place, yeah, that was a dangerous job. It seemed like the government could have done something. Gases and fumes, you know, and if it was that bad, seems like they shouldn't have allowed it, but they did. And then the trouble was that the men that they brought up here from the South were greenhorns and it was big money and naturally they took the jobs.

But there was another case. Take right up here in Bloomfield, about a half mile from here. They were paying $20 a day back there in the days of the war. They were making shells, live shells. And up there in Kingston, when they exploded up there, you know, men were running, they were running so far, by God, that they got lost. They didn't know which way to get home!

They were paying pretty well then, $20 a day and that was a lot of money. Some of them made as high as $10,000 a year working up there. It's the danger and the skill. They had trouble up there. One or two men would get killed every year. Now they're selling the company out, transferring it to Japan. That's true of a lot of plants around here. Take some of the big foundries that made the big castings. Some of them employed several thousand men. And most of the men worked in the molding and casting departments, and most all of those foundries like that hired mostly colored. See, they said that they could stand the heat better. I never worked in one of them myself, but that's what they said, the manufacturers, that they hired the colored because they could stand the heat better. It was good pay. That's a lot of money for a colored man, a man who's been a laborer. But that's the kind of jobs they had to take when they wanted to earn a little more than a laborer's pay.

There are several things that I feel I have to get off my chest. It's what I feel and I know a lot of my friends my age feel the same. I don't understand why the government ever took the prayer out of school. That's one bad thing. And another bad thing is this. A woman's place is in the house, to take care of those children. And if she goes out to work, when she comes home she's dead tired and she can't even think of her family. The kids have to take care of themselves then. They should make it possible for the woman to stay home like our mothers used to do.

But I really can't understand why they took the prayer out of the schools, because a child grows with the knowledge he gets from day to day. Now, if he don't get no knowledge in the church and the school and in his home, what does he know about the Bible? I think that religion should be a strong part of every child's growing up. That is the best thing you could do for them. Prayer would help them.

I am very interested in what young people do. My wife, you see, was a great church worker, and there were a lot of children there. And religious training sinks into them. Anything good will sink into them, I don't care what anybody says. Here's a little illustration. A man called me up for a moving job last fall. He said, "My daughter is moving to New York." And then he told me that she was moving to Greenwich Village. And it kind of hit me a little hard, after a while, that a man of his standing would have to watch his daughter move down there. And I said to myself, "Now that mother and father are probably heartbroken. They've probably talked and talked to that girl, and they couldn't persuade her not to. But they thought that the best way was to give in to her and help her, because if this thing don't work out they got a chance of her coming back home. Like the Prodigal Son." There's an example. Sure, there is nothing, no example better than the Bible. I don't care what anybody says. I have followed it all my life and still do.

One more thing I want to say. If my wife were still living, I would never have retired from my business. I would never have been wanting to retire. I would have stayed here and been taking care of things, but after she passed, there was nothing for me to stay in it for. I'll tell you, living alone is something. I never knew that you could miss a person so much. I never knew. People say, "Oh, it will wear off," but it doesn't. I can't shake it. You see, like this house here, I think that it might be better for me to get out of this house. I'll tell you why. Every time I do something, I can see her. That she used to do this, she used to do that. It brings it right back fresh to me.

A woman can make a man. If you get the right kind of woman, it can make a man. My wife never nagged me, she never tried to make me do something which she knew that I didn't want to do because I didn't think it was the right thing to do. If she could see that it was the right thing, she would always go along with it. The girl next door, an Italian girl, her people passed too, and we have been friends for 37 years. She told me the other day, "Mr. Edwards, I know just how you feel because you are going through just what I did." She's about 42 and her boy is about four years old. And she wouldn't get married until her mother and father died. She said, "As sick as they were, I didn't mind what I had to do as long as they were in the house there with me." And I stayed with my wife, she was sick for five years, you know, and I used to bathe her and everything. But just so she was in the house, see. That's all that mattered with me. That's why I guess I took it so hard.

Robert Moore

We've known each other so long it's a bit strange my telling about things that I know you know, but you want me to sum up some of my experiences, and I will just act as if you don't know things, some of which we even did together. It will give me a chance to pull some things together, too, and I have often thought that it wouldn't be a bad idea to write my story, except I never could think who might be willing to publish it. I imagine there are a lot of people who feel the same way. Lord knows, I have come a long way. I don't know whether it's been upwards, downwards, sideways or whatever, but it's been a long road. I never would have thought that it was going to end up the way it has, but I guess that it all ties together somehow. Even your asking me about it. I remember we used to talk a lot, those days back in

1941 when there were weeks between ports. There wasn't much else to do and it made the time pass a bit, and some of those weeks, when we were wondering just where the next submarine might be, they were just about the longest weeks I've ever spent.

You remember Red, the Swede. Couldn't swim a stroke and the gentlest fellow you ever saw, he would really sweat when we had those alarms. Poor fellow, I heard that he shipped out on a tanker that got it and they never found anyone. But that's the way it was. You remember that first engineer that used to be on you and Joe's back, meanest fellow I think I ever saw, but he really knew his job. He went on several of the worst convoys to Murmansk, and he got picked up several times after the ship went down under him. And then he's back in New York, blowing all that pay and he's drunk as a skunk, falls down an elevator shaft 12 floors. Can you beat that!

Well, the beginning was in the Virgin Islands. My sailor grandfather, the Scotchman, was a sailing ship master, but I never saw him myself. My mother always said that he had his captain's papers and he met my grandmother and married her and they had half-a-dozen children, including my mother. It wasn't at all uncommon for a sailor from Europe to have a wife on the islands. Maybe they had wives back in wherever they came from too. So I always knew that I was what you call mixed. It never made much difference, except maybe it explains why I always wanted to go to sea. Maybe it was in my blood. And I was determined that I would become a captain, too.

We had a pretty good life on the island. I never remember any hard times, and I guess anybody who was a child in the Caribbean always thinks that it was something like paradise. The schools were good, too. My folks and everybody I knew took school very seriously. I suppose it's pretty evident that we were brought up to respect reading and writing, to think that how you spoke was important. To this day I think that people from the islands have a beautiful way of saying things. Why my father and mother decided to leave for New York was never very clear to me. They said that there was more opportunity, more chance for advancement, and they certainly thought that their children would have more chance to get ahead. There was no doubt in their minds that we were all going to go to college and have some kind of profession. We heard that all the time.

But for us children, used to the island, it was a shock to find ourselves suddenly in Brooklyn. We soon found ourselves pretty well settled in Brooklyn. There is an old Negro community there, families that have been there for ages. And there were a number of families from the Caribbean who established themselves in that area. My father was a skilled woodworker. He had no trouble during the first years in finding work, well-paid work. I think that the families from the Caribbean were perhaps more ambitious, more inclined to go into business and to save. We were somewhat apart from most Negro families, almost cut off from southern Negro families. We moved in quite a narrow circle.

I was ten years old when we arrived in Brooklyn. That would have made it 1924, I think. I had no trouble at all in school. In fact, I think I was a little ahead of my age. We all, the children, that is, were accustomed to doing odd jobs, and in that I don't remember any trouble at all finding little jobs to do in the neighborhood where you could earn a bit of money. I can't recall that people made any distinction between white and nonwhite children, shopkeepers, and so forth who might have some work that a youngster could do. You didn't get paid much, but it was something to be proud of that you worked some after school and on the weekend. Things were smaller scale then, it seems to me, and there were more possibilities for youngsters.

I don't want to imply that we were always either going to school or busy working. There was plenty of opportunity for other things, and we sometimes got into trouble. But our attitude towards it was very different from what I see today. I remember once my friend and I went into a jewelry shop. Just for the deviltry of it we took some cheap watches while the storekeeper wasn't watching. Then we went outside. But right away we began to feel so troubled that all we wanted to do was to get rid of the watches, any place at all would do. Would you know, I told my father what we had done and he went to the storekeeper and paid him for those watches, I guess to teach us a lesson.

He could do that then. Later, when the Depression came, it wouldn't have been so easy for him. There was very little extra money in those days. In the first year or so I don't think I noticed it very much. I was finishing high school and concentrating on getting into college. I had my heart set on City College. That was the best, so far as I was concerned. In those days, you didn't think of places like Columbia. I guess that the tuition would have been out of the question. I got into City all right, but you know, I think that I had in the back of my mind that if I could get a college degree that would make it easier for me to become a captain of a steamship. Maybe it was living in Brooklyn and seeing the ships all the time. Maybe it was some memory of the islands. But I don't think the idea of being a sailor was ever really out of my mind.

It's hard for me to recollect early exactly what I thought then about the obstacles in front of a young man like me to becoming a sailor, let alone a sailing master. I knew that Negroes weren't officers on steamships. But there wasn't then perhaps the kind of awareness of discrimination that young folk have today. It was there, but I suppose that if we had all known how high some of the hurdles were, we might never have tried to jump over them. On the other hand, it seems to me, there was the idea that it was up to us to progress. Anyway it was something like a fixed idea, even then.

In those days in college, I was interested in getting an engineering degree. It was hard work, but I think I would have gone on to get the degree if economic conditions had not been so bad and it seemed wrong for me to add to the burdens on my father and mother. Even getting back and forth to school from Brooklyn was a problem. There were even times when the fare, even that nickel, was just too much, and I set off on foot—all the way up Manhattan, starting out across the bridge on a cold windy day. That is something to remember.

And it was no longer so easy to pick up a dollar here or there at odd jobs. In fact it was practically impossible. Storekeepers didn't offer much in the way of odd jobs, and what jobs there were were snapped up by grownups.

I hung around the docks a lot those days, and it just seemed to me that it would be better if I got a job somehow or other; and I don't know whether it was my being there so much or my age or even my color, but there came a day when a man asked me if I wanted to ship out. A tramp freighter needed a mess boy right away, and if I was ready to go they would take me. I ran home, told my younger brother that I was going to be a sailor, didn't even dare to tell my folks, I was that excited about it and I thought they might say no. So I told my brother to tell them that I would write to them as soon as I could.

I don't even remember clearly what that old ship was carrying. I didn't have too much time to find out, I was kept so busy. Those were the days before there was anything like a strong union, and conditions on shipboard were about close to being unfit for animals, let alone humans. You know all about it, I'm sure. But since it's part of the story, it should be told. The crowding, the filth, the slop that was called food, the brutality of some of the officers. It really was subhuman, and I think it was only because the original members of the unions had lived through these conditions and the pay that went with them that the unions had such strength and conviction. Today I hear that these new big tankers are like floating luxury hotels for the crew. They were pigsties for us in those years before the union. And I learned quick what my position as a Negro mess boy was. He was the bottom of it all, in every way and all the time.

You know, we still had troubles when you were shipping with me. White sailors, particularly the deck officers, believed that the Negro should only be mess boy. They really wanted service. It was hard for some of them to stand watch with a Negro at the wheel, I can tell you. Those were long frosty hours in more ways than one. But all that, that was nothing compared with some of the things I had to go through. Some times I used to work black gang. I suppose that if anybody is ever going to read about me, except you and me, they should know that a black gang doesn't mean a BLACK gang. They aren't black men, though I've known young folks to think that was what it meant. It meant the men who worked in the engine room, and it comes, I suppose, from the times they used coal, and they must've been really black then, I mean coal dirt black. And in those days I guess there were Negroes who were slaving away at the furnaces too, the way Conrad and O'Neill tell it. It was the kind of work they were thought to do. Sometimes, not often, I did work in the hole in those old ships where, if a person took sick, you could be moved around. I can remember one where they had me doing a wiper's job. That's the lowest you can get in the black gang. You just go around cleaning up and chipping paint and all the rest. Well, there was this mean, I mean really mean, old first engineer from Connecticut. He told me once that his family were all navy and the navy knew how to take care of the Negro. I swear, he used to urinate at night into the bilge, and then he used to enjoy sending me down there to clean up. Nothing you could do about that in those days. No such thing as a shop steward to make a beef to. You just thought, I'd like to hit that man over the head with a 36-inch spanner some night when he's taking a leak. It gave you murderous feelings, something like that.

By the time you came to know me in the forties, that had mostly changed. We had checkerboard crews then, white and black. And it wasn't unusual for whites and Negroes to bunk together in the same fo'castle, and everybody ate together, side by side in the same mess, and there were black shop stewards. The union, the National Maritime Union, took a real hard line on integration, long before most of the rest of the country knew what the word was supposed to mean.

But all that was in the future when I first began to sail. You know, I was always somewhat apart from the rest of the crew, it seemed to me. First of all, there were those two years at City College. I just didn't bother telling anybody about that. Most of the sailors then had little schooling, particularly the white southerners. And I wasn't about to tell them that I was a college boy. That could've spelled trouble, and they most would think I was nothing but a stuck up nigger, pretending. But I did read a lot, partly to pass the time and partly to better myself. I always did like to read, you remember that. A ship's a great place for reading, and I will say, the union did a real job in educating and improving us. Some of the ships had a real good little library by the end of the war. Anyway, long before I went to sea, I had taken up Joseph Conrad. I remember that I saw that title, *The Nigger of the Narcissus*, in the Brooklyn Public Library, and I was just attracted to it. So I think I've read almost everything he had to write about the sea. Sometimes I thought, when I was reading his books, that man knows my thoughts. He was a real sailor; that is the only way he could have learned what he says about sailors, ships and the sea.

Those were hard days then. It was hard to get a job. It was really hard for a young black man to get any place at all. So when I had a little experience at sea and knew the ropes, it was natural to stay at it. There were times when I was on the beach. But mostly I could keep afloat, but not by much. And I told myself that some day I would have my own ship, so I used every opportunity to learn the trade. There were fellows who took a shine to me, and, of course, if they were a bosun with more work than they could do, they didn't mind having a young strong fellow like me ready to help with some of the hard parts. Splicing steel cable, particularly when the cable is old and full of broken wires, can be one of the toughest jobs around, even when you know how to do it. Most people wouldn't even know what it means to splice. But that was one of the things that a sailor was supposed to be able to do. And I simply helped around until it was natural for me. I came to enjoy doing it so that it was really right. And sailors appreciate that. Those cables can mean your life. You're hauling cargo out of the holds with them. One of them lets go and it can take a man's head off.

One of the things about sailing is that you need your papers. Once you've been to sea, there's not much trouble getting them. But your papers tell what you are supposed to be able to do. A sailor can't ship as an able-bodied seaman unless he has AB papers. The whole thing is graded, like, from bottom to top. And you can work to get your papers. It gives you something to look forward to. I had gone as far as I could as a seaman. The next jump was to deck officer. Then you go up the line of the mates until, if you can get your master's papers, you're qualified to take a ship. Most of the first mates, chief officers, already have their master's papers, and they're just waiting. So that was always my ambition. Even when I was tied up in the union I had in the back of my mind that someday I would be on the other side as an officer. It's hard to explain just how that can seize you. I wanted the responsibility of a ship. Even when I was just an able-bodied seaman, I used to enjoy those hours in the night when I was at the wheel, all alone except with the mate and a few men on watch and the black gang down below. And then to feel the ship through the wheel, you sending a message to the ship to go a certain direction, even though it was just straight on course. You always had to make adjustments, particularly in a tricky sea. There's nothing quite like it, to my mind. It may sound boring to people outside, and Lord knows it is in some ways. Standing there for hours, except when you're spelled for a cup of coffee. But there it is, you and that ship, she's in your hands.

Anyway, those days during the war when I was studying for my mate's papers and when I believed that we were all fighting the war together for some kind of a better life after the war was won, those were, I suppose, the best days of my life, in spite of the danger and the long lonely days at sea on those trips to the Middle East and up to Murmansk. Just the thought of it all makes me a little sad. But it was a hopeful time, as I recollect it. You were scared all the time, maybe, but that made the times when we all joked about it and laughed about the danger, it made those the times you remember now.

I kept plugging away at the preparation for the mate's papers. It was a good time for studying, and I was sure that I would pass and start my way up the ladder to becoming a master of a ship. It was time when there was a lot of talk about firsts for Negroes—first pilot, first general, first of a lot of things. And I thought it would be nice to be the first skipper of a ship. I never even asked myself whether there ever had been a Negro captain of an American merchant ship before. I just took it for granted there hadn't. I knew it wouldn't all be so easy. But I felt that I was prepared for whatever it took.

Well, I took the examination for mate's papers when I felt good and ready, and everything went fine. No trouble at all and I wondered why I hadn't taken them years earlier. I was that confident, and although I was no longer a spring chicken, I could see a long and glorious career at sea ahead of me. There I was, not yet thirty years old and already with my mate's papers. Maybe not quite setting the pace that young Conrad did, but still more or less on track. That was just about the high point of my expectations. I suppose the rest of the story of my life is just why didn't the dream turn out and what did I do about it. It's always hard to tell about these things; that's what makes it, I think, so hard to cope with them and accept it after all these years. I expected to become a master. I didn't become a master. Why? Why did I decide that it was just not to be and that the best thing for me was to forget it? Why did I decide to leave the sea? There are so many answers that I can give myself that it makes my head spin sometimes. But I still hold to the conviction that I would have become a master if I had been any ordinary young white mate with my qualifications and my ambition and my experience. Nobody ever said that my work wasn't always first class. I never shirked any job. There was never any black mark against me. It makes me laugh to use the expression, "black mark," that way, because another part of me says that there was always just that "black mark" which set me off from the rest of the young deck officers. And then I sometimes ask myself, what if I had stuck it out longer? Was I just too anxious to make it? Should I have had more patience? Would it have made a difference if I had still been at sea during the 1960s when there was all this talk about civil rights? Or was I just caught up in what was happening in the merchant marine in general? A lot of other people had to give up their ambitions and they were white where I was colored. Some of them were just as disappointed, maybe, as I became. What answers do they give themselves?

The questions are a bit torturing, and I can't really answer them to my satisfaction. But there it is. I came close. I felt that I could have achieved my goal. It was that close, I could feel it. I knew what it was to be in charge of a ship. I knew that most of the men I worked for respected me for what I could do. I never had any trouble that way. You either knew your job or you didn't, you were either a responsible man or you neglected your tasks. Sailors are good that way. They're afraid of an officer who is incompetent or careless, and they appreciate the ones who do their jobs and care about their ship and their crew.

There came a time, not so many years after the end of the war, when I came to think that I was up the ladder as far as I was going to go. And of course there were family pressures too. I don't need to tell you that it's hard on a wife and hard on growing children to have the father of the family away so much. It's better to be a bachelor, no question about it, if you want to be at sea. Not that my wife ever really asked me to give it all up. She wasn't that kind of a person. But I knew it was hard for her and there was the question of the children growing up. Well, one day I said to myself, I have had my fling at the sea and that's that. I'll just call it a day and settle down. I had no doubt but that I would find something to do. I've never been troubled that way. You have to have confidence in yourself if you've had that responsibility of a ship in a heavy sea. You don't lose that, I believe. And you have to be able to make decisions. So once I had made my decision to give up the sea, I knew what I had to do and that was to find some kind of work which would use my abilities. I was just into my forties, and I knew that I would have good references from my employers.

Since I left the sea, things have been generally good. It took me a while to find my legs, but I finally found responsible work to do. And since that time I've made my way up through the company, so that you could say that I am in an important executive position with the company. My work involves supervising a large number of men, and the training I had at sea helps in that kind of work. You know how to give orders and to make sure that the work gets done. And the fact is that the company uses a large number of minority workers, blacks and Puerto Ricans, and I think they look up to me because I treat them fair. There's no place for favoritism at sea, and that is something you carry with you. You have to set an example and you have to care about the work being done properly, no matter what it is. I know that the company does the type of business that relies a lot upon a labor force that is recruited from the minorities in New York. But it does offer steady work and a chance for a number of people to advance where previously they might have been caught in the kind of revolving door work which so many people seem to get trapped in. I consider that one of the most important measures of my success as an executive is the low turnover rate.

I had to make a decision soon after I decided to stay on shore. We could have afforded to move, I suppose, into one of the suburbs. It would have been a hassle, I know, but we could have afforded it. But I made up my mind to stay in the community. Maybe being at sea for so many years made me want to feel that I had some roots somewhere and those roots were in Harlem. When we first moved there, it was a very quiet neighborhood. I had been brought up in Brooklyn but my wife was from Harlem, and I knew it from the time I studied at City College, and I liked the neighborhood around the College, so that is where we settled. And we have lived there ever since. I don't need to tell you that I am troubled about the changes that I have seen, and the changes seem to be getting more rapid in the last few years. It seems a shame. It's hard on us older people in the community. It's the decay of housing first. A good building next to several that are falling to pieces or abandoned. Shooting galleries for the addicts, fires breaking out, just shells of what they were, and you ask yourself why? Why did this building fall apart and this one stay together? How long will your own building stay even half-way in shape, because you can see the same signs of decay in your own building? It's like your apartment becomes a refuge from all the disorder and trouble. A little world by itself. I know that's what a lot of my friends feel. So they spend a lot of their energies on keeping their own apartment or house in just as apple-pie condition as they can. A lot of time and money too, and they don't seem to have much left for the community itself. Or perhaps they just feel that there is really nothing they can do about it. It's just too big a thing. And of course the problem of personal security or safety has really become a serious matter. More and more you don't go out unless you have to, if you are the age of my wife and myself. My wife feels it particularly. I have to get out because of my work, and I suppose I still feel that I can defend myself; and I think that you communicate this feeling so you don't have as much trouble. At least I can't say I have had too many incidents. Oh, one or two where there might have been trouble but I was careful. You do keep a kind of watch out for trouble, and that's not a pleasant thing to have to do.

There has been a breakdown of the proper relationship between older people and younger people. When I was a child, you knew that you might be watched by some older person if you did something really wrong. I don't mean little things. I mean something that everybody knew was wrong. There seemed to be an agreement about things like that. Some things were just not to be done, at all. And all the adults made sure that all the children knew this. I don't think the discipline was particularly harsh. I don't think it needed to be, because for the most part we were good children and young people. They talk a lot today about pride, but, you know, in spite of all the difficulty in being a colored child, I think our parents did train us to have pride in many ways. It was like there were two worlds then. The outside world where people had these beliefs about the Negro and your own little world where you knew that these attitudes were wrong and crazy. Sure, we suffered from the slurs and the insults and the obstacles, the whole crazy pattern of discrimination that I don't think young people today really appreciate or understand. But we didn't have to accept it, and when we heard white people talk about the lazy or shiftless or happy-go-lucky Negro, we could just compare that with what we knew about our own parents and friends. They surely weren't lazy or happy-go-lucky. In a way we could look down upon people who believed those things about us. The real injury, I believe, was that we couldn't become what we knew we had it in us to become. Men particularly were restricted to a certain kind of work, certain occupations and industries. You just knew that. As far back as you knew anything, that was the world you faced when you grew up. The Negro as porter, clean-up man, waiter, shoe-shine man—that is hard to face. And you knew that down South it was worse, much worse. The only road out of this kind of work you knew was education. At least that was what you were always told. But if you had to leave school, one way or another, then you might believe that you were just foredoomed to a life of toil and hardship. Knowing that you were just never going to get a good job at all. Now that's hard for a man to accept, and when you knew that it was just a matter of the color of your skin, why, man, that was a bitter cup. We had to be strong, you know, to drink it and still survive. You had to call upon all your pride, that I know.

Moses Clapham

I have lived here now for, let's see, about 38, 40 years, but I was born in South Carolina—Kingsley, South Carolina. I came here in 1927 when I was about 17 or 18 years old. I come up to my uncle. My uncle was living here. He was Reverend Henry C., and when he died I moved over to M. Avenue. I stayed there until 1939 or 1940 and then I moved over to 107 C. Street. I have been here ever since in this house, so I have been in the same neighborhood for about 30 years.

I'm 62 years old now. I'm an old man. I got all my schooling down in South Carolina. I didn't finish high school. I only went as high as the ninth grade in South Carolina. We had a college down there which my uncle orginated, and I am named after him, Moses Clapham. I'll tell you why I didn't finish school and why I didn't go to college.

My father, he was a big man in his county. He made a good living in South Carlina and he had everything. And he got into trouble down there with some of those white folks, and he shot one of them. He killed a man, and he had to leave home. First he went back to the West Indies where he come from, and he stayed there for a while. And then he went to Florida and he got in touch with me. And the white people started to give me trouble when the old man leave home. They started to give me trouble because I was, you know, a pretty bright boy myself and they tried to pin a lot of things on me. So my mother told me, she said, "I'll tell you what you do, son. You go up the road here with your uncle, meaning to Newark, until things get a little bit quieter and then you come back." And when I came up here, I liked it pretty good, and I never went back, except to visit.

My father was a big farmer. In those days, you see, my father had sharecroppers and had people working for him, you know. He was a progressive type of man. And these white people didn't like him because, you know, he had a big store and them kinds of things. A black man wasn't supposed to have that kind of thing, not in those days. And they do everything to double-cross him, and when he get enough of this, he told them, "Listen, I don't want no trouble but I don't want you all to be double-crossing me. When I say something, I want to do what I said I am going to do. I don't want to do nothing but what's right." And one word led to another and they had a gun battle. So my old man shot him. But my father, being a mason, he got out of it somehow. There were white people on his side too. And they put him on the chain gang. They give him lifetime on the chain gang. He stayed on the chain gang for a few days, and then they took him off the gang and tell him to go away and don't be seen in South Carolina no more for a while.

When he come on back to Miami, he bought a place in Miami and I still have that place in Miami now. Anyway, my father came back to Miami and he stayed in Miami for about 15 or 20 years, and then he got ill. When he took sick he wanted to come home so he came on home and he stayed there for awhile, but he couldn't feel safe there, because the white people, they had this against him. The son of the man he killed, he had this grudge in for him because this black man had killed his father and that kind of thing. So my father went back to Florida and made his home in Florida and so he died.

My father had only two children, my sister and me. But after my father left, my mother had about five or six more children. Seven of us in all, but only me and my sister are full brother and sister. So I have a large family down South and they are spread around some. I still keep in touch with them, particularly my sister.

When I came up to Newark, I found my uncle. He was a minister, like I said, so I worked around the church for a while. And then when I got to be a big boy, I wanted to go out for myself and I told my uncle so. He said, "Well, Moses, I tell you what I'm going to do. I'm going to look for a job for you." I said, "Okay," so he put an ad in the paper. I didn't like none of the jobs that came up at first. They were like the work I was already doing, clean-up jobs and things like that, and I didn't like that.

So my uncle put another ad in the paper and this ad run for about two or three weeks. And finally this man called up the old man, that's what I called my uncle, my old man. And this man said, "I see you got an ad in the paper for a young man and he's supposed to be a bright young fellow. Would you bring him over and let me interview him?" The old man say, "Yes." So me and him got in a cab and came over to Newark. And the man asked me, "Did you ever work in a laundry before?" I told him, "Yes," but I ain't never seen a laundry before. But I figured I could catch on pretty good. He said, "What laundry did you work in?" and I said, "A colored laundry down in Kingsley, South Carolina." He said, "Yes? What did you do? Did you pull clothes?" I said, "Yes," but I had no idea what pulling clothes was. I had never heard tell of it. He said, "I'll tell you. Now, I'm going to give you a try-out. If you do pretty good, I'll advance you. You look like an able young man." I said, "Yes." You know, I was about 18 or 19 years at the time. So then him and the old man, they make a deal about how much they going to pay me, and that kind of thing. And I said, "Okay," and my uncle said, "Now, son, tonight I'll pick you up and show you how to get over here, because I can't bring you." You see, my uncle called me "son" and I called him "my old man." His church was in Smithfield and my sister lives there now.

So that night he picked me up. I was working until about seven o'clock that night. We frequently worked late in the laundry. So seven o'clock that night, he picked me up and brought me out to C. Avenue and showed me how to get on the bus to S. I would have to walk seven blocks down from C. Avenue all the way down to the laundry, seven long blocks. So then he waked me up the next morning at five thirty because I was supposed to be at work at seven o'clock. But I was a little late. I'll tell you why. When I get up that morning I got into the bus and tell the driver to let me off at A. Street, but he took me all the way to Loving Park, and I had to blunder and find my way to the laundry.

I thought I had lost the job, and I told the foreman, "Now, listen, I got lost this morning." He said, "That's all right, Moses, come on in." And I went in and changed clothes and went to work and did pretty good. So when the week was up, the superintendent come and say, "Clapham." I say, "Yes." He say, "I want to see you in the office before you go home." I figured I had done something wrong. I feel scared and that kind of thing. When I go into his office, he says, "Mr. Clapham, I'll tell you. You's a decent kind of a fellow and you work good, you work better than these men, than my old help." He said, "Now, I'll tell you what I'll do. You do pretty good like you're doing now," he said, "next week, I'll give you a raise." Well, I was getting $18 a week and he was giving some of the old men only $17. He said, "I'll give you a $3 raise." So I went home and I told the old man, my uncle, and he said, "You see, the old man liked you. You go ahead and do your work like you should and you'll be all right." So I worked for about three months.

Then the washer, Spencer Harris, God bless him, he was a nice man, looked like a white man, don't you know. But he's colored and very decent. So he says, "Moses, you look like you want to learn something." I said, "Yes, I am here to get everything I can, as far as money, I need that."

He said, "Don't worry about that. I'll do everything I can." So that Friday, he said, "Do you want to come in tomorrow?" I said, "Yessir," you get a little more money for it. So that Saturday I went in, and me and him and the boss were in the office and we talk about what's done. Spencer said, "Now Mr. Hertz," he said, the boss man is Hertz, Spencer says, "This is a good man here. Now I'm going on my vacation. I don't want you to get nobody to wash here. I'm telling Moses how to do it, and anything he don't know, he can come in the office and ask you to brush him up a little bit and he'll do it." So three weeks later Spencer went on his vacation, and before he went he showed me how to do it. I did the work as good as he did or better. So I worked there for seven years, same laundry, same man, same superintendent. And about seven years later they moved up here to Belleville and I went back South for a visit. I did pretty good and my mother, and she did pretty good in South Carolina with the farm and everything, and she brought up my little younger half-brother. I sent my mother money every week. I told my uncle to send money, and I don't tell him how much, you know. I said, "You do what you see fit." When I get my pay, I would give it to my uncle and tell him, "You do what you see fit," because you know, I live with him. I get a suit when I need one. So my uncle took my money and he sent it to mom like he sees fit. And I worked myself up in the laundry. When I leave out of this laundry, I was making $100 a week.

I stayed in the laundry about nineteen years, nineteen or twenty years. So, I worked for this man about nineteen years, and then my health started going bad on me from staying inside so long, and the doctor said to me, "Clapham, I'll tell you what you do now. I went with you as far as I can. All I can do is tell you for your own goodness, if you want to live and have good health, you get out in the air where you can catch some air. You get out of the laundry." So I told the superintendent what it was all about. He said, "Moses, bad as I hate to lose you, suppose you take the route." I said, "Well, I don't like that. You got to meet all kinds of people, stand all kinds of abuse. I don't like to be abused." He said, "Now, I tell you what you do. Go on out there for yourself. And anytime you come back here and want a job with us, you know you're welcome."

When I leave the laundry I was making $100 a week. I had a good scene. And the girls at the laundry, they all liked me pretty good, the superintendent, liked me, the foreman. I got along good because I treat people with respect. So then I talked with some fellows and they say, "Well, Clapham, why don't you come down to the waterfront." So I went down to the waterfront, but that was too cold for me. I couldn't take it. I worked down there for a little while, handling cargo, longshoring. I had my union book and everything, so then I did construction from then on, you know, a little construction work from then on out.

I worked for this construction firm, and I worked up to be foreman there. And I worked until my health started failing on me. So now I am retired and I get some kind of disability check. Here's the check I get from my company. Lifetime disability. I get $160 a month, something like that, as long as I live. That's only from my local, my union in the construction industry. I was in the union at the laundry, but that union don't mean nothing. So, I get this check from my local, from 472, and I get a check from Social Security. I don't get any welfare. They wrote me a letter sometime ago. They wanted me to come down to see whether I can do any kind of work. And they want to increase my disability from the state.

Getting my disability, I had a little trouble. When I came out of the hospital, they give me a runaround for awhile until they get things straightened out. They told me that I got to do this, and I got to wait for about seven or eight weeks. It must have been about ten weeks before they take action. But when they take action, they paid right up to date. All this time I was going down to the office, they would tell me to come back at such and such a time, just come back. So I went back. I played along with them best I could. I was sick all this time that I was going back and forth, and I'm still sick. You see, the wife, she take off sometimes and she takes me down, and I get a bunch of my friends to take me down by car.

When I was in the hospital, I got unemployment benefits. They sent my check. I had no problem getting it, but it wasn't so much. They also took care of all my hospital bills. I stayed in my hospital about seven weeks, before I went up to the government hospital.

I have lumbago, arthritis. I couldn't even straighten out. They had to feed me for about seven weeks. I couldn't even turn my head. I couldn't even move nothing. I just could open my eyes.

When I came home, my wife take care of me for about a week or so. And then I was pretty good. I was strong enough to get about and walk around a little bit. Sometime, if I go out now and I turn my head, I can't get it straight, you know. Looks like I have a catch in my neck. I just can't do anything until my wife straightens my head. That's why she told the lady downstairs that if anything happen, I should knock on the pipe and she'll come up and check it up. But, once in a while, I goes out, goes down to the church, walks around the block. Well, I mean, I try to be active.

I do something with watermelon to occupy my mind. I have a truck come up from Carolina. Like I told you, I have a farm down South. So when my truck come up, I take off 25 or 30 watermelon and put them in my garage, and the rest I take down to the market and auction them off.

And I have a little place in Florida. Oranges. And I have a half-sister down there too. She take care of the one in Florida. Every so often I go down there, but I haven't been to Florida since I was in the hospital. But she came up to see me, to talk to me, and tell me how everything is, because I get so lonesome here in the day by myself. I get so lonesome, I do.

If you are on disability, every once in a while you have to be re-examined to find out whether you are able to work. And if they find that you are not able, then they increase the allotment. They wanted me to come down to Washington Street to see if I would be able to go back to work pretty soon or whether I ever would be able to work. And then they were talking about increasing my check. But I told them, when they give me this $310 a month for disability, I said, "What am I going to do with this kind of money? I can't do nothing with this." The man said, "Well, that's all the state is going to give you now, until we see further." If I were a veteran, perhaps I would be better off, but I was never in the army. I don't own this place where I live and I have to pay $95 a month rent.

There have been some points in my life when I had a hard time. I guess we all have a time in our life when we had it really rough. Yes, yes. When I first came here to Newark, my mother was the head of a family and I was the oldest boy. And she didn't have no income other than what I tried to make. And my uncle, he was pretty good too. And I worked to send the little money I could get home to her like I told you. And when I worked, I sent everything I could. I was giving my uncle everything I made. I mean sometimes I went out and shined shoes when I was not working.

I didn't tell you about how I got married. I went down South after I stayed here ten years and got married to a girl who went to school with my sister. We were all born and raised in the same neighborhood. So I went back down South and I see my sister, and my sister tell me, "Moses, here's a nice girl. Why don't you court her?" I said, "What am I going to court her for?" I said, "I'm in New Jersey and never had nothing, and she's here." She said,

"Well, that's all right. You don't want to marry no girl up there. Why don't you get a girl from here?" So I think about it, and my momma told me the same thing. She said, "After all, she want to get somebody who you can have confidence in, somebody who care for you." I said, "Well, that's nice."

So then I went over to see Hazel that night. She used to live on my father's place in South Carolina. We talked things over. Her mother didn't want me to come to the gate. She said to her daughter, "That man ain't going to mean you no good. He's just going to take you up the road and do worse, and beat you up and make you _____." That's what she told Hazel, you know, she told me later. So then I told her, "Now listen, when I go back up the road, I'm going to keep in touch with you and I'm going to write for you, and you and my sister can come up and see me some time." So she was willing, but her mother wouldn't let her come, you know. So I came back up here and I went back to working the same laundry I was working in then, and I keep in touch with her, and went back a couple of more times. And the third time I went back we eloped. I got married.

It was in June when the school closed. She told me, she said, "Moses, I tell you what you do. Now you come back here on the eighteenth of June. That's about the only chance I'll have of getting away," because, you see, they lived way out there in the country, you know, and the mother watched every chance she could get, you know. She said, "I will let Jean bring me to commencement. And then I'll get dressed and we'll go off and get married." So then I did that. On the eighteenth of June, I got things all packed, bought me a nice car. My mother helped me to find a pretty looking outfit.

Her mother said, "Where you going Hazel?" She said, "I ain't going nowhere. I got to go to commencement, don't I?" Her mother said, "Yeh, but how come you getting dressed up so much?" Hazel said, "I supposed to look real nice at commencement." So that night my brother Jean brought her to Kingsley, and we went about 23 miles to a place they call Florence, South Carolina, and we got married. And, oh, did her mother raise hell the next morning. She said, "That nigger come all the way from New Jersey to take my daughter. Now what you going to do?" She said, "Where's your license?" She thought we didn't have no license. So Hazel showed her mother the license. My mother was there too, and she said to Hazel's mother, "Tell me, why you going to raise all this Cain for, you know you don't mean that." "I don't want my daughter to go up the road," says Hazel's mother.

So I speak up. "Well, if you don't want her to go up the road, you can keep her here." She said, "What am I going to keep her here for? And you done keep her out all night." I said, "Well, God bless her," I said, "I'm going to keep her out all these nights." She said, "Well, okay." And her grandmother came up, she had a hell-raising grandmother. I used to wonder about these old people, you know. They always were signifying, you know; she's a signifier, like trying to make out the future. She said, "I know this man got a wife up the road, and he don't mean no one woman no good. He ain't nothing but a _____." You know what she said. I said, "Well, after all; this is my wife here. I have no other wife." I said, "If I had another wife, I wouldn't even have her. I wouldn't come down here for her." So my mother said to Hazel's mother, "No, Camille, Sonny ain't that kind of a man. I know him. He ain't never been married. And never was until he got married last night to Hazel. See, I know everything." She said, "Buddy, (that was what she called my uncle Moses, the minister) he calls up and tells me everything Moses does up the road. He's a straight, fine fellow," she said. "I'll tell you one thing, if your son was like him, you wouldn't have nothing to worry about."

Then she shut up, my mother, so my mother-in-law, before we leave, she said, "Now Sonny, I'll tell you, you know what I was raising all this Cain yesterday, I didn't know what I was doing, but now I think I was kind of high-handed over those kind of things. And everything is all right and any time you want to come back here, you come back." And they made me welcome and everything. Then just before I took sick, my mother-in-law, she's still living, you see, she's a very nice woman, too, she came up to see me when I was in the hospital, you know, to rub my head and all, to make me feel like I was in the family.

When my father passed, he leave me a pretty good little penny. My mother and I loaned money every once in awhile to get the farm straightened out. She still is doing things. My father-in-law died, but she married again, an old creature. He ain't doing nothing but sleep. So now she's doing all right. And I'm doing all right. So I mean, as far as me having a hard time, my biggest trouble was trying to help my mother. And before my father had to go away, she was the kind of wife, she had never had nothing to worry about. She didn't have any experience about anything, so I needed to help her.

I'll tell you how I feel about getting old. I don't take care of nobody's business. I try to do everything I can to make the neighborhood a better place to live. Everybody who needs help, I try to help them if I can, but some of these people don't appreciate it. But I just do what I can. I don't feel comfortable about growing old in Newark, so I'm going back South. Yes, I'm going back, when I get well. The wife and I were talking about it last night. I have a couple of houses down there now, but I'm going down and build a nice little brick home on my place down there. And when the wife retires, she'll retire in about two years, then we're going back down to live.

I want to get down there. You see, my mother and father, they all are dead and buried down there, and if I go, I want to go down there where I was born and raised, to see the church they's built on my place down there. It's the Baptish church. It's like the one up here. They names it Hickory Oak Baptish Church, and Clapham, the name is right on the cornerstone of the church. So I mean, that's where everybody knows me to be a decent kind of a fellow, and that's where I want to die.

I have friends, quite a few. Even from South Carolina, white people, they come up here. They come up here and they stay right here in my house, sleep in my bed, eat off my table, treat me good when I go down there. William Baker, he's a white man, he say, "Mr. Clapham, come back, stop by my house. I got something for you, because I told my wife how you and Eva treat me when I was up the road." They came up here and spent the night with us. So when we got ready to go, we stop by George over in Kingsley. He says, "Come right in, Mr. Clapham." Any of the other colored people got to go around to the back, you know, but he asked us in the front. We go in the front and sit down and we tell his wife how we treated him up here—what a time we had. And nobody in the world would never know that he had been a white man or a colored.

He was on the highway patrol. He said, "Well, Moses, do you still drink?" And I said, "Well, a little." He said, "What do you drink? Corn?" I said, "Well, I'd like to have a little corn." He said, "I'll tell you what I'll do," he says, "I'm going to Kingsley, but on my way back I'll bring you back a jar of good corn whiskey, being that I take home a nigger last week." So sure enough he go there and on his way back he got this whiskey out at his friend's and said, "When Moses come along, give him this. That's about the best corn whiskey there is."

I feel it is safer in the South because there is a lot of crime in the street in cities like Newark. You see, when I go down in South Carolina, I got a farm way back out, about 13 miles from Kingsley, 12 miles from Hemingway, way back out in the country, I mean way back out in the country. It's sleepy. You go out there, and there's nothing but trees and a house here and one there. And you go about three or four miles and you see a store. Somebody's house or store. And I think it is safer out there.

The crime doesn't bother me much. I used to be a rough boy, myself. Don't get me wrong. I mean, I had my experience about life. I've given that up now, and I don't want any more of this rough life. I told my wife last night, "I think we had better go back home. She said, "Why?" I told her. When she came up here, she didn't want to live up here, but now she likes it, now she doesn't want to go back. I told her, "I'm going to take you back home and put you on the farm, you know." I like Newark, I love it, it's the only home I know. Newark and Summit, but like I said, when I get ready to settle down because I'm not working anymore, I think if I go down South and get out in the country where I can get all the nice fresh air, all I want, I think it will add a couple of years to my life.

I don't like the way they are tearing up Newark—you know, you see the houses all torn down. That is rough. I don't like that at all. Newark is going to be a big old country pasture, pretty soon, if they keep this up. I think they are trying to get a lot of colored people out of Newark. I mean the white people are moving out. They are building up those apartment houses, packing them all into one, all the colored people into one. All into those tall buildings. I don't like that. Sometimes I say to myself, "What they going to do? Maybe they are going to pack all the colored people in these apartments, and put a torch to them and burn it all up. Burn the lot of them up. But I don't really think it will happen like that. But it has really divided the black neighborhoods, the way the city has been torn up. Where do these people all go? I really don't know. Some of them go packing into these apartments, and some of them go into the country, if they can afford it.

You take some of these people in this neighborhood right here. They are on the welfare, and they shouldn't be because they're working themselves. They got men laying in the house there, sleeping, like husbands, and some of them are working, and the state is giving them a nice check.

Of course a lot of people really do need help, and it's right for the state to help them, especially the type of assistance that old people get. They need to build more old folks' homes and get some of these old people off the street. For example, take that old lady out there. She needs to be in some place where somebody can take care of her. But she's right out there on the street and all messed up around her legs. She can't even take care of herself. She needs help. She needs somebody to look out for her. The state should have somebody come over there to her house at least, to take care of her, clean her up a little, and give her something to eat, talk to her and comb her hair. And wash her clothes and, you know, get her straightened out. It's ridiculous that she's left all alone. She needs help very, very bad. They have these senior citizens homes, but she just don't want to go into one. She owns her own home and she wants to die right here. When her husband died, she used to go to church every morning, every morning. But for the last year, since I came back from the hospital, she's lost interest. She can't hardly walk and she just sitting out there, with that big old dog.

You don't see too many in her position, but the government doesn't give them any help. I'll tell you that. She's a well-to-do woman. She don't need financial help, but she needs somebody to talk to and tell her these things. She's just let herself go to pieces.

Sometimes I think about my future. I think sometimes I should open up a nice business here. But I say, I'm too old now to start off. And you can't get nobody to trust no more, you know. All the people, they try to take advantage of you just because you are up in age. My nephew, for example, he said, "Moses, what are you going to do?" I say, "I'm going home as soon as I get straightened out." He says, "I'll tell you. Why don't you get a nice place here and let me run it for you?" I said, "What are you going to run it for?" He said, "Well, I got my band. I could play music. I could do this." I said, "Well, God bless you. Why don't you open up a place yourself? I'll back you." He said, "Yeh, but I don't want to be responsible for nothing." I said, "How come you want me to be up in the front of it?" He's a nice young fellow. He teaches school up here. But he wants me to go and spend my money and be a front man, and then he'll go ahead and do what he wants to do and he has no responsibility. So, you see, if I open up a business here, I want to see what's going on, you know what I mean.

I never bought any property here in Newark because I always had a place down home. And I always had my mind on going back home. And I just didn't get to the place yet where I was up to going back, that's all. But during my forty years here in Newark, I always had it in my mind to go back. Now, the preacher in this church, in Kingsley I told you about, on my place down there, he wrote me a letter last week, tell me he's building a kitchen on the church and he want me to give him sentiment for my uncle, so I sent him $50. I always had my mind on living in Carolina. I don't know why. It's just in me, I guess. I am just a home-loving man.

If I had my life to live over, what would I change about it? Well, I'd rather be down home. I'd rather be in Carolina, although you have a tough time down there. As a matter of fact I wouldn't have left Carolina if people had treated me with respect down there. If they didn't put on me what they put on my father. You see that mason banner on the wall. That's from my father. That's what got him from being lynched. There were a lot of people wanted to lynch him in Carolina, when he killed this man. The man he killed was a well-thought of white man down there. And they give my father a lifetime on the chain gang, and they kept him on it for about five days, and because he was such a good man, they said, "Well, we can't keep Sam in a hell like this." So the fact was they let him go and told me to keep this the rest of my life.

There's something else I got here. You see this pistol. It's what he shot this man with. I got that and I'll keep if for the rest of my life.

John Scott

I've been here ever since 1914. I come from Panama City in Florida. The 20th of September I'll be 73. I was just a young man when I came here. I was married down there, in 1913. I come to Newark in 1914. I moved here, had a push cart when I came here as a young man. Well, things was bad in Florida, and a lot of folks were coming up so I just thought I would come up too. I had never thought of Newark. I didn't have any family here at all. I can't really say why it was Newark rather than some other place. It was just one of those things. A lot of folks were leaving for Newark, New Jersey, so I just came along too. Those were hard times too.

Before I came here I was in the express business, hauling people, moving people. I was a young man. I worked for Dr. Lee for a long time. I see'd how I made a living for him, and I figured I would make it for myself. It was my own business, not his. I borrowed money to buy a hacking wagon in Florida. I used to meet the trains and carry people around.

I didn't go to school in Florida. I went to school in Alabama. I run away when I was 14 years. I didn't finish up school. I got through the seventh grade. I was born in Alabama. I went to Florida with a doctor. I stayed with him I don't know how many years. I was working for eight dollars a week, room and board. That was what I was working for. Carrying him around to see patients. I never did like the work. I was lazy. I always liked an easy job. I worked with the deputy sheriff. I drove him around when he went to arrest somebody. And many a time, he would go to somebody's house and he would throw the gun on the man and I would put the handcuffs on him. I put handcuffs on many a man in Florida. But I thought I had to do it. He was paying me, you know what I mean. You working for somebody, you got to do what he say.

After I ran away from home, I heard from my family all the time. I got a sister here in Newark. They knew where I was all along. In case something happens, I always did let people know where I was at.

When I got to Newark I got a job at the Ward Bakery Company. Guess how much money I had when I came here? Forty cents! How I got the job was this way. I said to a fellow, "I don't know how I am going to stay tonight. I ain't got but forty cents." He said, "Maybe I can get you a room where I'm living." And he got me a room and board. Room and board was six dollars a week. I didn't get but $12 a week at the bakery. I was a sweeper at the bakery, push a broom.

After the bakery, I got a job at Butterworth and Judson, testing acid. I kept that job a long time. I got that job by going out there looking for a job. I just went out there. I tested the acid by putting a little in a glass, and you got a thermometer, go down in it and see what grade it is. A lot of people who worked there turned yellow but not in the place where I worked. It was the sulphur. In other words, part of the work there would turn you yellow. But if you were where I was in it didn't. Those people who worked with the sulphur, they came from Alabama and Georgia, all over the South country. People came here at that time, they came in box cars. They shipped them up here. I heard they mostly come from Alabama, different towns.

I talked to them. Times were kind of hard when I first come here. Anybody who wanted a job could get a job, but they didn't pay nothing. They were just odd jobs. Jobs were really cheap at that time. That was during World War I.

I was never in the army. They ain't done nothing for me, why should I go in the army. I got a doctor keep me from getting in the army. Doctor Gordon, he was the doctor kept me from getting in the army. I forgot what I give him.

After I left the acid place, I worked at Crucible Steel. It's a place in Harrison. I worked there a long time. Worked behind the machine. They held a piece of steel about this long. After you got through working it, see, it went almost across the street. I was working in the hot mill. You didn't need any training for it. You just started on the job and that's how you learned how to do it. There was never any union there. I never heard of a union.

At that time, you could count the cars in Newark. There were hardly no cars in Newark. The job at Crucible wasn't the last job I had. I can't count the jobs I had. Mostly I was a night watchman, worked in garages. That was the most jobs. Night watchman, I did that for the Pontiac people and the

Nash people. I love to work nights. The reason I work nights is I don't like bosses. In the night you work to suit yourself. I worked from 1914 to 1956 and then I retired. I quit work in 1956. I didn't want to work till I go to the graveyard.

Since I been retired I been doing what I'm doing now, sitting. I get plenty of amusement. I know a lot of people. I look at television. I am just as happy as an old man can be, if he isn't sick. I get out of here, 9 o'clock. 10 o'clock, 11 o'clock, or 12 o'clock.

I never had a serious illness. I lost my wife in 1955, and then I got married again, like a fool. I stayed with her seven years, lost the shirt off my back. I was her third hushand. She divorced me, the other, Mr. Banks, he died.

My major source of income since I retired is Social Security. I get $176 a month. I don't have welfare, there's no welfare about it! I haven't taken any welfare since I was born. And I never will. What have I been doing all these years to go to them now they give me something to eat?

This is the only house that I now own. I sold two before my wife Julia died. I had more money in the house over on Bergen Street than I got in this one. I put a lot of money in that house over there. I got three floors in this house. Six rooms on the first, and ten rooms on the other two floors. I rent those two floors out. I gets $106 on the second floor and I get $110 from the other. That's pretty low rent today for all those rooms. The way I figure it is this. There are a lot of poor people, they ain't got nothing. I don't feel like just getting blood from a person because times is bad. I know I don't get enough money. People sometimes ask me, how did I manage to save up enough money to go into buying a house. If two people pull together, they can do a lot of things, if you got a good wife. Me and Julia bought these houses through the city for back taxes. You got them cheaper that way. So, me and my wife lived down here. When this house was bought, there wasn't no electric light or steam in here. We lived down here on this floor until we put steam on one floor at a time, till we finally put steam in the whole house.

I spend a lot of time at church. Every Sunday I go to church, unless I'm sick. If I leave for Florida, I leave on Friday so I can go to somebody's church in Tampa, Florida, on Sunday. I still go back and forth to Florida. I was back there in June. But I never think of moving back down there. See, I go to Dade City. My father-in-law lived in Dade City and when he died, he left us seven or eight acres of orange grove down there. And he willed that property to Julia. He willed this here farm to Julia, my wife, but when her mother dies, I get the property. I having trouble with that property down there now as far as getting somebody to look after it.

I look after this house. All I got to do is collect and rent, and take care of small things, unless there is something I can't do.

My first wife, Julia, was the third hair dresser in this town. She opened up a beauty parlor in 1916 at 319 Bank Street, right across from that drug store.

It's a shame the way they're tearing down Newark and ain't building. But it seems like I was talking to a fellow today. He come from Baltimore. Says they're doing it all over down there. I think this is aimed at the black community. I believe that is what it is. Don't you? I could be wrong, but it is a shame.

I hate to see a lot of things. Number one, you can't walk the streets safe today. That's bad. A white woman was robbed right here where I used to be. Two colored boys robbed her. I was the first colored person who lived in this block. I been here for 47 or 48 years, I don't know exactly which. I'm scared. I don't go nowhere without a gun. And I know that I ain't look for trouble. I don't go nowhere at night, except to my church. I didn't know in the old days what it was to lock the cellar door. But now it's just one big thing. People today, if they leave home for something, they don't know how they are going to find their home when they get back. It's just that bad.

There have been times I was so poor that I have walked into Harrison and different places, but I wouldn't think about saying I've got no money. I went up the welfare office last month. They wrote me a letter. Two or three people said, "Mr. Scott, you getting on welfare?" And I said, "No, and I hope I never will!" I been in this world a long time. What I been doing with my money all these years? And I ain't got no money to pay rent? And I got nothing to eat? What I been doing all these years? I ain't got a child in the world. And my health has been good. There ain't nobody but a fool going to work and throw away all his money.

There is something wrong with welfare. Listen, it's killing the country. I would declare it out today. There's young girls hardly twenty years old getting it today. Why don't they get a job? If old folks has to have it, then that's all right. I know that I never went there for nothing. The welfare is all right, but a lot of people are taking advantage of welfare. They don't want to work. A lot of young people are like that. They wouldn't work. Now I got to kiss somebody to get them to shovel snow here in the winter time. I asked a boy one time, I said, "Hey, I ain't got much snow. Sweep the stoop down." He said, "Mister, I don't sweep snow." I asked another boy, and he said, "Let me have fifty cents." I say, "I ain't going to give you a dime." I was painting that stoop out there last summer. I said to a young boy, "Go and bring me five White Owls." Then I heard him say to his friend, "I ain't going to bring him no cigars back." I said, "Bring my money back here, bring it back. I mean it, because if you don't you're going to get this paint brush right in your face." And I meant it too. I would have throwed it in his face. Before he got out of sight! "I ain't going to bring no cigars back. We going to keep this money!" Give him a dollar to bring me five cigars.

These young people mostly attack those that look old, like me. Those are the ones they beat up. Those young kids go looking for old people like me. I came from the bank recently. I went to the bank to cash my check because I wanted to pay the oil man some money, somebody else some money. A young man met me down the street. He says, "I just came from the Metropolitan." He said, "The Metropolitan just gave me $14,000." I said,

"Liar, you get out of my way." He said, "I'm from Virginia. My boss told me that you couldn't put money in the bank up here." He says, "You go home and show me three or four bank books. I give you a thousand dollars." I said, "Nigger. You go on get out of here. I'm gonna knock you in the mouth." You see, they're doing all the old confidence tricks to get something. He said, "You go in your house and show me three or four bank books. I'll know what bank you put your money in and I'll put this $14,000 in." I said, "They wouldn't give you, you fool, no $14,000 in cash." He said, "My brother got the check." I said, "They'd give you so much of that money now and the money would be put in the bank so many days before you could take it." I said, "Where you get that tune? You better get out of here before I call the law."

I like Newark, but I should have done left Newark years ago. Hard breaks as I've had, I ain't had it that bad in Newark. The only thing is I just lost my wife. I think that I have been very successful in Newark. I come here barefooted and I was able to get me a suit of clothes and buy shoes in Newark, and in other words I haven't done too bad since I been in Newark. Old man that I am, I consider myself doing good.

I had a source of inspiration, because a lot of black people didn't make it, you know. They just couldn't pull themselves up, sometimes. I'll give you an example. I told a fellow two weeks ago at the tavern, he came in there with two ladies, I said, "Lewis, I see one of your little girls yesterday and she needed shoes." I said, "You should go on home with your money." He said, "Mr. Scott, tend your so-and-so business." And Monday morning he hit the window and come in and said he didn't have money to go to Linden to go to his job. I said, "You cussed me the other day because I told you about going home and buying your kids things they need." I said, "I don't have a child in the world. I can go up there and spend five dollars in that gin mill with them girls easier than you could. And now you come here to get money to go to Linden." And he showed me a slip where he drawed $112 and come here Monday morning to go to work! I wouldn't give him nothing. He snapped me up and cursed me. His child was barefooted.

They ought to get a bank book before they gets the kids. That's what a woman told me in Florida. She said, "Mr. Scott, before you start a family, get you a bank book." So I told Julia, "Well, I don't want but two children. I ain't going to work hard to educate a lot of children. I don't want but two." She said, "Mr. Scott, I'm sorry but I can't have children." If my wife hadn't had anything, I would have quit her then when she told me that. I wanted children. My wife had her own home in Panama City. And I didn't have nothing. I just did have enough money to get the license.

A lot of we old people ain't going to have nothing nohow. I know I ain't going out tomorrow or this evening and make myself short. I am going to buy what I have to buy. I ain't going to run short. I am going to make it last till the first of the month. I know I'm supposed to get rent the first of the month. And I am supposed to get a check from Social Security on the third.

And I limit myself, I'm going to make it to the first of the month. I think you're living on the fat of the land to get a check from the welfare. I think that if you spend it right, you will have enough. Sometimes there is a lot of people don't know how to spend that money when they get it.

When I quit my second wife, I owed $986 oil and service. I owed that much on oil. I figured that Bea was paying that but she didn't. When I see'd that bill, I like take my heart attack. I gave the man $150, $100 a month, till I knocked that on the head.

There's so many of them who are on welfare, the welfare people can't do just what they want to do. Now I know that might be a big word to say, but I hope that the Lord never let Mr. Scott go down there to get nothing. I been in the world long enough, I know long as I am going to live, I know I ain't going to welfare for nothing. That ain't no big word for me to say. I know what my condition is, I know if I get sick, I have Social Security and Medicare.

But one thing does bother me. I told Mr. Jagger yesterday, I said, "I hope that if I have to die, I hope that I won't be around here two or three days before anybody knows." Mr. Jagger said, "You won't be down there two days without me knowing." Mr. Jagger is my next-door neighbor. If he don't see me today, or the day is gone or it get too late, he is going to come over and knock on the window to see if I'm home.

I know that I ain't going to get no insurance, I'm too old. I know that I'm not going to get rich. Some folks got money, just to set down and squeeze it. But I don't want to buy nothing. I don't care if I wouldn't leave a nickel at the end of things.

Another thing that bother me is I got a family up on the second floor here. He ain't no good. I want to see him out of my house so badly. He got children and it looks like he is going to kick them out. He just ain't no good. I tells him, "Why don't you lay down so much money each week for the rent so that you can give me all the rent you owe me?" He must be around fifty years old. There is some people old as me aren't never going to be nothing. You can't tell them nothing. Some of these people take advantage of you in this building because they don't pay the rent when they should. I bet you I would get them out of here quick if I could. There's nobody give me this shack here. A lot of these people think I got money. "You crying, Mr. Scott, you got money. Mrs. Scott left you money." Even if she left me money, you got to know how to spend your money. You don't know when you are going to get sick. You don't know how things are going to work out in life. I was able to dress myself this morning. I don't know whether I am going to be able to undress myself or not. I went to a funeral on Monday, widow I knew in the church. She had a blackout in the church.

My wife, Julia, says to me, at 100 Lark Street, "It's tough. You got to make it and you will make it." She says, "I'm going to buy what I have to buy. I ain't going to do nothing like a lot of other women do. Even if I see a person with something nice on today, I only going to buy what I have to have." She said, "Guess I will save to buy a house now." And when she said that, I cut out on spending, going where I used to go, you know what I mean. That's a good thought. When we got the first $500 saved we looked at a house on Howard Street. But I give Julia all the credit for telling me that. I used to go out, play pool at night, Saturday night maybe we would put a quarter or fifty cents on something. When Julia told me about saving some money to buy a house, you know, I went to pulling her way, I thank her for it. When you get sick and down, it's nice if you got a sister across the street, or cousin across the street, but it's nice if you can balance the scale with money and you don't have to ask nobody for anything. That's nice. I'm telling you the truth now.

I don't say that I had no hardships. But I had a wife who knew how to spend money. Number one that meant something. But there were times when I made but $3 a day and even if food and everything was cheap at that time, I wasn't paid but $15 a week. If I lost a job, I didn't have to go out and do the hardest jobs, like working with a pick and shovel. I went out one time in Irvington. They didn't have steam shovels at that time. The man had a lot of picks out there. "Get you a pick, big boy." I caught the same bus and came back home. And I had been without a job a long time.

That's when I went into business. Julia give me the money one time to go and pay the money note on the house on Richmond Street. A fellow had a truck to sell on South Orange Avenue, and I take Charley Gordon over there to get this truck. The fellow said to me, "You sell this truck for me, Mr. Scott, and I give you $10." I give Charley Gordon $40 and he paid $60 for the truck. Then I said, "Now give me $10 for selling the truck for you." I'm buying the truck but he didn't know it. He said, "Mr. Scott, you didn't sell the truck." I said, "If you don't give me $10 I ain't going to let him buy it." I said, "You told me that if I can get somebody to buy the truck, you give me $10." And I told Julia when I came back. I said, "Julia, I lost that money." She said, "How could you lose my money?" I said, "I didn't lose your money. I lost our money." I was about five weeks paying that note off. I got tired working for the boss down on 4th Street and got a license. I had nothing to put on the truck, so I went to the ice house and said, "Let me have six blocks of ice on credit." And then I sold ice, I sold wood. I used to be out selling to twelve or one o'clock at night. I would go out early in the morning, selling. You know that you make up your mind to do something, you can do it. That was kind of hard, but that wasn't too hard, as long as I could keep something in the ice box. We didn't have frigidaires at that time. You would put a newspaper on that ice and roll it up. So if you struggle you can make it. You're going to have misunderstandings, but if you got a good wife, you can get places.

When I look back on my life, I feel that I did the best I could do with it. I done the best I could do. The source of my inspiration these days, what keeps me going is trusting that man up there. I get down on my knees every night, like He said to. That prayer that you used to say in the same church.

We didn't have no seats in the church. If you trust that man up there, He will open doors for you. I know that some people is going to get so high when they get a bank book, so somehow that they can't talk to Him. I am going to live the best way. I decided that a long time ago.

Panama

Well, I was born in the West Indies, and I traveled ten years at sea. And then I spent some years of my life in Panama and come on here. I helped to dig the Panama Canal. And then I come on here. And from the time I come on here I been doing the dirtiest kind of work. When I come on here, no black people up in Harlem were allowed except in certain places. And many of the black people were down in Cherry Street, Montgomery Street, then they moved up to Railroad Avenue and people beat them up. That's where the black people used to live, where the train came on one side. Sometime when the train came, it used to set the place on fire. So that when people talk about Georgia seems we had a rougher time than in Georgia.

When I come here, I went for a job. I was an engineer when I came here. I used to run a tugboat, but first I used to run a dredging engine in Panama. And when I came here I went there to the employment office they had there on 14th Street. And when they go to call for an engineer, I went up and the man told me, "We don't want no porter here. We don't want no porter here. And then I said, "I'm not a porter, I'm an engineer." He said, "Well, all right, I didn't know that they had colored engineers nowhere here." Then I said that I was an engineer in Panama and then he said, "Oh, you're a foreigner." He said, "Where did you learn the trade?" I said, "Down in South America." And then he said, "Well, open up the engine." They had everything locked up for a test. And I opened up the engine and I put her to work. And I tested the valves, and he said, "I've never seen no one test an engine like that yet." I said, "Well, the engine is going and it started and the cylinder turning over, I timed her when the crankshaft was coming up and I timed her and I tried her." And then he saw that I timed her and she was running half speed, he said, "That's an engineer." So then when I was done, he said, "I'm not the man to hire you. I am only the superintendent. The supervisor is the one who has to hire you, Mister." When the supervisor come, the first man, he says, "Do you see the engine going? That young fellow has got it going, half speed and full speed." The supervisor said, "Mister, I will tell you. I must tell you the truth. If you wasn't a black fellow, if you were a white fellow, then you would have a job all your life here. But since you're a black fellow, I can't keep you here." I worked half a day there, and he gave me two days pay. He give me soap for washing the hands and he says, "Here's fifty cents for lunch." At that time fifty cents would buy a lot of food. He give me fifty cents for lunch and he give me two days pay. And he give me a recommendation. And he said, "If you weren't a black man you would have the job all the days of your life."

So then I get a job at a corner house at 93rd Street and Riverside Drive, as a handyman. Look after everything, little electric work, a little a-this and a little a-that. No, no, if you were a black man, you couldn't get a job as an engineer in this place here. You want them to kill you? For engineer, they were paying an engineer $35 a week. But you want them to kill you? That was a white-man job. Do you think that you could go near an electrician's shop? Do you think that you could go near a bricklayer's job? They kill you. Those were white man's jobs.

This here place was worse than Georgia. Man, you couldn't walk on the East Side and on the West Side. This over here was the Italian quarter. And the Spanish couldn't come over here when the Italians and Jews were here. They used to pay me every two weeks as a handyman. I got $35 for a half a month. So I got $70 a month. That was in 1912.

I was here in 1912, then I go back and then I came back here in 1914. And I stayed here from 1914 on. All the time people talking about how bad Georgia was. Georgia wasn't as bad as here. I was in Georgia then. For the black, it was more friendly in Georgia than here, because of the competition for jobs here. There was no competition in Georgia. The Georgia white man tell you what to do and you do it his way. And they were learning you and you didn't know it. But in New York they put you up against the white people and, you see, that's the difference. Georgia learned you how to do a job. The white man says, "Go over there, I don't want your job. I don't want no competition with you." But here in New York, the white man put you up against the wall. Up here you couldn't learn a job because no one would teach you. That's the trouble with people here.

And when the little black children had to go to school, and when they are coming home from school, they had to fight their way. The black children did. And they would get a bloody nose. I heard one time when a child said to his father, "Oh, my father, I don't want to go to school. The white children will beat me up."

When the First World War came, I go over to the court house. In 1917 they didn't take Negroes into the service in the beginning. We made them soldier us. We started work as sentries in the country. We now call them country guard. And we worked in the country and so got drill training and so they give us a dollar a day. Well, all right, when there are about fifteen thousand of us, the United States went to war. And when they get twenty-five thousand black soldiers, they sent them out to France. But when they send us, Wilson said, "You are going to save your country." He said, "I don't want to make the Negro go across the sea." And the Negroes say why. "We don't put them across the sea because when they come back, those niggers, who going to disarm them?" Some of them went across the sea. When they went, they put on them long swords on their rifles to charge and kill. But the foreign soldiers, they said, "We are foreigners. We are English. And French. We ain't so damn stupid to go up to the Boche." And the

Senegalese, they said, "We were killed by the British and we will learn to kill from the British. And we fought by the British." And the black man said, "We can do more than them people can do." He said, "We can go up to the line of Marny and turn back the German." He said, "We are going to see whether the Negro and the Senegalese aren't better than the Irish, French or British soldier." And they put in the 15th and the 15th was spent up there and damn, if they didn't turn back the German flank. Then when the Senegalese came, the flank was already turned.

And when they came back to New York, the President said, "You see, I told you." The black soldier said, "Take your foot off the black people here." So you see now, President Wilson, he didn't want that at all. He was just like Washington. Keep them in their place. Just use them for a tool. When they are armed, then who will come to disarm them. So after they come back, the soldiers started to raise hell. They went to Washington. What did they do there? They turned the water hose on them, that's what they did. On white and colored soldiers both! They went to Washington to get some money because their wives were in distress and they needed the money, and Hoover told them to turn the gun on them, turn the water hose on them. I know they nearly drowned them.

During the First World War, they drafted me to a place. I was making wooden steamships. Can you believe that? I was making wooden steamships. The first country ever to use wooden steamships in a war. You have to go up there to see them, see all them black things, them black scars there, those steamships, they're wooden. They were in a hurry and they built wooden steamships. Some of them just split in two. I worked on that job during the duration of the First World War. We started in 1916 to get the pier built and to get them wooden steamships built and we worked on them from 1917. We had Hog Island, and we had Cornwall making wooden steamships. And we worked from 1917 to 1918. We worked from 1916 on the pier and starting to get all the lumber and all that to make the ship. And in 1917 we put out all the boats, twenty-five of them, new wooden ships, steamships, and we were putting them out as fast as we could until the war finished. And then we start to pull them up and tie them up here.

After the war was finished, I did many types of jobs. The government discharged everybody. There was only one yard still building steamships and that was Port Newark. That yard was building ships, like the government yard over in Brooklyn. And they started, they begin to open up yards here.

The government didn't try to help you after the war. How was the government going to help you? The government didn't have no jobs for nobody. After that there was a break, a depression, because the country was so down that there was a break. They wanted the black man to go and leave off their tools. They want us to leave off this nice lathe and go down and pick apples on the farm.

During World War I, they was paying $125 a week. And up to $35 a day. When I was working in the shipyards, I seen more money in 1917 than I seen in the last World War, because I used to get $1.35 an hour in World War I. We worked all the time we could work. The regular shift was nine hours, but see, we worked nine hours extra. They didn't take any taxes out. Sometimes we carried home $200 a week, man. We made time-and-a-half on weekdays, and we got triple time holidays and triple time for Sundays. And a loaf of bread at that time was five cents. You could go into a restaurant, Mister, you could go to the beer garden—and put up one poor nickel and you get a mug of beer ten inches high. And there was plenty of food at the table. And they had everything, a ham, potato chips, and everything that you can eat or drink. And rent wasn't high. You could get a seven-room apartment for $35 a month, a real nice apartment, or four rooms for $25, for $20.

When I left the government work, I went to work in the shipyards as a caulker. We went from boat to boat, from yard to yard. I made $1.35 an hour. I did that type of work for about six or seven years. After that, when this crash come down in 1929, and people was out of work, then people made their homes out of cardboard. I couldn't get no jobs during that time. I don't know how we survived until Roosevelt came. After that they helped you. I was an electrician then and I could not get no electrician work when I went to the shipyards. When the Harlem Trade School opened up, I went there to get a job as a learner. I go there to get experience. When I went into Harlem Trade School in 1940, when I first go there, there was no colored boy there. In that school they were all whites. The instructors liked me. We were foreign boys, and the white boys did not work very hard, and they get to like us because he was a foreign teacher so we get along with them. And they continued to do so until we get all the white boys out of that school up there.

Now, man, I'm too old to work. I'm much too old to work. I was telling you that in World War II I was working as an electrician at Sullivan Yard, and at Atlantic Basin. We didn't have that during the First World War, because there wasn't enough electricity. A man used to go around with a ladder and light the lamp when I was young. He lighted the lamp in the park, and when the wind come the lamp would go out.

During the Great Depression, they had the NAACP, they had the Cotton Club, and they had the Workers Alliance. And they raised so much Cain that that's why they bring the WPA on. And they started in 1933. I was working for the school, for the Board of Education, as an electrician. We was remodeling, taking out the old lines and putting in pipes, the new pipes, and running the conduits through them.

I got hurt working during the last world war here. In Port Newark. They was building a ship out there, PT boats. I fell when one beam cut away. A beam cut away and it caught ahold of this foot here to keep me swinging until they rescued me. But they cut a part of my foot off. I was out for about six months. I got some compensation, yes, that one time, but the last time I get injured, I didn't get no compensation. I got an injury at

Atlantic Basin. I was outside measuring wire. We roll out the wire to measure it and right here something cut me. And after it cut me, I was laid up and they brought a marine case and the marine robbed me of the case and I didn't get anything. Robbed me of the case, me and the next white fellow. And we were going to court, but they say that they can't go up against the navy. And I was laid up for more than six months. I went into the hospital and I had to pay. I had to pay a private doctor. It wasn't so expensive then. They treated me very good, better treatment than now, because at that time the doctors had to struggle, so they give you the best. There were so many doctors, even some of them were home relief doctors. There was welfare doctors. When they had this WPA, doctors and lawyers were on home relief too.

Now I receive Medicare and I get Medicaid too because when I worked I didn't get so much big pay, because the pay they were giving in World War II was less pay in the shipyard than during the First World War. During the First World War we were getting $1.25. They didn't have no CIO. CIO was just coming in at the Second World War. And that's why I could advance more. And I had to wait until they had the WPA, because when you went to the AF of L they told you that they didn't have jobs and they wouldn't allow you to be a helper. All the helpers were white. I told the man at the union, "I'll give you a hundred dollars if you give me a job, a hundred and fifty dollars." I did that so that I might get experience for a carpenter's trade. And he said, "I wouldn't give you a break for a thousand dollars." You didn't get no break in those days. It was only when the Second World War come that all the electricians that come out of school got a break.

I don't know about the Medicare program. Sometimes it looks to me that it is very shaky, because sometimes the doctors say that they don't get no money. So if they don't get the money in time, some of them won't take you. Most of the doctors won't take you. I have had trouble with doctors refusing me as a result of Medicare. There's one up here. He's at 125th Street near Madison Avenue. He don't take you. Another one over there on 132nd Street, he don't take you. At 129th Street, he don't take you. I just go somewhere else. I go to my own doctor and he charges ten dollars. The last time I pay, that one up there on 127th Street, I paid him for three treatments and he charged thirty dollars because he see that I couldn't get it at my doctor's. Then I go to Slayne, on 125th Street, he charges $15 and he don't take you if you are on Medicare or Welfare. He don't take you without you pay money, unless you are covered by insurance, that big insurance—what do they call it—in the paper all the time, Blue Cross and Blue Shield.

I receive Social Security and I receive a pension from the state. But I don't get much. I have trouble making ends meet on my pension, yes, everybody does. But if they help me, I am able to get along. The Social Service people send someone to help me. She comes here to work three half-days a week. I live alone here. The only income I receive is Social Security.

I speak Hebrew and I keep myself occupied studying Hebrew. I can speak it now and I can read it now. Our Black Temple is on Pennsylvania Avenue in Brooklyn, I have been studying the Hebrew language for many years. I take care of the house, cook my food and everything, to keep myself occupied. I don't have any relative in the city. Other people come and knock on the door, just for the hell of it, and then they run away. This place is mostly Spanish and I have more trouble with them. I have been living here ever since this was built, six years ago. It would be all right if the people didn't molest me so much. The apartments are all right. But they molest me so much, night and day. They are so evil, man, they steal from old people. And I have so much iron on the door outside. That's to prevent them from opening the door. Otherwise they would jimmy the door. That prevents them from jimmying the door. They have robbed me about three times this year. They come in there and they come in through the open window there. They didn't try to harm me but that was because I wasn't here. One time I was here and they tried to come up and in, and I rushed out the front door and called and they ran. I called the police, but they can't do nothing. They can't protect you. Man, all these young people, so many are addicts. You hear them all the time. All over this area, they are buying and selling dope. The place is rotten with it. Before this I lived in private houses, in tenement houses. I never lived in an apartment. This is the first time I lived in an apartment. I wish I didn't have to live here.

Willie Booth

I can't understand why you want to talk to me. Come all the way you come, for what? It puzzles me that you think I got something to tell you. I got a million stories I could tell. But you say you are interested in what I done, what kind of work and so. What jobs I had. So many they all run together in a way. In fact I remember better the things I did when I was young, maybe because some of them last longer, and maybe because I was young. You say start from the beginning, when I first began to work. Well you know, seems like there weren't any real beginning. I always work.

I was born up in the country, pine woods and some cotton land. My pappy he had some land. Don't know whether it was really his. Maybe he just work it. But that's what we all did. Up and down those red clay fields, day in, day out. Course it wasn't all work. We were just young folks then. Of course, we were supposed to go to school, down the road a way. But it weren't much of a school and no one seemed to care much whether I went or not. Leastwise my folks didn't cause I don't think they had much schooling at all. No one ever read anything that I can recall. We were that far from town. We didn't see things like magazines or newspapers to speak of. I remember, come to think of it, reading newspapers pasted on the wall to keep the wind out.

But of course that's all a long time ago and all I knows is that I could read some but that's about all that I learnt in school. Seems that after I got big and strong enough to work a man's work, there wasn't much sense in sitting in that tiny school with all them children, just to listen to them and the school teacher. I'm kind of sorry now that I didn't go to school longer, maybe it might have made a difference, maybe not. You know, that time, I guess I knew so little about what things were like beyond where we lived. Just the next town and not much about that. I just thought I would be what my pappy was, a farmer. Come to think of it, sometimes it seems to me that it wouldn't have been too bad, that is if I could've made a go of it. I sure wouldn't be where I am now, middle of nowhere, sitting on a stoop.

At least they, I mean my folks, they had some place and they had kinfolks all around. We really did have some good times, no matter how hard it was. I mean get-togethers and all that. And Sundays. We knew each other, knew what to expect, who was good and who was bad and who was in between. Where I guess most of us were. But your folks would tell you, I mean really tell you, if you been bad or mean. Young people, they knew that the older folks, not just your pappy or mammy, were watching them even when they weren't watching them. That sure is not what I see around here. Nobody watches anybody, it seems, but what it really is, the way I look at it, we older ones are just plumb scared to say anything. We've just been pushed aside I guess, and finally you get so you don't even care. I don't know why I talk so much about those long-gone times. Seems another world and sometimes it's hard to know what comes between.

Anyway, you know that there's no sense talking about being a cotton farmer in the South the way my pappy raise cotton. That's all over now. And all the time I was growing, things were getting worse. I grew up into what they call the Depression. I guess we just slid into it where we were. Hard times just came naturally, it seemed. Looking from today, don't know how we managed to get through those times. It was just scrounge and skimp all the time. After some years things got a little better, but those years, we all just got by, and my family, I mean my brothers and sisters, we just all flew away, got scattered all over so I hardly know where they are today, if they are still alive. Got some addresses somewhere but I moved so many times they sure don't know where I be and I suppose they done the same. It's not right not to know whether they alive or not. If they died, not to be at the funeral even.

But you want to know what work I do in those days. Seems like any kind of work, so long as it took someone young and strong. There was that kind of work always, seems to me. Not much maybe, so we all kind of took turns at it, or maybe scrapped for it. But we did have ways of making do. By that time I was gone from my pappy's place. Spent time in towns and cities, first of all in Augusta. Those were the days before the big war. And I remember that things got better when the war came near. Course there wasn't any factory work or work like that. Not then. It was outdoor work or maybe cleanup work. There was work like on the railroad or just the highway and there was the sawmill, if you were young and strong.

That was real work. I don't think young folks today know what real work is. I don't think I ever work so hard. Seems like I can still feel it somehow in my arms. You had to be careful but you had to be quick. And those saws, they like a wildcat ready to take a bite, if you not careful. I remember a belt once, it broke and whack the fellow next me across the shoulder and he never lift his arm again, just broke something inside, a nerve they say, and I use to see him, his arm hanging all dead and cold next him. Not much of a mark outside. We were young then, we didn't think much about things like that. Never get us, we say. We too smart but I guess a lot of us weren't so smart as we think.

Before the war, that's how I divide things. There were lots of jobs and lots of times with no jobs. We all together, we young fellows, all together so at least you stay alive. One fella just about bound to have a job and we all used to sharing. But of course there never was anything left over. It was day by day then. That's why, when the war came, I said this is for me. Now I can go someplace and maybe make something of myself. It was the army for me, right from the beginning. I heard about the navy. Everybody knew what the navy was. But the army, there was the recruiting office and it just seemed the thing to do. The army, that's what divided my life, you could say. Before and after. It seem to me that, before the war, I knew where I belonged, were I lived, who I see, what I supposed to do. After, I really never came home. I never know the country was so big, the world so big. Just think, a farm boy from Georgia and he's in the middle someplace of Europe. Just the ocean itself. We all thought it would never come to an end. Thousands of us down in the middle of that troop ship, all sick, and we keep on traveling and traveling. That was something to remember. The convoy all over the ocean and we all wondering when we going to be blow up. And none of us can swim either. We use to laugh about it.

The army was something. You mention training. Well, we got some training in making our bed and how to salute and hold your rifle. But you know what training I really got from the army? You're gonna laugh. I learned how to do laundry, yessir, that was my specialty, as the army calls it. I know the army had schools, schools for everything, and I would've liked to go to some of those schools, like auto mechanic or cooking. But instead I learned how to run the biggest machine I ever saw. It could wash all the dirty clothes of a whole battalion at once. We were called a Quartermaster Battalion, Laundry.

And we were all black with about five whites for officers, and a few others for sergeants. And we go overseas to wash the clothes of all those white soldiers with rifles and tanks and things, so they can be clean when they out fighting. Not that I can say I really minded that much. We all knew that we weren't there for fighting, until maybe just at the end. I heard that some boys did go into the infantry but it was nearly all over then. So while the fighting was going on like I say, I didn't mind it too much, except you knew that you were just loading and unloading and doing cleanup work for the white man's army. You run that laundry unit day and night sometime, till you can run it in your sleep. I should have gone into the laundry business, I knew that machine so well, but of course, I don't suppose that's the way they run a laundry in civilian life. But that's the only training I ever did get, so help me, in the whole time I was in the army. How to put up and knock down and load and unload that damn laundry unit.

But the hard part, really, if you come to think of it, it came after the fighting was all over and we settle down in Germany. Seems that when the soldiers start packing their bags to go home and so on, there wasn't much use for us anymore, so we hardly have to operate the laundry. They saving us for the Japanese they say. So there we all were, about a thousand or more, all stuck in the mud outside Nuremberg. All the white troops in nice houses all around the city and we laundrymen out there in a swamp they must have looked for so it could be wet all the time, in little tents that leak and mud all around so you never get dry and clean in a thousand years. So we go into Nuremberg, all blown up and ruined, but the Germans they like us. They like anybody with a candy bar or some cigarettes.

So there we are with German girls in our arms and those MPs just looking at us like they want to run us in. And there were fights and things, so finally the army decides that it is going to move us out of the mud, but they still don't want us near any city so they move us to a German army camp in the mountains, outside of the place where Hitler used to have his summer place. Me and my friends went up there to look at it, right at the top of a mountain it was. We stayed there awhile, but the officers, they were in town so we just laid around. I heard about them schools, but I didn't bother. Wouldn't have done any good anyway. We just waited to go to the Pacific.

Then it was all over and we came back the way we came and there I was in Norfolk, and they took us to a camp in New Jersey to get our discharge. Honorable discharge as quick as they could get us out. I never seen the army move so fast. Sign that, and there you were, ex-GI, battle ribbons and everything, still in uniform and some pay in your pocket. And friends saying, let's go to New York. I guess I never thought about going back to Georgia. I was on the move then. Like I said, it was after the war then and I thought I was a big man, been in Germany, crossed the ocean, ribbons on my uniform, here I come, New York.

Maybe I'm talking too much. You say if I am. I'm trying to tell you the jobs I've did, but they're mixed with other things too so it isn't easy just to say what I worked at, and I can't remember the one without the other. I don't often think about what I've done, where I've worked. Like I said, there's been so many places and things I've done, it sometimes seems all mixed up and I have to refresh my memory about the times and places. I remember sometimes, when I was looking for work and they asked where I had worked for the last twenty years or whatever, I would think, there isn't room to put it down and anyway, I can't keep it all straight with the years and so on that they ask for. That was when I was looking for work at big places and they had these employment people asking you questions and writing things down about you.

It's funny to think about just now. It's been just about 25 years since I come to New York, big and strong I was, all set to make it. Here it is 25 years gone by and this is how you see me now, broken down and sitting here on a stoop with my friends, and you wouldn't believe what I was like then. My arm was thick around like a big ham and I didn't know what it was like to be tired. People even said, why don't you try for to be a boxer, you got the body. But I knew that I was too old for that and besides I never did like fighting that much. Didn't even like to watch it on TV, people beating each other's brains out and getting all cut up.

There I am in New York, looking at all the big buildings and hearing my friends say that there's plenty of work and we can get ahead. Plenty of work and plenty of women. Just reach out and grab, and you can have it. Me 30 years old, and ready to take it all in. In those days, I never had to think about a job. I had lots of friends and I made a lot of friends. You just knew where there was work to be had. You never had to think about staying too long at a job. And it's a fact that I never did stay long for a particular job. Seems like there always came a time when I knew that a job wasn't taking me any place and I had some money in my pocket and the best thing was to take off for a while and look for something else. Course when I got married, I did stay longer at a job, but that didn't last. Just came apart and there I was with some furniture and some payments due and nothing to come home for. That's when I came over here to Newark. Seems like I had enough of New York, about 1955 I think that was. I had an army friend over in Newark and he said I could move in with him. So I thought I would just forget all that furniture and those payments and the whole business. That's when I think I began to lose touch with my kin.

Sometime it seem to me that it's been all down hill since I come to Newark. I think it's been a bad luck town for me, but I never seem to be able to get away because I didn't want to go back to New York and I didn't want to go back to Georgia. Couldn't do that. What I do at my age? Try to raise cotton? Knew I wouldn't be any use on the railroad or up in the sawmill country. So I just stayed here in Newark and took whatever come my way, whatever that might be and some of it mighty hard. It's funny, the older you get the harder the job is, because you can't pick and choose anymore. I did work that I can scarce believe I did. Lifting things, carrying things, clean-up jobs. I can tell you that I took what came. Some of those jobs weren't so bad. Maybe a clean-up job in a yard, but some, well they just about took everything I had. I can't complain, never did complain really because what's a man to do? But it was sure downhill for me, and it was move from one place to another and from one job to another.

The funny thing is, a man gets older without really knowing it. Doesn't really feel it until he just can't do his job anymore. You think you can, you can't. It's gone, won't come back. People who work with their head, maybe the head gets better when it gets older but you see me, you wouldn't think that I could lift almost anything in my day. What can I lift now? Sometime I think that even a bottle of beer is heavy. Oh, it comes to a man sudden. You're young, you're old, and that's it. And to tell the truth, maybe you should just die away. You're worn out, just like a car's worn out. No sense trying to repair it.

I'm not alone. Don't know how many there is of us, on this street, this city, but there's a number of us. We keep together some. In the summer, it's not so bad. We talk, maybe somebody got something to eat, to drink. Maybe we just talk. We're all the same, you understand. We move around some. I in this house for two years, but that's a long time. It isn't much and some houses they get torn down or burn down or just plumb give out. No heat, no water, no landlord. The junkies move in and then it's time to be finding another place. The whole Central Ward, I remember what it was when I come here, seems to me it's falling to pieces. Like Nuremberg, just like those German cities that the old U.S. Air Force knock to pieces. Would you believe it? A whole city that looks like it's been bombed out, and they told us that it was going to be all new, full of new houses and, what they call them, senior citizen houses. I got to laugh. Here I am, how old do you think? But I'm worn out and ten year or more will come before I can get into one of those places and then they won't let me in because others will be there first. So me and my friends, we have to look for what we can get and we move here and there so we hardly have a place we call our own, or anything to go with it. How can you, you can't keep anything in your room, not if the junkies know it.

People around here, they're scared of the junkies. Won't go out at night if they can help it. But we get along. They know we ain't got nothing except a few dollars every week or so, the welfare, so what I do, I let them have a dollar or so, and I spend the rest as quick I can, so they don't bother me at all. Sometime they even give me a bottle or two of beer if I got nothing. We live and let live, like they say. But I don't blame people when they are driving at night through these streets. These young folks can be mean, real mean, and they leave us be because they got other things to do.

You ask how I go about getting a job when I haven't got a job. The answer is I don't. That's past for me. Oh, I'd take a job if I could do it and someone come to give it me, but I wouldn't know where to go to get a job. The kind of things I used to do, seems like that's all dried up. I never was for jobs in factories, though I had some in my time. But everybody knows the factories is going. Was a time when I might have thought of the unemployment people, they had odd jobs and such, but I haven't heard about that lately and I don't know whether it's worth the trouble. There comes a time when you just don't feel up to looking for work anymore. I used to hear about jobs from my friends. They'd pass them along. But now most of my friends are gone and the ones left they haven't any more job than I. All my friends, we're in the same boat. I sometime think that folks my age, have a job, a house, they just don't want to be bothered with us. One thing I know for certain, the church they can't be bothered. They build those big new buildings but they don't want us in them.

We're supposed to stay right where we are. This stoop, this is where you'll find me and my friends. Come summer it's not so bad. I don't care to think about winter. But I suppose I won't be along for too many more. You ask me about what I going to do when I get old. Man, I'm old now and I don't expect to be much older. You ask if I have Social Security or veterans benefits and all those things. I have what I get from the welfare. Once I had my honorable discharge but that's gone and maybe it would be just trouble to go to the VA. How am I going to get another discharge? They take one look at me and give me the runaround. I don't even know about Social Security. I know I once had a card and a number, but it's like my army number. It's just gone away. It belongs to the time when I was young and strong, when I was a soldier and after, when I had good jobs and money in my pockets. Now I just sit here and wait, and if I have a bottle of beer that's about all I expect out of life these days

COMMENTARY

What themes and variations are seen in the life histories of these six black men, who came originally from the South or the Caribbean but spent most of their adult lives in New York City or adjacent areas? Discernible in their adult adjustments are the influences of parental family, education, work experience, and marital arrangements-in addition to the impact of overriding social forces such as conscription, discrimination, and depression.

Some of these men were born and brought up in the South and their presence in the North put them into a special category. While there had been a steady exodus from the South starting shortly after the end of the Civil War, eight out of over ten American blacks were still living in the South on the eve of World War II. There was something different about these early emmigrants who were affected by forces ranging from the hostile pressures on them to leave their birthplaces to the pull of relatives who had earlier made the transition and found the new environment supportive.

Also worth noting is the hold that the South continued to exercise on several of them, an attraction strong enough to draw them back to finish their years in a locale which had rejected them initially. Only part of the explanation is to be found in the sentimentality that most people feel for the surroundings of their childhood and youth. In the stories of these men there are clues that the hold of the South goes deeper and involves such wide-ranging factors as the salubrious climate, the slower pace, and, unbelievable as it may appear at first, the personal relations between whites and blacks within a segregated social structure.

One of the high costs involved in migration is the loosening of family bonds, weakening, if not severing, of important supports by the loss of propinquity. Therefore it is not surprising to read of the substantial efforts that several of the men made to keep in touch with those whom they had left behind, and the anguish that one expressed from having lost contact with his siblings.

As one would anticipate, the young southern black man who relocated to the North came with relatively little education or occupational skill. Only two later acquired extra preparation, one in the form of engineering know-how and the other, two years of college in New York City. Considerations of racial discrimination aside, their modest preparation for the world of work foreshadowed at best modest career development advancement.

This line of argument must not be stretched too far. In the early decades of this century, formal preparation for the world of work was of lesser importance than it is today. The number of good jobs reserved for the educated was relatively smaller than in the era after World War II, when professional and technical positions enjoyed the most rapid rate of increase.

Discrimination took a heavy toll. The electrician was repeatedly prevented from finding work in his trade. The local union was closed to all black men. And there was so little prospect of the ship's officer ever getting his master's papers that he finally decided to settle for a managerial position on land. The most telling evidence of the pervasiveness of the subtleties that obstructed blacks, even in the more open sectors of the economy, is revealed by the harassment suffered by the small trucker who fought for everything he gained—a license, insurance, and customers.

A correlate of racial discrimination is the health hazards connected with the better-paying jobs open to black men. Blacks could find work in the foundries, chemical plants and munitions industries that experienced rapid expansion during World War I and the prosperous twenties. But the risks of taking such jobs came high, with accidents, occupational diseases, and premature death all too frequent. In our small group, two of the men suffered adverse health conditions as a result of being employed at low-paying jobs.

If a man's job and career establish dimensions of his life, his connubial family plays another key role. One of the group remained single and another's marriage failed, but the remaining four had good marriages from which they received much support and satisfaction. What is striking is that only one of the long-time married had children. In the men's stories, both they and their wives found much meaning and satisfaction in close ties to their churches which, together with socializing with neighbors, provided the principal arena for interpersonal relations. There was little crossing of racial lines, on or off the job.

This brings us to the last aspects of the life histories, the financial and emotional problems connected with the men's aging, including their forced or voluntary retirement from jobs.

To consider the matter of income first, only two were dependent exclusively on income transfers. Booth had deteriorated to a point where he was unable to follow through and apply for Social Security, much less enter into the more arduous process of seeking disability payments for which he might have qualified.

The other four men reached their older years with some modest economic resources, including the ownership of a slum house or two or property in the South that had been left by a close relative. Not one was affluent, but all were able to maintain their customary standard of living, especially with the help of their Social Security checks.

Those who had recently been widowed after long and good marriages found their old age a lonesome burden; they missed the companionship they had had for so long. The loneliness was greater because they had no children and because their friends had died or had relocated out of the neighborhood.

Neighborhood deterioration was associated with increasing crime, theft and attacks on older persons by young delinquents. Scott tells us that he always carries a gun when he goes out. Panama lives mostly in his room which, despite its multiple locks, has been forcibly entered three times within the last year.

To see one's home, block and neighborhood transformed from a pleasant and serene area to the opposite represented an additional burden for these men in their later years. Several remarked that they should have escaped when they still had the opportunity but they were now too old to pull up roots and start now. Only Clapham, who had kept his ties with his family in South Carolina, had an alternative: he is going home.

The pride of accomplishment of work well done, of money earned, of a good marriage, of a clean record, of economic independence—the knowledge of these accomplishments proved a source of strength in the years when their lives had turned downhill—through the loss of health, wife, job, friends, the deterioration of the neighborhood, the vulnerability to attack, and the lack of respect of the young toward the old. The world which they had known and which had not treated them well was being rapidly transformed, and not for the better. This was perhaps the most difficult burden that these older men had to carry as they came closer to their ends.

BLACK WOMEN

Mary Crowell

Most of my children, they got up here before I did. We lived in Alabama, me and my husband, but my oldest children, they had all come up here before we did. We first moved from Alabama to Covington, Kentucky, in 1922. That's just across the river from Cincinnati, Ohio. Then we left Covington in 1927 and moved up here. When my husband died in 1932, we was up here just five years. I been here ever since. 'Course I was born in Melinda, Florida, where I was brought up, but all my children were born in Alabama. Same town my husband was born in.

Well, you know my husband worked at, what's the name of that place where Mr. Baxter was working at, that's the place he was working at when he died. He was working on the railroad before he came to Newark. That was in Alabama and in Kentucky. He first worked at the scissor company in Newark. I know that the last place, he had to go to work at five o'clock in the evening and he worked until seven o'clock the next morning. And he had to punch the clock every night. That's where he was working when he died.

Sam, my son, was living here when he died, and Sam stayed right with me. His name was Edward Cecil but we nicknamed him Sam. When he was a little boy, Sambo. He was born in Alabama, like all of my children. I am the mother of twelve children, eight girls and four boys. And Leland was my oldest boy and Porter was my next oldest boy, and Sam was my next oldest. And then Beau Jay, the one you saw at school, he was my youngest. He lives in Washington, D.C. His name's really Richard Leconnier, but we called him Beau Jay when he was a little boy. And we still go by that. Most of my children now are running pressing shops, cleaning and pressing. Fortley runs a pressing shop. Sam was working when he died, he died in 1958.

I am a hundred years, 25th of this last July. If I live to see the 25th of next July, I'll be a hundred and one. They had a program for a birthday party for me at the church, the Metropolitan Church. And now I am just living on. I can't see now to do nothing for myself. But I have lived all over Newark.

Since 1932 I lived with Sam, me and Sam. And all of my children they were living with me until they got married. When we first moved up here, we moved the horses with us. And we stayed with them. Then we moved up to 157 Camden Street. Then we moved from there, me and my husband, 'fore he died, we moved from there around to Wallace Avenue, Mr. Cass Kane's house, and that's where we were living when he died. And then I moved from there, I moved back to Camden Street. We lived all over the place on Camden Street. Then we moved to 13th Avenue and then down to South Orange Avenue. Goldie Mae got married there and her and her husband were living on Huntington Street and we moved from there down to Huntington Street. Cause Charlie died in 1932, and so I just moved all over Newark after he died. When Leland died we were living in the Scudder Homes.

When we moved up here my husband was working for the railroad company in Kentucky, but he didn't like Newark. Just before he died we was fixing to write to the man he worked for in Covington and go back to Kentucky if he could have gotten the same job back, because he was working for the railroad company in Covington. And then if he couldn't get that job back, he was going to write to Mobile, Alabama, and get the job he had there back. And if he had lived, we would have been living in Covington or Mobile.

He just didn't like it up here much. 'Course he used to work at crowds and meetings himself, when we was down to our home. Because we owned our own home and then he had a restaurant, colored and white, and he sold the ice house. And then too he was an undertaker, when we was in Parlor, Alabama, where he was born and raised. And all my children were born in the same town he was born in. But I was born in Florida, not far from Pensacola.

He run the business and he worked at the mill, the sawmill. That how come he left, because they moved the sawmill. And there weren't no work there for nobody, that's how come he left there and come to Covington, Kentucky. He worked the sawmill. Martin Lindsay was the man that owned it. And he moved from Parlor to Mobile, Alabama, when all the work there in Parlor had closed down. And nobody didn't have nothing to do. So that's the reason why he left there and come to Covington, Kentucky. He worked at Crotter Mills there and then he had a restaurant. And a place where they cleaned clothes, and a place where they fixed shoes. All that was in the building we had down there. And the men would bring their clothes there to be cleaned and they had a man there to clean folks' clothes and a place to fix shoes. Oh, he had a nice business down there.

In Newark during the Depression, well, both the boys were going to school here in Newark, at West Side. But Beau Jay, he hadn't graduated when his father died. 'Cause Charlie used to look at his record and he would say, "That boy, if I live, I am going to put that boy through college, if I have to whip my arms off." He sure did like Beau Jay. Beau Jay is my baby boy, but Rosalie is my baby. She's the last one that lives here. Beau Jay was my youngest boy. Anyhow, all of them was children when their daddy died. Rosalie was going to a school here in Newark, that big school down there where they all used to go, white and colored was going there. Robert Treat. That was where she was going when her father died, Robert Treat. I'll never forget it. That morning she was going to school, that was when she was 15 years old, and he called me, he said, "Well, I've lived to see our baby 15 years old." That was in April and he died in May. The next month he died, in 1932. Yes.

During the Depression, he still had his job working. We were living over there in Goldie's house over there in Huntington Street and I didn't suffer 'cause Beau Jay had a nice job shining shoes, and Sam, there was some laundry where he worked at, when he died. He died in 1958.

Beau Jay lived with me before he ever married. After graduating from Morgan State College, him and Beebe, the wife he's got now, they both graduated at the same time. He's only got but one child. His name is Ricky, and he's about 22. Beebe was living in New York at the time. Beau Jay, he used to be a mail carrier. Now he has some other kind of job, some night job. When you get old and blind and disagreeable, so that you depend on children, and old as I am, you know your mind is gone. I can think of things better way back there when I was young, than I can now.

Well, my life begins a long time ago. Mine began when I was in Florida, a little bit of a thing. My mother died when she just had two children, me and my sister. My sister was younger than I was. And when she died, that was how come we come to Alabama, because all her people live in Alabama. Her oldest sister come down there and got me and my sister and brought us to Bruton, Alabama. And we lived there at Bruton, Alabama. She was living with her daughter, and her daughter's house burnt down, and then my mother had a sister that lived in Parlor, Alabama. She had a sister and she had a niece that lived there. And her niece and my auntie take my youngest sister. And we lived right close together and we weren't separated because we were right close together, the houses were. And we were raised up in Parlor. And I was married and that was my husband's home, where he was born, and all his children born in the same place where he was born.

I got so many grandchildren. I got the goddamndest gang of grandchildren and a gang of great-grandchildren and a gang of great-great-grandchildren. There is no use trying to count them. I have given up long ago. Goldie Mae, how many grandchildren? (Goldie: "You have six living children and you have nine grandchildren, ten great-grandchildren and four great-great-grandchildren.'') Sam lived right with me until he died.

What bothers me is that I can't see. Can't get around to do nothing for myself. I would like to be up so that I could cook and do for myself and wash my clothes, so I wouldn't have to bother people about nothing. Because I love to cook and I just loved to work around the house. Oh, I could cook most anything. When we were down in Alabama, I cooked for the whites and colored. We had a white dining room and a colored. We sold all kinds. We used to have a soda water fountain. We made our own ice cream; made all our ice cream and soda water. We would just buy the flavor. Could I cook chitlins! Oh, yes, Lord. And soup. And, Lord, I used to make the finest rolls and fried chicken, and beef and we used to have venison; people used to kill deer and all, and then in the market they had all kinds of meats you don't ever see up here. Rabbits and squirrels,we used to cook. Them white people, they were crazy about our restaurant. They say, men used to come down from Montgomery, Alabama to fish and they would come to my place and eat all the time, white and colored. We had a nice place. Down to our home we used to make all our ice cream. We had a big old five gallon ice cream freezer.

My oldest daughter used to teach. She taught school seven years. Rosalie was a teacher and one of my grandchildren lives here on the first floor. Lois, she graduated from A and T College. And Rosalie graduated from A and T. And Beau Jay graduated from Morgan State College, and now I have a grandchild in Brown University. That's Goldie's boy. And another boy at Rutgers University. Then Roger and Louis, my great-grandchildren, they are in college.

I used to have to go to a doctor very often, but I haven't been for a long time. See, I've got sugar diabetes. I had been to Washington to visit Beau Jay and his wife and I was crazy about sweets. I used to eat so much ice cream and candy. So when I come from Washington that day there was a man who sold ice cream and candy and I just couldn't get enough of them. I eat all the way from Washington to Newark. So I said, this is bad. And I went to Dr. Haynes and he told me, you are just full of sugar. So he sent me to a diabetic doctor and he said you are just a regular sugar baby. That's the first I knew I had diabetes. It's been a long time. I stay on a diet and I have to take insulin every morning. It's given to me in shots. Rosalie gives it to me every morning. I can't eat nothing sweet and my son had it. My oldest boy. But that's the only thing that I have had to go to the doctor for. I have always been pretty healthy. I was always just as healthy. Nothing didn't bother me. I eat anything I wanted to eat. Ain't nothing bothered me. I was always just as healthy as I could be.

I've been on Social Security ever since Sam died in 1958. I have to pay the rent out of it. Don't have much left out of it then. The children take care of me. I can't do nothing by myself. The church helps me out too. They had my birthday party down there and they give me some money. Altogether two hundred and some dollars. Then, you see, I had terrible bad luck. All my things I had, I was leaving over to Goldie Mae, and her house burned down and I lose everything I had when the house burned down. I am just asking the Lord to give me a home in heaven when I leave this world. That's all.

My name is wrote down up there. I have seen that. My name is written down. I have seen it. My name is written down up there. I've been up there, in my dreams. And wrote my name. That was when I first got converted. That's when my name was written. So I just prays to the Lord to save my soul. Because there is nothing else in this world. I just put my trust in the Lord. That's all. That's all I can do, because there is nothing in this world now for me, because I can't see. I can see a little out of this eye, but I can't see at all out of this one.

Lord, I used to sing. You know, Miss Grayson, she used to have a singing group, and we used to go all over New York and sing over there. And the bus would come and carry us over there. No dancing, though. No dancing. Down home you dance and you get turned out of church. I used to dance when I was young. But I don't do no dancing now. 'Cause I used to go to church every Sunday, when I could see. Nobody had to come and carry me because I would just get on the bus.

You want me to pray for you all? Well, I says, good Lord, to help you all and take care of us. Yes, most of my prayer I do, you know, silent prayer. But I'll pray for you all. The Lord will help these gentlemen who are so nice to me to come and see me. Take care of them. And I give them into your hands, our heavenly Father. Please to hear my prayer. I'll just give you all up into the hands of the good Lord. And this gentleman here. I mean the one who 'caused my boy to go to school. Cecil Cox, Mr. Cox, I'll never forget you, God knows, and I'll pray for you for the Lord to help you. And you still live in the same place. Well, I declare. And I am so proud that you all come to see me.

Helen Barbour

I can say I had a kind of hard childhood. I was raised with a stepfather, but that didn't stop me from trying to be the best that I could. So that when I became a certain age, I tried to explain to my mother that instead of my doing housework for folks around that I could care for her better by getting a better education and being able really to do something.

I grew up in Florida, and I stayed there till I finished high school and one of the junior colleges in St. Augustine, Florida. What I studied there—I started to study a course in home economics but I found that would be where you wouldn't get a degree. So I took a teacher training course and I finished a teacher's training course there. I worked my way through high school there and then back through junior college and then took a teacher's training course. And with a brand new state certificate I came out and taught one year. And I found that the children, you know, unnerved me so badly. I had been working so hard and the doctor said that by working nine years and going through two schools, high school and junior college and teachers training, I should have had a break. But I was that eager to work because I wanted my mother to go buy a little house there. She needed a little money so I went to work to help her get this little home started. And after this I left Florida and I came up here; this was in 1936, to get in Civil Service work.

I didn't have a job when I came up here. I had taught one year in Marianna, Florida, and I gave the money to my mother to start a home. When I was growing up at school, that was the very time of the Depression. When Roosevelt stepped in everything was closing up. It was very bad. My family had it pretty hard like most families. My family didn't do anything to help me. You see I worked my way through school.

I wasn't afraid to come to the big city alone because I had a cousin who lived out in Long Island. I stayed with her until I got myself situated. I used to do housework, still applying for Civil Service. Finally I stopped doing catering work and service work and day work, and I got a permanent place with a rich woman, the sister-in-law of Richard Rodgers. I know you heard of Richard Rodgers, the great songwriter. I met her out on Long Island while I was out there with my cousin, and I was her housekeeper for four years and a half. And that's when I got my start of getting into the Civil Service. When I left her, I applied for Civil Service work. I didn't apply for Civil Service when I first came. I was afraid; I was too timid to branch out. But I started to get myself prepared. I took those catalogues for training. I would buy everything I could to study.

When I got my first job in the city, not the Civil Service job, I was doing day work. I got that job because of my cousin. She was accustomed to those kind of things, and I went to agencies, and, you know, I could use her for a reference. I didn't have any problems getting day work. In fact, to tell you honest truth, maybe it's because of the kind of person you are, maybe it's the kind of pushing and determination you have in you that you are not going to go down, I could always find work. Oh, I had hard days, but it wasn't because I couldn't find work. I could find day and hourly work, I could find plenty of it. And once I did a job for somebody, I got recommendations more than I could use.

Before I started working for Civil Service, I took several exams. I didn't get into Civil Service either until I was married and up in age. In 1942, after I finished with Miss Rodgers, after four years and a half, I started back to doing catering work, but I wasn't satisfied, because I figured that I was due for something higher. I wasn't satisfied. I picked up catering very naturally. My mother was a good cook, I guess from birth, and my aunt was a good cook from birth. And it looks to me that it is just in the family. They used to cook for people and I used to do the serving. This was for people who were giving dinner parties and I would serve. And by being around people who served and cooked, I guess, by observing, by doing what you learn, you learn while you are working, you know, to do those kinds of things. So I served very efficiently, satisfactorily, I would say, in those capacities. I mean, I didn't hear any complaints.

But, you know, being as how I had gone to college two years and all that, it bothered me to do catering work. There is nothing wrong with catering work, but it still bothered me. I felt I was doing that work as a stepping stone, but I wasn't satisfied. I wasn't happy; I felt that I was due for something better, so I kept studying everything that I could find, and I talked to people. Everything that I could see was Civil Service. I would read it and study it, you know, trying to prepare myself so that when the break came, you know, I would be ready. I thought maybe I could go into being a file clerk or anything except housework, that's the way I felt. Even at that time I was interested in taking care of sick people.

I didn't get into Civil Service work right away because you had to take Civil Service tests and get onto waiting lists. So I took the tests and I was put on the waiting lists. I didn't have any problems when I finally went to an interview. The first Civil Service work I did was for the city. That was for the Board of Transportation during World War II. They were short of manpower. Well, I worked six years for the city, for the Board of Transportation. I was a railroad clerk. I would get down in the hole, that's what they call it, for the Independent, IRT, and then I was transferred to the Third Avenue before they took it down. And that was where I got terminated because then the men came back from the war. That was about the best-paying job and they seemed to want those jobs, whether they were able or not. The women were just terminated. That's why I call it kind of hard. It wasn't just me. All the women were terminated. Then they said, "You have to take another examination to be classified ahead of the men from the army," so I didn't bother to take it.

After that it was tough. I had to go back to the same thing that I had been doing, day work. I went back to that, back to serving dinner parties and cleaning and doing day work. In the meantime I was trying to find other kinds of jobs by making applications and so forth. I went to the New York State Employment Agency, and I was still studying to try to be prepared for the Civil Service because this was one thing I learned—that if you just came from the South, you have a drawback and you have to try harder than other people.

When I went back to catering, I went with some very rich people. These people had a couple of stores here in New York so when they didn't have dinner parties and I wasn't working there, I would work in the store as a stock clerk. They had several stores and I used to go and put away hats and lay out stock for the girls and go get certain hats. And you get the clerk to mark hats, to tag them, and put them in stock, and keep the stock straightened out, and put stock back when the sale days got through. I didn't mind that, but I was still trying to get a Civil Service job.

I had a number of different jobs, but I always was trying to get a Civil Service job. It was the fringe benefits that I was looking for, why I wanted a job like that, because then you would get certain sick days off; you would get paid for your sick days, and I knew that when you become a permanent employee, you would get a pension, after you had done satisfactory work and stayed there long enough. And you got a vacation with pay. And I found that the fringe benefits weren't as good on private jobs. In some private jobs, when they were booming, you know, you really had to work hard, and then there would be months when the work was slow and I would only come in two, three days, and then for a few months you might not have any work at all. I had a son to take care of because I had a bad marriage, you know, and I had a son that I had to take care of. And I needed to be making enough; I needed to be making a steady salary.

In 1951, when I had a final break with my husband because he came to be a bad alcoholic, he wanted me to sign with the welfare to get a check, you know, like charity, welfare. And he wanted me to go down with him so they would give it to him. This was after I got off the city job, and I was doing this catering work, you know, day work. But it wouldn't have been welfare for the family. It would have been just for him to cash it in a bar. He couldn't keep a job because of his drinking. He went to the Veterans to get help, you know. He used me; I had lost my job, so he went to them to get help because I had been laid off my job—terminated, as they say. So they said, "Well, we can't give you anything unless you bring your wife." So he brought me, and after learning the circumstances under which he wanted to get help, well, I felt that wasn't true. I mean it wasn't fair. So I told them that I was a healthy young woman and didn't need welfare. I said, "I want a job. I would like to have a job." I said, "If you got a job to offer me, then we'll talk." So they tried to change him and tell him, "You got a wife you could put up on a pedestal. Boy, you got some wife here. So why not straighten yourself up. We'll send you to one of those Alcoholic Anonymous, you know, and straighten you out and you come back, and then, if you don't get a job, well we'll see what we'll do." And they still told me that if I needed it, I should come back. They gave me a name. I guess I was too busy to call back, because I wasn't interested in what they were talking about. They said, "Mrs. Barbour, if you need us, come back." And I said, "When you have a job to offer me, I'll come back."

It was 1951 that I started to work at the VA, the Veterans Hospital. At first I was nursing assistant, because they give you 90 days training as an aide. It's up to you to build yourself, to show them some aspect of study and then prove yourself, to show some extra aptitude for being a nurse. They wanted to send me to Harlem Hospital to become an RN but I told them I had a son to educate and I couldn't go in residence, you know. I needed to make a certain salary. I found out after I got into nursing that it was something I really liked. It was something more dignified. I was helping somebody and helping myself. I was better satisfied. That's what I have been doing since 1951. And I haven't had too much trouble. I figure this, that everybody can't like everybody. And I have come in contact with some people that wasn't too crazy about me. I guess I wasn't too crazy about them. But that didn't keep me from making it. I got four outstanding performances from the inspectors. And I have gone back and got extra training for extra duties. But I am still a nursing assistant because I could never go in residence, not even for practical nursing.

I can't complain about my salary. I make about $6,000 a year. My salary had just kind of increased over the years. You improve yourself, as you go along. I think a lot depends upon the push we have in ourselves. I was determined that I wasn't going to just sit back and expect something to be dumped in my lap. Because if there is anything worthwhile that you are going to get, you got to put forth some effort yourself.

My son is 32 now and I live here alone. I like to go to church. I suppose it is one of my major outlets. I try to go on Sunday outings, and there have been times when I have gone and talked to people who live alone like I do, to try to give them encouragement, but they are a lot older. I try to find out their problems and bring it to the attention of the Catholic Charities. Anyway some of them would take sick people to their appointments in hospitals and clinics, and some of them would go out shopping for them or cook a meal for them. You know, they had different people who signed up for different things, but I took the ones that you go visiting and talk with them.

I have found that when you have the right attitude, and you put forth your best efforts, there's always somebody that's going to be with you. God will never let you down that much, I believe.

Sometime I have had trouble with people I worked with, some supervisors, because I worked at such speed and was so exact that I wanted everything to be done so exact and perfect that I showed up everybody. You know, I wouldn't do that on purpose, but in all the private jobs I did, the recommendations that I got said that I am very diligent and that I put forth my best efforts and I work very hard. I don't meet any prejudice at my work, because the people who stood by me when I got my first couple of outstanding citations were both Irish.

I belong to the Rosarians in the church and I go to their meetings and their outings and their functions and that's about all. Because you see, right now, doing hospital work, you don't have much free time, you know. I have a lot of friends in this building and I use a lot of my time to help them. When neighbors have problems, I go in to help, like there is an old lady about seventy-some years near this apartment. I have a key to her house and I go in and check on her, because she was sick two or three times. Her sister said to me, "I feel very satisfied to know that somebody is checking on my sister, because if her roomer is out, she is there all alone." So I go in, and I do her shopping sometimes and I go in and get her food ready and I clean up, clean up her bathroom and kitchen because she's so tired out or something. And now this other woman had a death in the family and I offered my services to answer the telephone and take messages, you know, and do what I can. And if she needs the house cleaned up or some dishes washed, or her kitchen straightened up, I try to go and do that. I keep myself involved with people.

The only way I would consider going back to the South would be if I have a little place all my own and I'd be retired, but to tell you the truth, right now I have the idea of retiring before I get so I am just walking on a cane, while I can still go around. I learned so much about the needs of people, especially people who are older than me and people who are helpless or handicapped, maybe not as old as me, but handicapped. People say that they don't know what to do with themselves when they retire. But of course I have learned, maybe it's because I have worked in the church, that there's so much that you can do. There's so much that is needed that you can do so long as you have got health enough to walk around on your feet and use your hands and you got your good mind. So I don't think that I will really ever have a lonely day.

Older people are really forgotten. That's why I don't know why people say they got nothing to do when they retire, because when you see people sit there in the hospital all alone, they are going to get lonesome for their homes. And many of the people there don't seem to have anybody. Their families don't bother to visit them. If they are sick a long time, their families keep putting meetings off, until maybe you do good if you see them once a month, if ever.

I have been very sick a couple of times in my life. When I was working with this Miss Rodgers, I had a tonsillectomy. It first started with a strep throat, and naturally penicillin was just beginning to break, and from the streptococcus I had diseased tonsils and I had to have them out. But being that this lady's husband was a doctor, I didn't want for nothing. I had beautiful care. It's who you go to, it's who you know, believe me. And I can say that before you get old, it's good to build a nice personality and try to say a prayer, for example, "Make me an instance of your peace," that's a wonderful prayer. And instead of pushing to be understood or be cared for, try to care for somebody instead and try to understand why the lives of some people are what they are. And then make people care for you. So that's what I have tried to do. And I haven't been able to see this problem of prejudice and discrimination in my job as far as I can tell. Maybe it's because I haven't been looking for it. I work with some people who are looking for it, and every little thing can be taken as an example of prejudice when maybe it's something that is just a natural difficulty.

I am not taking out a lot of insurance, or saving a lot of money. I believe in the saying about the laying-up of treasures, but I think you should prepare for your old age, because when you get really old, when you get over sixty, you need someone who you can count on, if you need them. So about three, nearer four, years ago, I joined this savings plan, and every month money goes into that saving plan, and that's not to be touched. I will have a pension from the time I started on Civil Service. Three years after I became a Civil Service worker they started taking applications and if you are a qualified employee and you leave you draw a pension according to the status of your salary for the last three years.

It seems to me that some of the people who need assistance from welfare have a hard time getting what they want, unless they perhaps expect too much. And then I hear a lot of people panning it, that it's not operating efficiently as it should. I think it would be a good idea if the whole welfare system was better explained to the people, what to expect out of it and what they are supposed to get out of it, because I have had old people coming to me asking me, "Why do I have to write this letter and why do they want to check up and ask me if I need somebody to come and clean my room or go to the store and buy me something, why do they ask me?" They don't understand. I think that people should be better educated to what to expect and what the agencies are really supposed to do and have to do. So I try to explain to my old friends that it's not because they think that you are so helpless. "I am not helpless. I can go to the store, I can cook what I want to eat," I says, "It's not that. And if you are in need of that," I say, "because maybe they are finding that there are so many people who are left uncared for and are really suffering and are in need for things to be done for them."

Some of these old people, I think they especially resent being on welfare or Medicaid. I think that some of them feel that just because the welfare gives you that little money, they think you are a dog or something. Old people should be educated to appreciate what the agencies can do for them if they are very old and unable to do themselves. It doesn't mean that the agencies think that old people are down and out or outcasts. Old people are sensitive and some have got old and childish, and some of them didn't always have good dispositions anyway. You see I work with them too; I work with older people, older men, very few women, older men, and as they get older, their dispositions often don't get any better. They often get worse because you get more sensitive and more touchy. You come across some people on the other hand, who have an understanding and gentleness even until death takes them, as old as they are. And then you do have some people who are in those social agency positions who don't have patience for anybody. What bothers a lot of people is that they don't understand, a lot of them. Maybe they can't even read a lot of this literature that comes from the social agencies, this legal stuff. And it frequently is hard to understand. And it is hard to get it through to old people, and social workers get very annoyed at old people, very impatient, and they may hurt their feelings. And I have really heard some of the older people say they dread to have to take it, some of them suffer a long time before they will even go in to the agency and try to get it. I have had people talk to me, old people, about that.

They do have a union at the hospital but I don't belong to it. I figure it this way, that there's only so much that a union is going to do with the federal government anyway. In some instances, I think that unions are very good. But the suffering I have gone through at the hands of unions and the way the unions have been behaving lately makes me think that they are really outliving their goodness. I mean unions in general. They have really gone to such extremes that I think that they have really outlived their good deeds. In the beginning, before they passed the bill where you have to pay a person a minimum wage, it was good to have a union, because I really believe that employers would have kept on working you at this low wage longer. But I do feel that unions have gone to extremes.

I got put out of the city job without the union raising up a fuss for all these women who served wonderfully during the war when there was a shortage of manpower. I don't think that these women should have been thrown out without at least calling them together to say, "You did a wonderful job. We thank you. We did as much as we could to make you stay on these jobs." We didn't get any thanks at all. This is the way they spoke to you. They called your name, and your number and they said, "You're terminated and you have to go to the office and turn in your badge." That's the way we got the news. And no thanks for good service. Sometimes they would ask me to double up two or three times a week. I could do this because I lived near where I had good neighbors and all my boy had to do was walk around the block to the St. Charles School. I worked my vacation three years in a row, and I worked my day off until sometimes I would tell them, "Well, I'm going to have to take the night off because my little boy and I are very close and I promised him that we would go down to 42nd Street and have some entertainment."

I belonged to the union then and I will admit that Mr. Quill did make them raise us, because when we started down there I think we got $.58 an hour. And he did get us a decent salary. By the time the war was over we received $60 a week with overtime.

It's because the union didn't do anything for me then that I still feel this. They said, "It's Civil Service, what can we do?" So I said to myself, "If it's Civil Service and they can't do anything, then why should I pay my money to them?" So I feel the same way today. I work for the federal government now. And because I take care of sick people, I wouldn't strike anyway. I wouldn't strike and let so many people die. I don't have that kind of heart. I couldn't because I work in cardiology. My brother dropped dead from a heart attack, he went into cardiac arrest and I know what it is. When a person has a cardiac arrest, you've got to work and work fast, and with God helping you in his corner, you may save him but you've got to work and work fast. And look how many people would die, if you weren't there. No, I couldn't do it. I couldn't strike, not in a hospital. That's why I think that the union has lost interest in people.

And those teachers let those children stay out there for months and months and months and months and months and lose their credits, how could they do that? The unions have gone too far. And they are not satisfied with this. They ask for more and more money and what is it, just a vicious circle. You get that big salary and things go up higher enough to pay for that salary, and the very poor people who are in the low class, they are having a hard time, and the unions keep giving them a harder time, because they have got to go into the store to pay those higher prices that those who are making that big high salary are responsible for.

I often thought about going back to college and finishing the last two years, but I also thought about the time it would take from my little boy. And he needed me and he would grow up to be a man and he's got to take care of a family. And I didn't want him to say sometime that he wasn't able to take care of a family because he didn't have the right training. So I stuck with him and I didn't even finish the practical nursing. After I didn't get the RN, I started taking practical nursing, but I didn't go all through that. I have worked always as a nurse's assistant but I do know my work, or I wouldn't have received all those certificates. I knew that if I had gone ahead and finished the other two years, I might have had a better opportunity to get into something better, but I still felt that it was more important to spend my time with my son until he was grown up. I felt that I should really push to have my son get a good education. I didn't want him not to have the chance anyway. If he didn't take it, then I couldn't help myself, because he couldn't say, "Well, I had to help my mummy by going out to work before I finished school." I wouldn't have that.

I myself almost stopped school completely when I was 13. There were four of us children living at home, and my mother lost three. So she cared for four mouths instead of one. So they died babies, you know. I was the oldest of all, I had to give her a lot of help. I just had to make my opportunities, just with the help of a few people who I went to. You see, I went to a teacher, she's dead now, but she used to teach me in the evening after I finished my little housework. I had house jobs, you know, and all that money went to my mother.

I haven't had much experience with social service agencies. And I am trying to make it so that when I do retire, that I won't have to. Some help is due you because of your age, and I don't think that if you need it you shouldn't go to those agencies, but I think you should only go if you really do need help.

I think that the only problem you have when you get older is trying to stay well enough, even though you are old, trying to stay well enough to maneuver and help yourself. And if you can't help yourself, you must have enough resources to have someone help you. If my family aren't able to assist me, I don't mind going into a Catholic Home. And they would have those two checks, my pension and the check from my savings plan, to take care of me. I don't mind giving up the money, because I am not going to pile up a whole lot of money in the bank, so that it tempts people to walk in and grab it while I am allowed to go down the drain. That's why I have got that savings plan. Because as long as I have got my good mind, I can say where I want those checks to go. They may be able to take my bank book and get that money, but I can say where I want the checks to go for me. And if they don't want me, then I can use my money as I see fit. And in that case I would go into a Catholic Home, or to another home, and let the home have the money to take care of me.

Going in and out of the house sometimes at night, I do feel, you know, concerned. But then I go back to God again. I go back to that. Some people seem to think that the criminals just want to hurt old people, but I don't think that. I think this whole generation are vipers, what the Bible said was coming. I think that this generation are vipers, going around with all this dope and stuff, doing their thing, and getting their kicks. I don't think that it is just aimed at old people. I think that they think that old people got their little bundle, carried close to them, more than somebody young, and they think that they can take that easier. I don't think that they just prey on old people. I don't think they care who they take. But they just figure that old people are getting that old age assistance or that old age pension and they do have a little change with them. And they can get it from them easier. I know that some older people think they are just after the older people.

I definitely think that there should be a heavy hand on these kids when they do something. And I think that they let them get away with too much of this militancy and won't pass any laws to shut down on them. When they do destructive things, I think that they should be punished for it; letting them get away with this just makes them go do more, and more, and more. I think that there should be laws made to deal with it.

The streets are very unsafe. But I am not one to just hang out on any street at night. When I go on the street, I am going somewhere. And I go there. Or I am coming from home, and I come there. I am not one for standing around. But it is terrible out there. It's like a jungle. And my apartment has been broken into twice and I have been robbed.

I have a friend down on the fifth floor. Somebody went into her mother's house down South and strangled her to death, and took all her valuables because she lived alone. All the rioting and carrying on that you hear about up here, it's spreading; it's going down there too. They hear about up here and they do the same thing.

But as far as feeling afraid of growing old, all I worry about is not to let the generation of vipers get me so upset and weakened that I lose trust in God. I want to be ready for him when I reach my time.

Eliza Mason

My home was in Norfolk, Virginia. I was raised there and went to school there. I trained in Hampton, Virginia. I finished my training at the hospital there. But I went through high school in Norfolk. My father died when I was a child. My mother, she did domestic work up until the time I came out of school. And I used to work when I was going to school. I had a couple of jobs in the afternoon all the time I was going to school. I used to go to these jobs when I left the school at three o'clock. The lady would send her butler for me and I would get in that car and go there and fix their supper, wash those dishes, put their kids to bed, and they would bring me all back home. I did that for years and years for that family.

The Depression came on but I was working then. My family were poor people. I had an uncle and a brother and grandparents and all, and they all lived home. I wouldn't consider them, no ways, nothing else but poor. I mean we were able to eat and dress and things like that, but I couldn't do something like go to college. I went to nursing school instead, because at Hampton at that particular time, I think they paid us around $5 or $10, something between that, and, well, I saved up my money and I entered training by myself. My family helped me all they could. I worked that summer, little jobs, and then you were supposed to get so much money at the end of the term, but you don't get that money because by the time they take out for books and for your uniforms, there was little left. You didn't have to pay for them until after that time, so that made it much easier. In some of the hospitals up here, you used to have to pay before you went in.

After I got out of nursing school down in the South, I worked in my home town. I can't say that I had any problems getting jobs there, but it was the money. They made a difference in the salaries between the colored nurses and the white nurses. That's why I didn't like the St. James Hospital. The white nurse had a car and the colored nurse didn't have a car and she didn't get as much salary. And you had to work beside the white nurse every day. That used to upset me terrible, because she was a graduate nurse and I had passed the state board just like she did, but we didn't get the same salary.

So I decided to come to New York first of all because of that, but also because at that particular time I decided that I wanted to adventure out more. I also came to New York so that I would be able to pick out some special course or something. I saw this advertisement where they were advertising for nurses, because at that particular time colored nurses were getting very few jobs. As I say, I didn't have that problem. When I was home, I was always very busy. Then I went into public health work and did that about six months. Then I worked as a private duty nurse, and I worked in a hospital. So I did not really have too much to complain about as far as getting work. But just the same it wasn't what I was after.

Anyway, after I came up this way, after I saw this advertisement in one of the magazines, I think it was the *Nursing Journal*, and I saw that they were going to take colored nurses, I came up to try. I came up here in 1931 and from there I moved to Newark when I got married. I'm 66 now and I came up here in 1931 so that means that I was in my late twenties when I came up here. As I said, I had no problem finding a job when I left Norfolk to come to New York.

My problem, once I came up here, was this. I wondered why nurses from other states weren't getting the same amount of money as the New York State nurses were getting, so I went to the different meetings of groups of nurses, and finally we interviewed someone from Albany and they began to investigate why we weren't getting the same salaries as New York State nurses. We found out that a lot of these people in Albany thought we weren't registered nurses. They thought that we were practical nurses, but we were really registered nurses. So then after they found out that many of these girls from other states were registered, well, then they began to get us to take the examination and to take the state boards here. It wasn't just a case of black out-of-state nurses. Anybody who was from out-of-state at that particular time was not getting the pay of New York State nurses. I came to Newark in 1935 or thereabouts after I got married, but I continued to work in New York until 1953. I used to commute after I got married. I have always lived in this same district. We lived on N. Street for a short time. Then we moved to 8th Avenue until we could get this house.

My husband was a tailor. He had a business on O. Street. He had a cleaning and pressing shop attached to it. But a major source of income since my retirement is my apartment. I rent out one floor of this house and it brings me $125 a month and then I get my Social Security check. My Social Security check calls for $179.40 a month and one dollar is taken off now. So you can see how important the rent from the apartment is to me. Each floor of this house has six rooms so I rent a six-room apartment for $125. It is a source of security for me. Of course, I don't want to have to raise the rent, but taxes have gone up and I guess I will have to.

My husband and I, we always believed in putting something aside for our old age. In fact I think that the average person always puts something aside if they can. I always believed in that. Even if it is just a little bit, you can have something, you know, because you never know what's coming up. I do not get any Social Security from my husband, but I do have Medicare, oh yes. I never have had any problems getting things like Social Security and Medicare. And I haven't had any problems, to speak of, with my health since I stopped working in 1967.

As I said, I have been retired since 1967, but I have been doing some part-time work and I have a lot of things to keep me busy and to amuse me. In the first place, if you really keep house, you can find something every day. Seems like there is always something to do. Now I haven't vacuumed through here today, and I declare that I have to get the vacuum after you all leave because it looks so bad. But to amuse yourself, there is plenty for you to do, if you will only look for it. You can take an active part in your church, an active part in these various sewing circles, anything you want. Then you have your friends. If you have made good contacts before you get to retirement age, I think that the average person will have no trouble.

There's plenty of things for you to do. You can always go in and do volunteer work with people. I love many people that I know. If I hear that one of my friends is sick, I'll go in and help to take care of the house and do whatever has to be done. I have a certain number of people that I call every day. If they need me, or if they want someone to help them out, to talk to, or to give them a bath, or something like that, or just to stay with them, now I'll do that. Now I just stayed, about a month ago, with the mother of a friend. She was so sick that I stayed with her night and day. So you see, there's plenty to keep a person busy.

I don't have any immediate family here in Newark although I do have one brother who's still alive. I do have several in-laws but I guess my friends take the place of a family to some extent, although of course they are not the same. But as far as growing older in a city like Newark, I feel wonderful. I don't have any complaints. That's because I have so many good friends and so much to keep me busy.

Since I don't think that I will marry again, I feel that my friends are my major source of satisfaction in life. And I feel that I have quite a few good friends. And I believe that some of my friends, if I call them any hour and say that I am sick, I feel that they will do everything possible to get to me, because I will do the same for them.

Another major source of satisfaction is my house. I know that I am just like the average person, and if something needs fixing, I'll blow my top and say, "Oh, I'm not going to fix it, I'll go to the senior citizens houses," but I know that I am just lying to myself because I put my money into this house and I am going to stay here a little longer. I can't see anything troublesome in the future, well, maybe the taxes or something. They have gone up quite high, but probably I'll get along and if I haven't any bread, I'll ask my friend, Cecil, what to do. Growing old doesn't worry me. The only thing that worries me is my health. If people would stop thinking about growing old and try to make the best out of life that they can, eat good food, get plenty of rest, exercise, and say their prayers, I think we would be better off.

Church is a vital part of my life. I like to go to church. I think that every person ought to go to church. I was brought up that way, to go to church and Sunday school. And when we were children, if we missed Sunday school, we didn't go any place that afternoon. We stayed right on the porch. But I do feel that church is part of my life and that I should go to church. Yes, I do, because I think that knowing Christ is a great comfort. I feel sorry for people who don't. And I think that Christianity is really a great thing. I don't say that I live up to everything, but I think I am not the worst person. So long as I have the church, that's really enough.

In fact, it's because of that that I am not the type of person to sit down and worry what's going to happen to me, because I'm very busy all the time. I'm always going some place. And I spend as little time as possible alone at home. I'm always out and enjoying myself, even if it is just visiting a sick friend or helping a friend who needs some help.

I have been on quite a few trips. I am going on another trip this coming December. I am going to five ports in the Caribbean. I always go to the Caribbean. I like it because the weather is so nice and you can always enjoy yourself. But I've been talking about the good things in my life, my friends, my home, and most important, the church, and when I think of these things, I can say truthfully, like I said, that I feel wonderful and I don't worry about growing old. But that doesn't mean that there aren't any problems for me and my friends, because there are.

One thing is the way urban renewal has torn up the city. First of all, a lot of people who used to live around here have gone to East Orange and different places, in fact to any place that they can get. That's my idea, of course, and I think it comes from tearing everything down so quickly. This destruction of so many buildings all at once hasn't done too much good, because there is one thing about it. Newark is a terrible looking place now, as if an atom bomb had hit it square in the middle, it sometimes seems to me. I think if they had just torn down some places and then started to build and then torn down some more, I honestly think that it would have been better than to tear down all the places at one time. And of course doing it that way just simply makes the tax rate go up more and that drives some of us out of the city, and that makes it just that much worse. This tearing down has been going on so long. I think it started around 1967, and they haven't really done too much building, as far as I can see, but of course I don't have a car so I can't get around to see like some people can. There has been some building, but very little I think, for poor people. For people who can afford a fancy building, there is a lot of building and it's all right for them. But many people in Newark cannot afford to go into those different various projects. So that's one thing off my chest.

Another thing that bothers me is the matter of crime. I just don't go out at night. Anywhere that I want to go, if I don't get a cab or someone doesn't take me, I stay home. And I try to make a habit of coming back early. It's not only Newark that is like this—New York City, Pennsylvania, all down in the South, even in the southern districts, all around Norfolk. My brother in Norfolk, he didn't used to think about locking his door until he got ready to go to bed, but he locks it now because it is just like anyplace else. It's just not only Newark, it's all the places.

I have come to just accept it as something that is there and that you have to expect. I have to, because what else can you do? There is nothing else for you to do. Sometimes I think it is because we are getting so many people in every day from other places that nobody really gets a chance to settle down. I can't blame the people who come here. I guess they must be tired of one place so they go to other cities. And of course at the same time a lot of people who can move out of Newark are moving out. It's mostly whites who are moving out, but some of the blacks are moving out too. I don't know what their reason is. I guess some of them are just tired of Newark, but I know that some people don't like Newark any more because they say that Newark is rough. I suppose that in those districts it is real rough. I know that it is worse than around this neighborhood. And I know that every place is bad. You just have to be careful, that's all.

Considering what I have heard of other places, I don't think our police force is up to all they could be, especially in answering your calls quickly. I can understand the problem of the police and still you wonder what to do. So many of those places are torn down. Those halls are dark and everything. The policeman has a family too, and he doesn't want to get killed, so it's really tough on them.

And I am bothered about the whole question of what the social agencies, like welfare, are doing. I think that most people don't have too much trouble getting assistance. I have only heard of one person who had a hard time getting social assistance, and that was four or five years ago. A friend of mine told me she had tried to get some assistance for her mother and she couldn't possibly get any. About six months later, though, she told me she had finally got it. But the average person, so far as I know, I haven't heard anyone complaining, and it seems to me that they do get help when they need it. But I will tell you one thing that I feel about these social agencies, something that I wish they would stop doing, and that is that I wish they would stop taking care of these girls that every nine months they have a baby and then they get more money. Then I think that they would have more money for people who really deserve assistance. Let those girls go to work and take care of some of their children. I think that there should be a law that would make those girls take care of themselves and any more children they have. I really don't think they should be given so much help when they behave that way. It's terrible. It means taxing people so heavily to take care of something like that.

Then there is another thing that naturally disturbs me. I think that if you move into someone's apartment or house, you should try to help that person, the landlord, to keep it up instead of breaking it down. You see, that's one of Newark's big problems. I do feel sorry for some of these people, but then sometimes I don't know whether I feel so sorry or not, because when these people are sometimes in good apartments, they still tear the apartments down like that. In the houses that I am talking about, these apartments were brand new and the people broke them down. It's not a case where apartments were allowed to run down by the landlord. I know that in some cases that too can happen. The landlords sometimes keep up a building so long as white people live in it, and then as soon as the blacks move in, they don't fix things any more and just let the building keep on deteriorating. But I am not talking about that kind of situation. I am talking about places where a perfectly good apartment building is wrecked by the people who live in it, particularly by the children.

And there's another thing. I don't live over across the way and naturally I don't have many friends that live over there, but there are parts of Newark that have an awful lot of fires. I know that. And I do feel that some of those people over there, those dope addicts and alcoholics, they just come into those houses and they light a match and they throw it down on the floor and so naturally the place just goes up in smoke. I don't know what people can do to protect themselves against that.

There are a few homes for older people, some in Newark and some in East Orange, and these homes are very pretty and well taken care of. They are really very nice, but it's the location that is bothering the average older person. Because of the location of some of those homes, people are afraid to go down there at night. Of course I wouldn't dare to go down by L. Street and all that at night. Quite a few older people are living in these homes but there are nowhere near enough of them, as far as I can see.

In some of these senior citizen projects they have people to look after some of the older people. For example, take the one that I know about in East Orange; there's a lady who goes around every morning to find out if Miss So-and-So is all right. Each door bell is punched every morning and if she's not well and can't come to the door, they ring for the janitor and he comes up and opens the door. This kind of service is very reassuring to older people who live alone and are afraid that they might fall or something and just lie there with no one ever knowing that they were in trouble, maybe even just dying on the floor or in their bed with no one ever to know.

The senior citizen home in East Orange is very nice. I have a friend who is living up there and she is looking so well since she got in there. She calls me up and she says, "Eliza, child, I am enjoying myself so much here. I am not bothering myself or worry. I lived in Newark for 40 years and I worked hard for almost all that time and now I am getting some reward." She says, "Now the Lord has taken me here and I am going to be all right." As I said, some of those senior citizen homes are very pretty, they're really beautiful. The one in East Orange just opened up about six months ago and this is about the most beautiful one I have been in. It makes you feel that some people care about older people.

They have somebody on duty 24 hours a day. Of course for those who are actually sick, I suppose it is a little bit different for them. But if they have lived all of those years and when they were making a little money, they didn't put some of it aside and didn't look out for themselves, well, that's just too bad. Of course the little money that you manage to save is not going to last you forever, but you will have a little something to take care of emergencies. Although some older people do have real trouble and need a lot of help, some other senior citizens are all right. They're not doing so bad for themselves. Don't you fool yourself about that. They are looking for the same thing I am looking for, good health and a decent place to live in. But some of these older people don't have to do nothing. They are not so bad off because they have provided a little something so that they wouldn't have to be so bad off when they got old. But as I said, the situation for some others is bad enough. You know, everybody is not alike. For one thing, there is the difference in a person's attitude. That counts for a lot. Now, of course, if you are just going to sit down and worry a lot, that is not going to be good for you. When you get older you have to learn how to keep busy and at the same time take life easy and not worry too much. Of course, that's easier said than done, I know.

I think of years ago, of our grandparents. They suffered hardships, poor jobs, all sorts of things, but with all this they managed to save a little something. But, you know, it's according to how you spend. You have to be kind of thrifty to know how to save, because some people are not going to save regardless of how much money they earn. Of course, in order to save money these days, I found, even when I was working, you have to learn to do without. And you have to learn to say, "I am going to put this check in the bank." And you have to walk out of the bank and just forget about the money you have put there. That's the only way I know I used to be able to save. I used to say to myself, "I am going to put this check in the bank and I am not going to touch it at all. A real emergency has to come before I touch it." And I would just make myself walk up to the bank and do it. That's the only way you can do it, because if I had run downtown, you see, to Bamberger's or some other store, I would have brought myself a new dress, or a pair of shoes, like any other woman. But since I have gotten to my present age, I have not changed my attitude towards a lot of things, including saving when I get an opportunity. And still I like to go out and I like to enjoy myself. I will take a drink once in a while and I don't mind people around me drinking, so long as it's kept in moderation.

Being that I have been a nurse all my life, I have a few ideas about what's wrong with hospitals. First of all, they don't have enough help. That's the number one problem. They don't have enough registered nurses, they don't have enough practical nurses. They don't have enough aides. They don't have enough people to take care of the patients. That's the number one problem. A lot of older people who are not working could be very helpful in the hospitals. They talk about public service employment. This is one place they could begin.

The people who are working in these hospitals, they are all tense because they are too busy and trying to do too much work. When they come home, they are all knocked out. My friend, when she gets off duty, is really beat. She works with newborn babies and she's really ripped when she gets home. The nurses try to do all the work that is necessary, but it is just too much of a job. I was there in the hospital last summer. I was there every other weekend, but I have never worked so hard in my life. So many patients, so much work to do. They didn't have enough things to work with and it was just terrible.

Virginia Thomas

I'm pleased to help a friend of my friend. Mrs. Moore told me when she arranged that you come see me that you are talking with a number of older people in the black community about what problems we are having, particularly whether we have any problems with work. My only problem with work is I can't stop working. No, that's not a joke either. That's the

Lord's truth. I sometimes think that life and work are meant to go together. And I am Christian enough to believe what it says in the Bible about work. Maybe if man hadn't been a sinner he wouldn't have had to work, but we all know how much of a sinner he is, and he doesn't show much signs of changing that I can see. But later I want to tell you a story about that.

First I want to begin at the beginning and tell you a little of how I first began to work. I was born, along with five brothers and two sisters, the second of the children in the family, and the first was my brother Jefferson, so I was the oldest girl. My father had a small farm, don't ask me how he ever managed to get it, which was just enough to keep us going so long as everyone pitched in and helped. He was a good farmer and I remember he could do just about everything. He was well thought of and he had plans for all his children. I think that he wanted us all to go to Hampton. My mother, I know, she was anxious that we get all the schooling we could get and that we always remember the importance of helping the race to progress. When I think of those two, working the way they did and sacrificing and worrying over us, how they made the most of their opportunities, I wonder what they would have done today when, for many young people, college is just there for the asking. They never had that kind of chance, but they always wanted us to have whatever we needed, no matter what it cost them. My mother had some schooling and she was proud of the way I took to schooling. I always had a nice dress to go to school, and I did well at school.

In those times, families were generally pretty big and children came one after the other. So by the time I was old enough to help around the house, it came to me to do a lot of the work that had to be done. It didn't seem like work either. It just had to be done—the stove lit in the morning, biscuits to make, laundry to help with, sewing, all the housework which a little girl like me would help with. My older brother, he did the same with the farm work. He was up to milk the cow and to help in the fields. I suppose children today don't understand how natural it was for us to work whenever we were needed. I think it made us feel good and we certainly learned to do many things. And we were taught that it was only right. When I think of it, I think what a nice childhood I had. I scarcely remember any trouble or sickness or unkindness. We were, if I do say it myself, a nice family.

But the Lord giveth and the Lord taketh away. Not that I knew what it was at the time, and maybe you never heard about it, but a terrible disease, like a sudden storm, it just swept through our family. Later they called it the influenza, 1918 was the year, and when it was done with its awful work, my father and my older brother were in their graves along with my baby brother. As quick as that without any kind of warning. You probably know about that time. Seems like any number of families lost someone, but I think we were about the worst hit. So that was the end of many things for us. The farm—we had to leave it and to go to live with family in Richmond.

School—it was the end for me because there wasn't room for me, the oldest anyway, where we moved to in Richmond, and since I was handy with housework and well brought up, it was easy to find a place for me with a doctor and his family in Richmond. Today, it hardly seems natural, but in those days it was quite usual for a family rich as the doctor's family to have several young people in the house. My main responsibility was to look after the two children, young as I was. But of course, I was busy from morning to night. You'd be surprised to learn that I was paid for working every day of the week, and, it seems to me, probably at least 12 hours each day. It was only a few dollars a week. But, of course, the important thing to my mother was that it was a place for me where I was fed, and the few dollars were a great help to her. And most of the time, I think, I enjoyed what I was doing. The only sad thing was that it meant an end of schooling for me, even of reading itself, which I was quite good at. I was just too busy each day to keep up with reading, and by the time I left the doctor's house, which is a story in itself, I had most forgotten what I knew of reading. At least I have never enjoyed reading since then, and I think each year I seem to read more poorly, so that now it seems that I hardly never read at all. So there went any hopes for Hampton Institute and what I could have learned there, perhaps to be a nurse or a teacher.

I said that my leaving the doctor's house was a story in itself. After I had been there for six years I thought one day to ask that I be paid more. I was now a grown young lady and it only seemed right to me. I was like a second mother to the children, indeed almost more than that, because the children really didn't see all that much of their own mother. I thought that I was almost one of the family, I had been there so long. You wouldn't believe what that mother did when I asked that I be paid a proper wage. She screamed that I was ungrateful and said that I must leave the house at once. So I said I would. The children were in tears when I left. It was the end of that part of my life for me. But maybe it was for the best. Otherwise I might never have left that family. I was that close to them except for the mother.

It seemed time for my family to move too, so we all went to another sister of my mother who lived in Philadelphia. I never liked Philadelphia. And I didn't stay there for long, even though that was where my mother was to settle. You'll know what I mean when I say that his seemed to me the time for me to make something of myself. New York was in the air. Everybody was talking about how exciting it must be. I was a grown person now and I thought that I would just go up to New York to see what I could find for myself.

I knew that I could always get a place with a family that needed someone who could do housework and was willing to work hard. Sometimes when I think back to that time, I wonder that I didn't think of other things that I might do. No, it seemed to me that I was fitted to do housework, and I don't think that I ever thought of anything else seriously. Of course, I always felt the lack of schooling. Maybe that just about shut off any idea of anything else. Sometimes I did dream of being a nurse, and even to this day my mother tells me that I should have been a nurse. Who knows, but anyway that's not the way things were to be for me, and if I had been a nurse I wouldn't be what I am today. You can't look back.

I didn't come to New York all by myself. My younger sister was with me and we found a place to stay not far from where we are now. It wasn't hard in those days. My, when I think of it, Harlem was a nice place in those days. You wouldn't believe, to see the way 125th Street looks now, how it was all bright and full of people and not at all the way it is now. We left our doors unlocked and never thought about walking at night. Everybody did. There were pushcarts and all such things. It was just as nice and friendly a place as you could want.

I found a job right away with a big family over on Riverside Drive, and I used to take the streetcar to work. It wasn't a live-in job but that was because I thought I would try to have my own place. Well, I worked there for more years than I like to think. Even worked there while my husband-to-be was courting me and when we got married. That was a long time ago. Seems to me that I was just a girl then.

My husband-to-be, he was a church-going man, when he could go to church, because sometimes he couldn't because his work wouldn't let him. But when he could he was there and that's where I met him. He was a porter on the railroad, used to make runs to Cleveland and Chicago. He worked steady until he took sick. I don't think he ever missed a day's work. He was that kind of a man. But we had grand times together then. We went dancing and did all sorts of foolishness and then we were married. I never thought about stopping work when we got married. It just seemed natural to keep on working, and we waited for children that never came. It was God's will, I suppose, and I have to think that all the children that I have taken care of, they're partly mine. I really do believe that. And I could tell you stories about how those children, some of them when they were grown up, they came to see me and they told me that I was like a mother to them. But Lord knows, some of them needed mothering, they saw so little of their own daddy and mummy. They seemed to rattle around in some of those big apartments, some of them 12 rooms or more.

My husband, he had his work, but I knew he would have been a good father to a son. He was that kind of man. Maybe it was harder for him not to have a large family, but he never complained. He had been a soldier, and he always said that you had to take the good with the bad and that for him, in spite of everything, things were mostly good. He had many friends on the railroad. People he worked with and some of the people who traveled on the train, they would especially ask for him. So he got to know many people, some of them famous in their day. I suppose you wouldn't know their names today, but then he would say, last night there was so-and-so in the car and sometimes in the middle of the night he would say that these famous men wouldn't be able to sleep and they would talk to all hours.

He was a funny man and I remember he said to me not long before he passed on, "Ginny, you know, some people might say that I never got very far in my life, but every year I must have gone about as far as the moon and back, and not many people can say that." I don't know as if he really went that far. Another thing about him, he felt that his work was a good steady job and that he could always take care of me. They had the union and the retirement benefits and all that. He said that not many people could say that their future was as well taken care of. I seem to be rattling on about all sorts of things, but he was just a good man. We always had a dog. And when he took sick (it was his heart and he wasn't all that old) he wasn't ready to retire; but he just couldn't go on with that night work, he needed steady hours and plenty of rest, the doctor said. Anyway, it was the dog that meant most to him then because he had to stay home, and the dog would keep him company until I got back. Then, of course, I had to keep on working. By then, I had more work than I knew what to do with.

I recall you asking me how did I get work if I didn't have a job and I wanted one. Well, one thing I will say, I never did use one of those so-called employment agencies, never did and never will. You should know something about the kind of work I do. If you do your work good, I mean if you are responsible and people trust you (they have to trust you because they leave you alone in their house and they ask you to take care of all sorts of things for them), then if somehow they move or something happens so they can't use you any longer, then they make sure that they let their friends know, and like as not one of their friends is looking for someone like you. I sometimes say that I have been passed back and forth. But another thing happened in my case which might interest you.

First of all, I would work for just one family. That is the way they wanted it, but like I said, those were always jobs where the hours were very long and you had to work most days of the week, Thursday afternoon usually off, but Saturdays and maybe even part of Sunday. So it was a long week for me.

Once a family I liked, they decided because their children were gone away to school and perhaps they didn't have the money they used to, who knows, well they asked me if perhaps I might like to work for them for just part of the week, because they had friends who would like me to come to their house for the rest of the week. At first I was doubtful about the arrangement, but I said that I would try it. It was the best thing I ever did, really. I'll tell you why. First, it put me in charge of how long I had to work, for the first time in my life. Today, for instance, I don't really work a full week any longer. I don't need to, and sometimes I don't even try to work a full day. Now, instead of a family to work for, I have what I call my clients. And there is always more clients than I can handle. All my clients have friends who would also like to have me take care of their apartments. Many of them are single, bachelors or single ladies, some are couples. I almost never work for a family with children anymore. But that's all right. I figure I've taken care of enough children in my life, and now it's quieter and more orderly if I don't have the responsibility of looking after children and doing the housework. So I can pick and choose the times and the people I work for. And I have cut down some over the past few years, but I still have enough work, and I know that I will always have more people asking for me than I can possibly take care of.

One thing I think I should tell you. Some people think that the work I do is lowering. And I can tell when a person who wants to be one of my clients thinks that way. Let me tell you a story. Not so long ago, I had an open day and one of my clients recommended that I take a friend of hers for a day. So I went to interview this friend. It was a nice apartment, I could see that, and only her and her husband and everything just so. We talked a while and I was thinking that perhaps I would take the job. But the lady of the house, she looked at me and she said, "I hope you don't mind polishing and waxing the floors, I mean, getting down on your hands and knees to wax them." I said, "Lady, maybe I once used to work on my hands and knees but that's a long time ago. I'm too old for that now. If you want your floors done that way, you'll have to get somebody else to do it, or do it yourself, because that's not what I consider to be my work."

I just got my hat and put it on and walked right out of there. Later the client who had suggested this person told me that she got a telephone call about me, and we laughed and laughed about it. That's what I mean. The work I do, it can be low if you let it be or the people you work for make it that way, but it doesn't have to be. I know that a lot of young people today, they look down on what I do, and some of them even tell me that they would never do what I have done all my life. Isn't that a nice thing to say to someone? Well, it's all in how you look at it. Lord knows that there's a lot of cleaning up to do in this world, straightening up and keeping things in order. That's what I do and have done all my life, it seems to me, since I was a little girl back on the farm. But it never seemed to me that this was something to feel shameful about or shirk. What would the world be like if we never took care about our surroundings or our belongings? There is such a thing as being treated like a servant, do this, do that, all day long. But since I've grown up, that's not been the way I've been treated. And if anybody, like that woman and the floors on your hands and knees, if anybody started treating me that way, they either stopped or I left. But I do think that it is a good thing that I work for a lot of people, not just one family. I see more people that way and it keeps the relationship what I want it to be. Just as friendly and close or as distant as the situation calls for. I decide which it will be.

Now you asked me to talk about work in my life, and I have saved what I think is the most interesting for the last. I told you about my husband being sick, it was his heart. Well, one morning I got up and I went to wake him up and there he was, gone. He went in his sleep and I never knew it. It was a time for me. I don't know how I got through those days. My friends were very helpful and there was the funeral, and afterwards there was just me and the dog. Both our hearts were broke and I didn't think mine would ever mend. And there was all the trouble with the Veterans Administration and the railroad people, and that's a separate story. I kept on working after the funeral, but I wasn't myself. People were nice and considerate, but it was such a lonely time for me, I really can't say. After a time I noticed that I had a kind of trouble sometimes, swallowing and a cough, and I felt too much tired. One of the people I work for, a lady whose husband is a doctor, she insisted that I do something about it all. So finally it was arranged that I go to the New York Eye and Ear where they examined my throat. I'm old enough to be told the truth and so they said that it was something that was malignant, which means cancer, and that they would operate, and they hoped that they would be able to remove all the cancer and I would be all right. Well, they decided not to operate at all because they said that it had spread and it wouldn't do any good.

I thought to myself that that was that. But they said that I should take some medicine and they hoped that would take care of the problem. So I took this powerful medicine. It must have been terribly powerful because I felt worse and worse, and I think everybody thought that I was certain to die. People came to visit me and I could hardly get up. I seemed just to sink away. But I kept going to the hospital for the medicine, and the doctor was very good to me. He said, "Virginia, we think you're much better. You're not completely cured yet but you're much better." And then he said, "I think you can go back to work if you want to. And I think it would do you good to try to, get you out of the house and you would see your old friends."

Well, I let my old clients know that I wanted to come back and they were all delighted, so back to work I went. I took it slow at first and there were times I was so tired. But everybody understood. Well, you know, that was four years ago and I feel better and better and everybody says, "Virginia, you're looking younger and younger," and I do believe they're right. I still go the hospital once a week for the medicine. And maybe this is just extra time for me. But I feel good and I work as much as I want to and I know that I am needed, and what more can a person my age ask? When I come home, I have the dog to look after and be with. I have my house to take care of.

The problem is, and you can look out the window and see it. You know that I was worried about you coming over here to visit me. This neighborhood used to be beautiful. A park next door, the wide avenue, nice houses, churches on 125th Street. And now it's got so I just can't bear to look at it sometimes. Houses abandoned, young people standing around meaning nothing but trouble to old folks. I can't have any mail sent here because likely or not it's stolen before I get to it. It's just a crying shame and it plagues me. I don't know how many times I lost my pension check which come after the death of my husband. After all the trouble that it took to get it, all that red tape and runaround, you wouldn't believe. If it hadn't been for a lawyer friend, a former client of mine, I believe that I would never got what I was entitled to and what my husband worked his life for. It's hard for an older person like me, and I told you that I have some trouble reading and understanding complicated papers and instructions. Well, going into all those offices with all sorts of papers belonging to my poor dead husband, his discharge and his railroad papers and all things like that which he kept so neat and careful, I thought I would never be able to understand what I was supposed to do, and I would go from office to office, never seemed to get any further. I had come to believe that I would never get the pension that was coming. That really scared me, because what would I do then if I couldn't work myself? It wouldn't do to think of welfare. I couldn't think of that!

So when I despaired of ever finding out what to do or where to go, I finally told my lawyer friend that I didn't know what to do and he said, "Don't worry. I'll take care of it," and he took those papers and me and we went through those offices with no trouble at all. But I think, what of all the people like me who don't have a lawyer friend to show them the way, how many of them just finally give up, the way I almost did.

So there we are. I have my pension, which helps, I have my work, and I put something away so that I have more in saving accounts than sometimes I can really believe. I worry some about prices, and it makes my heart sad to see what is happening to this nice old neighborhood. But I have my church, my friends, and I have the people who need me and so long as I have all that, I thank the good Lord. Now, let's have some cake. I said that I learned most of what I know when I was a little girl. Well, this is a cake which I learned from my mummy and I don't know where she learned it, but I suppose it goes back a long way. I've taught it to a lot of young people, and I suppose it will be baked long after I'm gone to rejoin my husband.

Carrie Blossom

I came to New York in 1919, from Charleston, South Carolina. I'm 63 now. How old would that make me when I came here? About 13, I guess. I came here with my aunt, and we lived in Jamaica, Long Island. I left Jamaica in 1934 and moved to New York. I went to school in Jamaica.

My father took me and my two brothers and a sister and brought us from the country; we was living in, I think they say it was, Clarendon, South Carolina, some place down there. I don't know much about *that*. All I know is that my father brought us from our mother's house and brought us to Sumter, South Carolina, to his mother. My mother took sick, that's how it was. I can remember only a little of my mother. I remember her when she took sick. Mostly I lived with my aunt. Now my aunt was living in Charleston. My grandmother she had begun to get sick, so she sent for my aunt from Charleston, South Carolina to get me because I was the only girl—the baby girl died in the meantime—so I was the only girl left. My grandmother said the boys could take care of themselves but the girl couldn't, see, so she sent for my aunt to come and take me, and my aunt brought me from Sumter, South Carolina, to Charleston, and that was around about 1912, because my grandmother died in 1915. So I lived in Charleston with my aunt.

I stayed with my aunt till I got married. I didn't go to no high school. I just made through public school, the grade school. I don't think it was lack of opportunity. I believe if I stuck to it I could have had an education, because my aunt *wanted* me to go to high school, go to college, get an education, but it was just one of those things, that's all. My aunt was in a position at that time that she could afford to send me to school.

After I got married I worked awhile. I had, you know, the babies in between working. I had four babies. I was 17 when I got married. I first started working, I did housework, the same thing, day after day. I went like to an employment agency and I got, you know, different jobs. At that time it wasn't too hard to get jobs around here. In 1924, 1925, 1926 you could always get some kind of housework, like day's work mostly. I couldn't take a full-time job. It wasn't easy to manage to even work at all, with these kids, but I had someone take care of them for me. Sometimes my aunt took care of them. I didn't leave them alone. Sometimes I had a girl to stay with them. There was very little money, but we kind of managed. My husband worked on the race track, and he gambled a lot, so that was the reason that I had to, you know, try to keep things going, keep the children together. And I'm still doing domestic work now. I work part-time now. In 1934, my first boy got killed by a truck. He was going on five. He was getting ready to go into kindergarten or first grade or whatever they call it and suddenly he got killed by a truck.

It was pretty hard for us during the Depression. Yes, it was. I had a *hard* time. I'm going to tell you it wasn't easy. I went through *plenty*. I didn't have too much trouble with the jobs I'd work on because people was always very nice to me. I could always go back to each one, but the pay was very little. Mostly the food we lived on was very skimpy. Like with a pound of liver, a pound of pork chops, you make ten yards of gravy. You know. But it wasn't easy, I'm not going to say it was easy, but through it all I'm thankful that we came through. Many days I'd sit and think I should have paid more attention to my aunt and went out and got a good education and I probably would have been someone today, you know, someone that somebody else could look up to. But at that time, well, there wasn't much opportunity for them anyway and that was the reason a lot of people gave for not wanting to further their education. I could have gone, but you know—young girls, they think more of boys than of education, so that's where the education went.

Nowadays I make $140 a month at the part-time work I do. I got Social Security for a while, but I haven't got *that* in three months. I get Social

Security from the work I did. When you pay into Social Security, you are entitled to receive Social Security. On Social Security you can work and earn up to $1,680 in a year. That's all. My job that I'm working now, I get $140 a month. I get it like the first and fifteenth. And I still have to pay them Social Security out of that. See, I come home with—uh—every two weeks $64.35. I don't know *what* I'm going to get now from Social Security, but the time I did get it, I got it for December, and I got it January, February, and March, I got $80.40 a month. And I haven't gotten none since then. I don't know what is the problem now. The last part of April, I think it was, they sent me a check for $482, so I took that and I put it away, because I didn't feel like I was sure I could keep it. When I was signing up for Social Security, they didn't tell me that I was going to get any—what do they call it—like back money. They didn't tell me that I was going to get anything like that, see. So when I got it I took it and I put it up. I says that soon I might have to start using it. And that was all that I have gotten since March.

Right near here they have an office. I've been there about four or five times, and the lady, she said she was waiting to hear from the people she wrote to. And I don't know who she had to write to but it's in the office, that is the excuse they give me. She wrote to them and she's waiting to hear from them. Then as soon as she hears from them, then she'll let me know. She says she didn't think I was entitled to the lump sum check. But it's kind of strange although she knows that I got this check, she's just not bothering. She just said that she has to write some place. I don't know, to tell you the truth, I don't know. I'm just sitting waiting.

As long as I can work, I don't *want* welfare. They are hard on people on welfare. Listen, honey, I've *been* on welfare. I was on welfare also with my children, 'cause when my husband and I got separated, course we was on welfare before I leaves him. So welfare, I guess there's nothing wrong with welfare. But I feel that as long as I can work and *earn* my money, I don't *want* no welfare. Leave it for when I can't do no good for myself. That's the way *I* feel about it. And I think a lot more of these people if they would feel that way about it, they wouldn't be so hard on people on welfare.

I'm not 65 yet. I got a little bit more to go. I haven't had any problem with any illnesses, where you had to have a lot of medical attention. Once I had an operation and Father McCann took care of that. I went to St. Vincent's Hospital. He took care of that for me so that didn't cost me nothing, but otherwise I suit myself, maybe once in a while I see a doctor for something. Nothing serious. You know, they take a lot of money.

I live here alone by myself. I have one room. This is it right here. It is a studio, whatever you call it. I have my own little kitchen. I have my bath. So that's enough. I don't like to go out, in fact. Just once in a while I go to St. Charles Church, to take a bus ride, or something like that. I'll go on the bus ride. I'll maybe go to a dinner, if they have a dinner. Something like that. I like to stay in the house. I like to sit with the TV and listen to the radio. I don't watch all the daytime series. Not the give-away things. I can say I'm very much a loner. I don't like a lot of people hanging around. It makes me kind of nervous. I guess maybe it's stupid. Every once in a while I go to a dance. I like that. Something that someone has given and I know them well and it's a group that I like to be with, then I'll go. But to go see something strange, I'm not for it. Sometime people tell me it's stupid to stay in here by myself, but that's what I want. I like to be home.

I don't fear getting old. Really and truly I don't think about it. There's no sense in my thinking about it. I try to keep myself as young as I can. I like to drink occasionally, and if I find that a drink is going to do me some harm, then I'll leave it alone. But I'm not going to do anything to tear myself down. I try to keep myself up. I try to save a little bit. When the time comes that I can't work, I will find out if I can depend upon these agencies that are supposed to help old people. That's what I will find out when I have to go to them.

I think that most people now are pretty much aware of the agencies that are supposed to furnish services, because I know there was a time when especially a lot of black people didn't really know what they could get, where to go, you know, they were very confused about who to see and so forth. It is not easy to keep informed, when there are so many different things, you know, every year, something different going on, where they can get help. From what I see every day, on my job, they go mostly to the priest and the priest directs them. They tell them where to go, what charities are available, the Catholic charities. I don't consider myself a very religious person. Not at all. No, I am not going to say that. I don't forget to ask the Lord to have mercy on me. I go to church on Sunday, and maybe once in a while during the weekdays, but I am not going to say often. Sometimes I'll get a spell and I'll go, say, about two or three weeks, and then I won't go for a while, but I go to mass.

Some people sit around and imagine that all kinds of things might happen to them. There might be some good things that might happen, I don't know. But I wouldn't want to get like that, you know, just sitting. Now that is the first thing that people think that would happen to me, you know, that she's sitting home all the time, looking at TV, doing nothing. You have a whole lot of time to think a whole lot of nonsense. But you know, when I find myself beginning to think stupid, foolish things, then I always just take the Bible and read a little passage in the Bible and that pacifies me, or I take my rosary and say my rosary. You know, it kind of washes that out of my mind. Because you have no right, you know, to think things like that. If I see a spook in there in the closet, you know. Uh-uh, no, I ain't got there yet.

I imagine that some of the older people are really forgotten people, but it seems that the older people that I know, when I see them each day, they look like they doing pretty good. But I don't get around that much. You know, I don't do a lot of visiting. In fact, I can't visit sick people. I get sick myself. I don't like to go to hospitals, and that's one thing I can say that I should be ashamed of, that's an awful thing. But to visit the sick people, or go to a hospital like that, I come on and I get deathly sick in here all by myself. And I care very little about going to the undertaker and seeing a dead person. That's another thing about me. That works on my nerves. But so far I have been very healthy. I haven't had any major illnesses. So I really haven't had to depend on any of these things, like Medicare and Medicaid. And I hope that I never have to. Some people have opinions about these things, these agencies, that they are not what they are supposed to be. But, you see, I haven't had no experience with them so I can't say whether they are good or whether they are bad.

A lot of people that I have talked to, and especially some of those that are older, tell me that one of the things they fear in getting old is the whole problem of crime in New York. And it is not only in New York. And I feel terrible about it. I got held up not so long ago. My daughter and I got held up going into her house. I was going up the stairs with her and these two boys came by and, you know, because I walk slower than my daughter, and you know, we were talking, and she was ahead of me, and I heard this running in the hall, and when I got to the steps and now there is no sense in my trying to get up before anybody else, so I just stepped aside. My daughter was up a couple of steps, and this fellow rushed past me, you know, so I'm standing there waiting for the other man to go by, and I turned around and this boy had a knife on me. I says to him, I says, "Is this what you want? Take it!" I gave him my pocketbook.

So the man turned around to my daughter. And he was trying to do something, there was something he had in his hand. And I looked and he was after her, and I screamed, so she said to me, "Oh, momma, don't scream, don't scream." She didn't know that the guy down below had my pocketbook because I had given it to him. Oh, yes, took hers too, but she didn't have anything in hers. But she had just given me $20 and I had it in there. I shouldn't have put it in there. I should have put it in down here. But you know, it didn't really frighten me, no, because they weren't violent, and I looked at the boys, and two clean-cut boys, you wouldn't think. You'd think, my son, that's what I thought of when I looked in his face. I said, "Gee whiz, he's just like my son, a nice clean boy," and I said, "This is what he's doing." And I did not get frightened until I got home.

When I got in the house, I started shaking, see, and since then I have been a little shook up, especially coming up on the elevator; I won't get on it. I wait until there is someone in the building that I know, and lots of times when I come in there are a couple of women down there doing the same thing, waiting, you know, for someone else to come up. But, I'm telling you, it is a problem. This problem seems to have gotten out of hand, it certainly has. It's way out of hand. A lot of older people seem to think that these people prey on older people. And so do I, because, you see, the older people can't put up a fight. The only thing that an older person can do is just to let them go ahead and take what they want. But a lot of time they will beat an older person, knock an older person down. You know, she don't want them to take her pocketbook and she will put up a little fight, and that's how they get hurt. And I say, "Just give it to them." I'm not going to fight over it. If they want it, then take it. But I hope it don't happen and I hope it don't happen to anyone else, because it is really no fun.

I have lived in this neighborhood since about 1940, because I used to live on 143rd Street, and when they tore that down to make housing, I came here. So since I left Queens, I have been in the same place, or somewhere in this general area. If I have to live in New York, I prefer to live around here, where people know me. Back in 1938 or 1939 at that time I lived over on 123rd Street. I was on welfare. I had been on welfare in Jamaica. That was when I first got on welfare. The people at welfare would take your insurance policy and turn them in to the insurance company, mostly Metropolitan, that was the only one that I had, and they got about $80 from this thing, and the insurance people mailed me this check.

I thought this check, when I got it, I could use it any way I wanted, so I spent the money, paid some bills, which was wise, you know, so a couple of days later the investigator came by and she told me about this check that I had got, you know, so she asked me, did I have it, so I said yes, so she sat there and she asked me where the check was, and I said that I had done spent it, paid my bills, bought food and stuff for the children. Eighty dollars was nice at that time. And she sat there and she deducted that eighty dollars out of me, and I didn't get a check for about a month, and that money was deducted from that check, and you know, I had a tough time for a whole month, because you get the check the first and the fifteenth. I had a tough time making ends meet.

But then I moved from Jamaica to New York. And I was living on 135th Street, and that's when the investigator came to my house and told me about finding my husband. I was still on welfare. So, she told me, she said, "Do you know where your husband is?"and I said, "No, I don't." She said, "Oh, yes, you do. You know where he is." I said, "I don't know where my husband is." She said, "Well, you have to go find him." I said, "I'm not going to find nobody," I said, "because when I left my husband, I told him I was not going to sleep under the same roof with him again, and I meant it. See." I said to her, "Now, if you find him, *you* live with him, because I am *not* going to live with him." "Well," she said, "you won't get no more checks." I said, "Okay," and sure enough, she shut me off.

I didn't think she was serious about it. But she shut me off. So I went to the place where you had to go to, the office. At that time it was on 135th Street but they were in the process of moving. And they were fixing up this other place. So for three whole weeks I sat there with other mothers waiting to get checks, and they had their children. Of course the poor little kids were crying, you know, because they were hungry, they didn't have no milk. Nobody could never see you but supervisors. So you just sat and sat there and sat there, from nine o'clock in the morning until they closed up, and you go home and you come back the next morning and you just sit there and give your name at the desk and sit there. And you sit there. And so this is what I did for three weeks.

And I was sitting there and something say to me, "Get up and go home and get yourself a pencil and paper and envelope and ink and write a letter to Mayor LaGuardia." So I did that. I went to my girl friend's house and I borrowed an envelope and a sheet of paper and a two-cent stamp. And then I went home and sat down ahd I wrote a letter. That's one letter I would love you to see. I should have kept a copy. I didn't have sense enough to do those things.

I just poured it out. I guess it was some *bad* English and some bad spelling, and everything. There was nothing fancy in me like that. I just needed help. And I told Mayor LaGuardia about all the other mothers who were sitting in the office with their children, about how their children were crying, because they're hungry, and sitting there from nine o'clock to five o'clock every day and nobody give us nothing, nobody tell us nothing, and I said that these women come up in their fine cars and with their furs and dressed pretty and walk over to the desk and get a check and we are sitting there starving and our children are starving.

I put all that in that letter and I sealed it up and I mailed it to Mayor LaGuardia. So in the meantime, this was on Friday afternoon, a friend of mine gave me the number for the mayor's office. I told the person who answered who I was, and she said, "Oh, Mrs. Blossom," she says, "I have your letter right here in front of me." That was the quickest action I ever had in my life. Well, anyhow, so she says, "I'll tell you what to do. You go to the 131st Street office and you ask for Miss Davis," and I said, "Oh, I been trying to get to Miss Davis for three weeks. And nobody can get to her." She said, "I'll tell you what you do. You go there and *I'll* call her. And when you get there, you'll see her."

And sure enough, when I got there, I was met at the door by Miss Davis. And I said, "Miss Davis," and she said to me, "You Mrs. Blossom?" I said, "Yes." "Why did you write downtown?" I said, "Because I couldn't get to see you and my children are starving, and getting ready to get put out of their home. And the rest of those mothers are sitting over there the same way. Their children are crying and they are hungry. I *had* to write downtown." Well, she took me in her office. And she raised Cain with me, but it didn't make any difference. She had to give me a voucher for food and for my rent. And I didn't have no trouble out of them until I decided to get off. I started working at St. Charles. I got myself a job that was paying me, you know, enough that I could pay my bills, then I got off.

My children were pretty well grown up then. The boys could go out and earn a little change, delivering groceries, they were working around a grocery store. I could have stayed on welfare, if I had wanted to. I could have stayed on, but I didn't want to. In all I stayed on welfare about ten years, but only because I had to. When the children were old enough so I could go out and work, I got off welfare.

Deborah Smith

I came to Newark as a girl. I came from Richmond, Virginia. I came up here in 1909. I came here as a nurse, a child nurse. I didn't finish schooling but I decided that I wouldn't finish. I dropped out of school. I was already employed when I came up here. I came up here with a job. I don't remember exactly who I was working for. I know her name, but I can't think of the family's name. She got married up here. She married this man and he was Jewish and he had a very unusual name, a name that you don't hear very often. And then I left them and I went to another family. And then I came back to Newark. And then I went to Hackensack, I was there about three months. Left Newark for a job, a better salary. I was looking for more money.

Good money in those days was $25 a month, and, well, I was working long days too. You could get along with $25 a month in those days. Frankfurters were $.16 a pound and pork chops were $.16 a pound and fish was two pounds for a quarter, and all that stuff. And look what you got to pay now for that. You got to pay $1.10 for fish now, more than that. It is different, but you don't feel no different, you know what I mean. Because you know how much you got to spend so you spend that and no more. You have to budget yourself, I don't care how much you make.

And then I met my husband in Millington. I went from Millington back to Newark and then to Hackensack. And then I came back and I got married when I was in Hackensack. It wasn't for money so much. I wasn't so much in the money part, but I just liked to get around, you know. Get around and meet people and learn something.

Well, I met a lady from the 13th Avenue church. She was from Virginia and she was a teacher. So I met her and I always, after I left this lady I told you about, I made my home with her. And she lived in Newark, she lived on North Broad Street. She didn't have no children, just her and her husband, and so she took me in as a child, practically, helped find me some jobs. And then I used to take music. I'd taken music before I came to Newark. And then I told her that I would like to continue music. So she gave me Mrs. Gaines' number. So I took music off of her.

And then at that time, Dr. Edwards, he was pastor at the 13th Avenue church, he came to my house, after I got married, because this lady that taken me as her daughter, she was taken sick so she went to the hospital. She came out of the hospital, but she didn't know where to find her husband, so I told her to come and stay with me and so she did. And she lived with me and Dr. Edwards came to see us. And so he asked me to play. I had my piano. My husband give it to me for my anniversary because we had married. So I played, so he said, "You come down. You come over to the church and play for us on Wednesday evening." So I went over and I did. So he said, "Now, that's your piano, you play just as long as you want to." And I taught for a while here in Newark.

I taught music at the third grade. It must have been in 1925. I didn't teach right through the Depression, because then I started to take on other things, because I can do a little of this and a little of that, see. So then I started sewing. I make powder puffs. I make powder puffs for a long time. A powder puff is to powder your face with, so they wouldn't give them to any other colored person but me, 'cause I knew this white woman that was doing this work, see, and she taught me how to do it. And then she said that she would get me a job, which she did.

I didn't sell them. I sewed for a factory. And I used to make a gross a day. Yes, a gross a day! I had to sew by hand because you couldn't make one by machine. And then I sewed that for a long time, but then after that they went out of business, so I got another job. Sewed doll dresses. So I sewed doll dresses up until I lost my sight. That was in 1946, or 1947. My sight got pretty bad on me then, so I give it up. The doctor told me to.

I never got bored. I didn't have time. 'Cause you see I had my children. You know, I had to look after them, and I couldn't take a steady job on account of me having the children, you see. I just took these little jobs. That powder puff job, that was at home. I brought the work home with me, and sewing my doll dresses I bring them home too and do it, and they would come and pick up the work. The way I got this job, well, I'll tell you. I used to do dressmaking and I got this job through a lady I used to sew for her. I used to make her children's dresses and school dresses and so forth. And I used to make dresses for other people, and so that is how I came to get this other job. I never used an employment agency. No. No. No. No. Never been in one of their offices.

You asked if I worked right through the Depression. Well, if you know people, you get around, you know different people, you see. There are a lot of people that know people, but still they have to go to the employment office. Got to have references and all that kind of stuff. So I didn't have to do nothing like that.

Since 1946, well, I have been taking care of my home. Yes, and I haven't done anything special, outside of taking care of my home. I live here by myself. Yes, I am here by myself. I haven't cleaned up this week, because last week I was going out. I was going to see some friends of mine, the first people I met when I first came to to Newark. She's got, I think, seven sisters and brothers. They are all living, but the mother and father have passed on. They are my oldest friends. They live out on Long Island. They have a home down to the shore. So she had me over to her house on Sunday and Harry take me over. She knew me long before I was married.

I was married nine years before I had any children, I was married on December 8, 1910. I had three children, Donald, Charles and Patricia. She works in the Veterans Hospital and Charles works for the Internal Revenue. He was in Newark, but they transferred him to Brooklyn. He has lovely children.

My husband was a musician, but he worked for the Essex County Park Commission. He used to be a watchman there. He was with them 28 years. I guess you know what the Essex County Park is. You know Bedford Park. Well, that is all in Essex County Park. Well, he worked over in that direction, so that's why I moved here. I lived in 5th Street and then we was looking for a house.

Well, we came over here one Sunday, going over to the park, over to the bench there, and they had music, a band over there to play on Sunday. So we was walking out one Sunday with the kids and we come up this street. And that Sunday, I said to my husband, because where we were living then we only had three rooms, we lived on the third floor, "That would be a nice little shanty to get in." I looked at the yard, and I said, "The kids, they could play down there." So we found that the house was for rent. An Italian woman, she saw me at the window and she and her husband opened the window and she said, "Do you want to look at the rooms?" I said, "I wouldn't mind." So she told her husband to get the keys So she came and opened the door for us and we came in and looked around in there. At that time it was nothing but an old dump but we went all around and looked at it, and I said, "It would be better if it were a whole house." And he said he would see about it. And I said, "All righty."

And so we had to go down State Street and see the landlord. He was down in his shop on State Street. So that Monday my husband went down to State Street to see him and when my husband came back he says, "He want people to come up next Monday and he will permit me to see the house." So we did, and he said, "I give him some money on deposit." So he says, "The house is for rent or for sale." So I told him, "Well, it is a nice neighborhood, but I don't care so much about the house." We stayed for awhile, then my husband, he says, "Well, if we go to East Orange or Montclair, I'll have to get up so early in the morning, especially when the weather get bad, don't you know?" And so, I said, "Well, you can walk from here to your job."

And so I said, "We'll take it on account of your job, and the neighborhood, it's nice." There were no colored people in the neighborhood. And so I said, "And I would like to get the children in a nice school." So then we took it, and my son was graduated from Garfield Grammar School and Donald and Patricia from Barringer, and Charles was graduated from Art High. So we were looking out for their education. And I didn't want to bring them up in a strictly colored neighborhood.

So I didn't come here to stay, but we just stayed. We just stayed and stayed. We bought it and we fixed it up. And so it turned out all right. We have been here 46 years. We've seen a lot of change, but still there ain't but two colored families on this block, that's all. One time there was about eight colored families here, but after the Bittlemens sold their houses, all the Italian people bought them and made the colored people get out. So the colored people next door, her and I are the only two colored people in here. So she passed away in February, and her granddaughter rents the house out. Her granddaughter lives up in Boston. So she just rents the house out and I haven't seen her since her grandmother died.

This is primarily an Italian neighborhood. I think the woman next door is Italian, but her husband's Spanish. And Germans down the street a little further, and next Italians. And across the street is Italian and down further, and I think there is some Irish around here somewhere. And some Polish. Next door she's Irish and her husband is Italian. So we are all mixed in, you know, and they all look after me. They are very nice to me.

We don't have any black and white trouble because we are all just like one family. Yeah, we are just like one family, yes, indeed. They come in here and want to know, "Is there anything I can do for you?" They watch and see that nobody come in and see how long they are going to stay. Yes, they are watching me all right. Yes, indeed, so they're very nice. And if I say that there is anything I want, just call them. They watch the house and they're watching me.

I belong to the Red Cross. I did belong to the Mothers' Club, and the Doxie Club, and I belong to the Guild. At the blind school, we makes novelties and little things. You see, I made those things over there. This is ceramic. We have that once a month. Every Saturday we have something. And every third Sunday we have open house. And the third Saturday we have sewing, and the fourth Saturday I think that we have jewelry. I go every week and every third Sunday of each month. And we have Thanksgiving Dinner, and then we have Christmas Dinner, and we have George Washington's Dinner and then we have Lincoln's Dinner, and we have spaghetti dinner, and we have bingo one Sunday, and we have the white elephant sale, auctioning off things. 'Cause we make a lot of things that we don't bring home. We leave them at the Guild. And people who want to buy them can have them. And they give us the money, but I don't accept any. I let that go to the Guild. And we have music and singing, oh, we have a good time. Oh, we have dancing. Every Thursday night, they have dancing.

We have time for other activities because, you see, dancing is in the evening. And we take up Braille because it is kind of hard for me. I don't know how to read something. You have to be sensitive to letters, you know. And so I haven't ever taken an interest in Braille, although it would be very nice if I did learn. We have cooking class. And we can take cooking and we can take up nursing.

The way I get down there is that on Saturday I call up for a ride. And different ones volunteer their services, and if I want to take a spin or two, I'll call them up. I never have any trouble, although sometimes it is hard to get a ride because a lot of people are busy, you know, 'specially men folks. They have their work to do. But we get a ride. I very seldom been left. Our school opens at two-thirty. From two-thirty to four-thirty. This is right in the heart of Newark, near the Penn Station.

You ask me what my children are doing. Well, Patricia, she married James Perry in 1941. And she has four children. James Perry and Thomas and Betty and William. Thomas, the second one, is a detective in East Orange. And he has two girls. Those are my grandchildren. I have a little boy four years old. Mary, my granddaughter, she is married too. My daughter works in the County Hospital. My son-in-law, I don't know where he works. He's sickly. He can't work steadily. His heart is not good. He's been overweight.

And my son, Donald, well, he graduated from Barringer and then he went to Winston-Salem, and then he went to Georgetown University Law School, in Washington. I am very proud of my children.

Other than my eyes, I haven't had any health problems that required hospitalization or anything like that. Only my eyesight. That's all. And I had to have an operation on them. And then I had a hemorrhage in my head. But up until that time I was in perfect health. My health is perfect, excellent. I never got any assistance from any government agencies when I was ill, and not now. I don't get Social Security either. I don't work so I guess that is why I never got it. I mean, the work I did was at home. All I get is my husband's small pension. He paid into Social Security, but I don't get no Social Security. Anyway, I just get along with what I have, don't you know? I don't have no expenses. I can't go to any expense, I mean, with my house or household. I don't have the money to do that.

We did not get to Charles. Now Charles, he works for the Internal Revenue in New York. He finished up school; he graduated from St. John's College. And then he worked for the ODB for quite a while before he went into the service. And then he went into the Internal Revenue and he has been there ever since. He's married now, and his wife, she's a teacher. And they have two children, a boy and a girl. The girl, she takes music.

There's a lot of music in my family. Yes, my people on my mother's side, they were all musicians. They lived in Macklenberg, Virginia. My grandparents came from there. It's not far from Richmond. Yes, but I was never out there.

I've been to a camp meeting. Oh yes indeed. I used to go there when I was a kid, 'round about ten years old. We used to have them after they get through with preaching, on the camp ground. Everybody had their table set up and you go around there and you could eat all the food you want—fried chicken and corn pudding and watermelon, anything, marvelous.

They start in August, see. The first Sunday in August, they'll have it at this church, and the second at this other church, and then the third Sunday, they have it at another church, that was the church my mother's people used to belong to. And people would come from far and near, and I remember that my mother used to kill chickens. She used to kill ten chickens and my father used to kill little goats and they would be cooking that for all week. And I tell you, they would have some food. And my mother and another lady, a lady name Lucy, they used to get together and they had their tables set together, and my father used to set up that table, as long as this room. And they had that white tablecloth on the table, and they had that food set up there, so that when you came out of church, after the church service was over, and everybody would get around and start eating. And all the watermelon was on and you used to have watermelon on the ground, and they put them under the table. And, after they finished eating the food, then they started cutting the watermelon and then start slicing the watermelon, serving the watermelon. It was good.

You ask me if I get lonesome? You kidding? I got the piano there; I got the phone. I can't see, but I just feel the keys on the piano. I don't get lonesome; I got my work to do. Sure, I have got my work to do. How can I get lonesome, all the work I got to do? I keep this whole place clean and spotless by myself.

COMMENTARY

The women, like the men, were born in the South and migrated in their late teens or early twenties to New York City or Newark. Most of them had had disturbed childhoods as a result of the death of a parent and subsequent hardship in their family. Several were raised by relatives. Like the men, most of the young women reached New York with little education and less training. One had worked her way through high school and junior college; another had managed to graduate from a neighboring nursing school which she had been able to attend because of the low fees.

With little to offer employers and facing a labor market that was highly discriminatory, it is not surprising that most of the newcomers had to take jobs as domestics, an occupation from which they could not readily extricate themselves. The junior college graduate sought, however, to improve her job and status and her story reveals the breaks and disappointments that she encountered. World War II enabled her to get a job in the city's transport system, formerly an all-male enclave. When the veterans returned she lost this job, as the union turned its back on its recently enrolled female members. There were subsidized training opportunities open to women in nursing, but faced with the responsibility of supporting her young son, she could not enter upon a course of full-time study and had to settle for a less attractive job in the Veterans Administration structure.

Welfare plays a critical role in the life histories of several of our women; it is a story with roots that go back to the Great Depression. One respondent reported that without money to feed her young children and threatened with eviction, she and other women who were single parents sat day after day in the local welfare office unable to talk with the supervisor and unable to convince the social worker to provide them with some support. She obtained action only after writing to Mayor LaGuardia. There may be many wrongs in the welfare system today but, at least in the northern states, children no longer go hungry because the welfare staffs are under instructions to withhold funds until they have proof positive that the families are in dire straits.

Most of the women feel it is better to have nothing to do with the system since many workers treat welfare clients so inhumanely. None of the women, at the time of their interviews, was on welfare, nor had any one of them been for years. They, like their generation, took pride in being able to care for themselves, even in old age when they were no longer able to work.

In the families that remained intact, the husband was employed as a pullman porter, a tailor, a park attendant, or a factory worker who had once worked in the South on the railroads, in saw mills, in his own restaurant, and in a dry cleaning shop. The pullman porter's pension was not easy to collect, but his widow, through the help of a lawyer friend, got what was due her. Another kept going with the help of the pension from her husband who had spent three decades as a park attendant in the Newark area. One widow reported that her financial circumstances were eased by the fact that she and her husband, when he was alive, had put money aside to buy a house from which she now received rent to supplement her Social Security benefits.

While two of the women were childless, several reached old age in the midst of children and grandchildren from whom they received both pleasure and emotional support, and possibly even some financial help. The presence of relatives was one important cushioning influence that helped them deal with the loss of their spouses and with the other hardships of advancing age. Others found much comfort in their long-term relations with neighbors and friends. Religion and local churches provided a further source of support. It is worth remembering that several of the women were Catholics, although most older American blacks were reared in and remained attached to one of the Protestant denominations.

The quality of a person's older years is affected much not only by money and ties to family and friends but also by the condition of one's health. In this respect, these women were on the lucky side. The centenarian reported that she was free of infirmities except for a diabetic condition which grew out of her liking for sweets in her younger years. Mrs. Smith had lost her eyesight but was able to manage her home and play the piano despite this disability; these activities occupied all of her free time. The others did not mention ill health or disability and apparently were functioning effectively despite their advancing years.

Deteriorating neighborhoods and the loss of financial security added to the burdens of these women as they entered old age; one of the respondents remarked that violence is all over and this is a "generation of vipers." Several reported that they would not go out at night or stay out late.

If one contrasts these black women with the black men whose life histories we reviewed earlier, one finds no counterpart at the low end of the curve. No woman, with one partial exception, is living a marginal existence, waiting for the days to pass sitting on her doorstep or locked up in her room with no ties to the outside world. These women had fuller lives with goals, interests, and activities from which they derived considerable satisfaction. Nothing about their later years especially depressed them other than the loss of a beloved spouse. In most regards, they know how to cope.

PART II

Young Puerto Ricans

INTRODUCTION

Young Puerto Rican men and women tell about their lives and experiences from a point of view very different from that of most older blacks. While the black man or woman often looks back over a long life and attempts to sum up its meaning, the young Puerto Rican looks into the future and tries to understand whether his or her experience, or the experiences of parents, provides some way of understanding and coming to grips with what the future may hold. In particular, these young men and women want to understand what scope they have for fulfilling their desires and ambitions, what options face them, and what forces, both internal and external, will influence their choices.

Both groups take it for granted that they are minorities, part of a recent wave of migration to the North, even if individually they may have been in New York for generations. They also take for granted that they are *not* like earlier immigrant groups in New York City, and that they should *not* be compared to other ethnic groups. They find no consolation in being told that earlier groups suffered, were packed into tenements, became sick and died, and were unemployed or underpaid.

Here much of the similarity between blacks and Puerto Ricans ends. For one thing, the older blacks who migrated from the South either made the decision to move on their own or wanted to come, regardless of the heartaches the move might cause. Secondly, almost all older blacks take it more or less for granted that their destiny is inextricably linked with that of America, in the sense that they are more American than any immigrant of the nineteenth or twentieth century. Their argument is about their status as Americans, not about whether they are Americans in the first place. Finally, many of the older blacks have been in New York or Newark much longer than have the Puerto Ricans. They live in communities that are much larger in population, and they have achieved some, even if slight, degree of influence and political power. Puerto Rican youth are apt to realize that, bad as the lot of the ordinary black in New York, the lot of the ordinary Puerto Rican is worse.*

To many young Puerto Ricans, it is important to understand why their families left Puerto Rico and other events that occurred before their births. The past is part of their present in a way that is simply not the case for almost all other immigrant groups.† But that past is also unique in American experience. Regardless of their feelings and beliefs about Puerto Rican independence, almost all young Puerto Ricans feel that the presence of the United States in Puerto Rico is forced and alien. Thus, they consider 1898 a critical date and the early decades of the twentieth century, during which the United States was rigorously trying to transform the island and its population into an English-speaking Americanized people, a critical period that determines, to some extent, their own development.

While most young Americans have almost no concern about what may have occurred during their grandparents' eras, many young Puerto Ricans have a consuming interest in what happened on the island during that time. Their understanding of that period determines what they believe themselves to be and what they believe they ought to strive for. From their point of view, moreover, the critical forces and events that determined the character and experiences of their parents and grandparents are directly related to their own characters and lives. Two examples may illustrate this connection.

When the United States took control over Puerto Rico, one of the primary objectives of the U.S. policy was to raise the educational level of the Puerto Ricans, and to transform the language of the island to English through the medium of the school. The policy of the U.S. authorities in charge of education was to use teachers with no Spanish accent; the school curriculum was carried out in English. Teachers were imported from the mainland, and no real effort was made to give them an understanding of Spanish culture or behavior patterns.

The predictable result was, with some exceptions, an educational disaster. It was impossible to turn the island into an English-speaking territory. Puerto Rican children usually resented their teachers and were, in turn, often treated with contempt and harshness by school personnel. The

---

*It still comes as a shock to many young Peurto Ricans to learn just how much worse that lot is. A recent publication of the Regional Office of the Bureau of Labor Statistics, "A Socio-Economic Profile of Puerto Rican New Yorkers," gives some details of the position of Puerto Ricans, emphasizing that a relative decline took place between 1960 and 1970, a decline which has almost certainly continued and probably accelerated.

†Perhaps recent young Irish or Israeli immigrants, living in America, also have something of the same sense of inextricable involvement in a part of the world which is not part of the continental United States. The attachment, in the case of young Puerto Ricans, is reinforced by a number of factors, not the least of which is the ease and frequency of travel between the island and New York City.

long-term consequence was that several generations of Puerto Ricans, including the parents and grandparents of Puerto Rican youth now in New York City, went to school fewer years than did mainland Americans, and during these years were unable to achieve the reading and computational skills in English equivalent to the mainland average. Usually their ability and incentives to use English were minimal, and of course their education in Spanish was neglected, except when the family itself was able to provide it.

Young New York Puerto Ricans know that their parents emigrated with relatively poor educational preparation, a language handicap, a feeling that they were educational failures, and a lifelong sense of inferiority because of their school experiences. They also feel that their parents can give them little or no guidance in school and sometimes have little interest in what they do there. To many Puerto Rican parents the school remains an alien and forbidding institution which emphasizes their lack of power.

The second example of a process occurring in Puerto Rico, which has a profound relationship to patterns of behavior and self-concept of contemporary young Puerto Ricans in New York City, is the transformation of the Puerto Rican economy which took place in several stages following the American seizure of power.

It might be well to note parenthetically that much of what took place would have occurred in any event, but the American presence may have accelerated the pace of the process to a considerable degree. Puerto Ricans, particularly the young, often believe that the suffering and displacement that occurred was the result of a deliberate American policy designed to exploit the island's natural resources and its supply of cheap labor.

One stage of the process of economic transformation, well under way before 1898, took place in agriculture. Plantation cultivation of sugar on a large scale was expanded, and many of the smaller farms disappeared in the process. At the same time, the island experienced a sharp increase in the rate of population growth. Low wages, underemployment in agriculture (the field worker in sugar cultivation worked scarcely more than half a year), coupled with increasing unemployment produced mass poverty in the countryside. Specialization in the cultivation of a few cash crops reached a point where the island was to a significant degree dependent upon food imports for its day-to-day sustenance. In 1965, less than one percent of land in cultivation in Puerto Rico was devoted to vegetables; almost 80 percent was in tobacco or sugar. The continuing crisis in Puerto Rican agriculture is vividly illustrated by the fact that between 1965 and 1969, a time of generally booming conditions in the world economy, the amount of land cultivated in Puerto Rico fell by 37 percent!

The response of government was to push the industrialization of the island through Operation Bootstrap. Since the middle of the Great Depression of the 1930s, industrialization and urbanization have proceeded rapidly. One result has been a significant increase in per capita income. In

1969, per capita income (in 1967 dollars) in Puerto Rico was about $170, one-fifth that of the mainland United States. By 1975, it had risen to about $750 (again in 1967 dollars), somewhat more than one-fourth of the mainland figure. At the same time a much larger proportion of the population was urbanized and therefore much more dependent upon the market for goods and services.

Although incomes did go up on the average, a high rate of unemployment was also a feature of island life, particularly among those whose earnings were lowest even when they were employed. In 1960, after a generation of Operation Bootstrap, one out of seven men was officially unemployed. A decade of economic expansion reduced this high rate to only 11.5 percent by 1970. In 1972, the rate was almost as high as it was a dozen years earlier. It comes as something of a surprise to an observer who is used to mainland rates of unemployment to discover that the rate of unemployment for women in Puerto Rico is significantly lower than it is for men, a reflection of the demand for service workers, and women operatives in light industry, coupled with the relatively low labor force participation rates of Puerto Rican women.

Since New York City is only a few hours and a hundred dollars away by air, and since Puerto Ricans, American citizens since 1917, are as free to move to the mainland as any mainland resident is free to move from state to state, it has been inevitable that movement between the island and New York would be considerable in both directions.

The most powerful force motivating movement to New York has always been the prospect of employment. For the overwhelming majority of Puerto Rican men who came to New York from the island, this has meant employment in low-paid service jobs or as operatives and laborers in plastic factories, toy factories, metal-working plants, and the garment industry. Educational barriers, language barriers, and lack of experience combined to channel Puerto Ricans into a relatively narrow and low-ranking sector of the city's occupational hierarchy. Coupled with these factors and underpinning all of them was a pervasive network of discriminatory barriers, strongest in just those areas where upward mobility might otherwise have been possible.

Once the Puerto Rican family was located in New York, any economic or personal crisis could push it into the welfare system. Unemployment, ill-health, or the break-up of a husband and wife, in short order would usually lead the family to welfare agencies because the family unit had few other resources to fall back on. Although the Puerto Rican culture traditionally placed severe sanctions upon idleness on the part of an adult male, the differential between welfare payments in New York City and those on the island ensured that some Puerto Ricans would choose to stay in the city when confronted with a choice between welfare assistance there or in Puerto Rico.

Although many Puerto Ricans fell back upon welfare assistance, the great majority of Puerto Rican men still continued to be attached to low-paying service, operative or laboring occupations. Proportionately more Puerto Ricans are members of the labor force than is the rest of the population of New York City. In 1969, for example, 78 percent of all Puerto Rican men *living in poverty areas* were in the labor force compared with 75 percent for the city as a whole.

This is partly due to the fact that the Puerto Rican population is relatively young and that a large proportion of the young population is in the labor force, not in school. But even in the prime working age groups, from 25 to 54, some 93 percent of all Puerto Rican men in the poverty areas of the city were in the labor force, as compared with 94 percent for the city as a whole. It is only when we look at men 55 and over that we see a sharp distinction between Puerto Ricans and the rest of the population. In these older age groups, the labor force participation rate of Puerto Rican men is indeed lower. It is significant that one of the major reasons for not working given by these older Puerto Rican men is ill health, a reason seldom mentioned by the rest of the city's older nonworkers. A lifetime in low-paying occupations as laborers or operatives has undoubtedly contributed to this pattern of debility and chronic disease.

We have detailed some of the economic transformations which have taken place in the lives of the parents of Puerto Rican youth in New York City because of the general feeling among the young people with whom we talked that they can expect little guidance in their own search for a livelihood from their parents' experience. When parents have supported a family by working at low-paying menial occupations, their children can often express admiration and appreciation for their labor while resenting and rejecting the pattern of work experience which has led to the parents' long years of hard unremunerative work. When a parent has been unable to stay employed or has left the work force, any attempt by that parent to inculcate his children with a work ethic which places primary emphasis upon the value of work is apt to be greeted with derision.

Young Puerto Ricans reject the kind of work that their parents usually performed, and they are aware that the city is not going to offer as many of these jobs in the future. The sharp decrease in factory employment in the last few years has hit the Puerto Rican worker very hard. The loss of many more low-level service jobs looms ahead. Young Puerto Ricans in New York realize that only through increasing entry into white-collar occupations can they expect to break out of the pattern of low income, chronic unemployment, and underemployment which beset their parents.

That is why it is so critical for them, both as a matter of survival and of self-definition to be able to answer the question, "Am I American or not?" It is significant that all the young Puerto Ricans with whom we spoke often used the expression, "they." When asked whom they meant by that term, they answered, "White Americans," and when asked whom they meant by "we," they said, "Us, the Puerto Rican." They did not pause to think about

PUERTO RICAN MEN

Ramon Gonzales

I was living down on East 5th Street, between Avenue C & D. I used to shoe shine. I was quite good at it. You could do it some place where people get together like in restaurants, or cafes, where they would have to stay for awhile at least, you know, and then while they're eating a hot dog or something, why not shine their shoes, or catch them when they're coming outside?

I'd say to my friend, "Why don't we go outside and play or do something in the back yard?" It was the slums, and it was almost like a jungle, a big play area from building to building, and he'd say, "No, no, no, I've got to get some money." It was some toy that he wanted, and he went inside, pulled out his shoeshine box and he went out and he got some change, and I was fascinated. I said, "Hell, I want to do this too." At the time I was in the third grade, I think.

It was never steady money, nothing you could really keep a tab on. Really all you had was hope, because you were so inexperienced that you couldn't realize certain things, you know. I'm amazed that we were even able to analyze the problem: well, this is a place where you have to stay, to get a customer, and just now I am even amazed at the fact that you just hoped to get $.15 a shine. That was kind of expensive, even though sometimes you used to hit them for $.25 if they looked like they didn't know any better, but some knew that was too high. I only got caught once, and I said, "Okay, okay, $.15." There was standard price for a shoeshine and you kind of kept to it, and if you saw a guy raising it to $.25, you know, you never bothered him about it. You just knew that he was wheeling and dealing and that something was going on, and just watched to see what went on. I stayed more or less close to home, because we were on welfare and to get caught by the caseworker—it was stupid.

We were all on welfare, the whole area was. The caseworker would not want us to shine shoes. It was considered an "added income," and they said that it was illegal and you couldn't be caught doing it. East 5th Street was a slum area and my family was on welfare. I was on welfare till I was 21; that was last year. They kept you until 21; they don't care what you do, whether you're in school, or whatever you're doing, and then they cut off automatically. It was nothing you thought about, it was so natural.

In a way this struck me because even though everybody down there knew that everyone was on welfare, some would try to put you down for something they were into too. Maybe you'd come in with a pair of socks or gloves, and they'd say, "Hey, did the welfare check come in?"; or else they might be cursing at somebody, they would be calling his mother everything, and all of a sudden you'd hear, "Your mother's on welfare," and I'd think, "Why don't you drop dead; your mother's on welfare too. Everybody's on welfare; what are you talking about."

I couldn't understand what was going on until I'd got to about sixth grade and I said, "Oh, wow, welfare isn't such a hot thing, is it; I mean, to be on welfare is really bad." And so from then on—I never denied it, I just never had to say it, I didn't have to tell anyone that I was on welfare. It was almost like you were a lesser something or other. It always gave me a scare. Somebody would be up there, and I'd be down here. That's why I never tried to deny it, because that would be stupid, but if somebody didn't have to know, there was no reason to tell him.

It had an effect at school. It never came up directly, but you could feel it. The students, even though they were living in the same area that you were, who weren't on welfare, they were different, you knew it, they seemed different—they talked, acted differently, and it seemed like they were treated differently. They responded to things—like they were the most studious types, they were the more neatly dressed, they seemed more sophisticated, more advanced, and they seemed to be the ones that were always closer to the teacher than yourself.

My family spoke primarily Spanish—the first language I learned to speak was Spanish. Usually the tiniest thing will give you some of the real story about the man. Pronouncing the word "Oh" slightly different from "O," that's the Spanish influence. So you know that the major language influence on him has been English or Spanish.

When I first went to school I could handle both languages, but English was still somewhat of a problem to me until, I think, high school. The first school I went to was a public school. I went to parochial school when I came to live with my aunt and uncle, to Corpus Christi grammar school. Before that, I'd taken some religious instruction when I was a kid down around East 5th Street. But in the first years of school I didn't have any feeling of success or failure.

I don't even know how I passed the grades. I don't remember taking books home. I took my notebook, I remember that, but I did have this feeling of achievement. I can remember even the words and the first book, but that was not reinforced very much by my family.

First of all, it was a big thing to be able to read. Any time I did it successfully the teacher felt satisfied; there was a really good feeling about it; I guess that was what was reinforcing it. I never felt that I was classified by the teacher as some kid who couldn't read, or a dumb kid, or anything like that. But I did not feel that the teacher was encouraging me either. No, it was that when I did it correctly, I felt good, and I knew I was doing it right, by the teacher not saying anything, you know, that you should have pronounced it this way. When there was a lack of instruction or correction, that to me was okay, and then I'd say, "Oh, wow, I'm really doing good at this. I can't read too fast, but I can do it." And then the picture was there, and here you were getting the idea, reinforcing it even more, like if you can read all of this, you know exactly what's going on in the picture, you don't even have to think about it, it's right there.

A number of children are classified by the teacher very quickly. There were the "in" students, and they'd be primarily the white, middle-class students, and then there'd be the rest of the students in the class who would just be put on one side. There were six different classes in grade three. If you were a three-one, you knew you were bright. I was in three-five, so that gives you an idea of where I started.

There were two testing grounds for you—school and your friends. With your friends it meant how well you could survive, how well they liked you, you know. There was always clear proof of liking, "Hey, let's go over here," and you knew you had some pull with them, or else, "Do me a favor, if you don't do me a favor, I won't talk to you," and I'd say, "Get out of here, go drop dead, I don't care, I'll kill you," things like that. And in school because we already knew that we weren't part of that little clique that was just teachers and favored children, the testing ground was, "How much could you get away with, what can you do?" With me it wasn't so much how much I could get away with. It was what I could do behind the teacher's back without anyone ever realizing it. I was not the prima donna of the class, at least not one of those that was directly put down by the teacher. If I got that feeling, it was never direct. Every time I used to see my friends get pissed or something (I mean get caught by the teacher), I'd say, "Oh, somebody's gonna get mean. I'll throw something at the teacher."

Getting caught by the teacher meant, "You did this, and you *know* it, young man. You *know*." I got caught once in first grade, and I didn't even do what she had accused me of. And after that I said, "Okay, I'm gonna fix wagons around here and I'm gonna fix them good. I catch a little girl like that I'm gonna break her face open." I was mad, and I said, "I'm gonna start doing things."

Now, it's not too easy to remember good experiences in school, but in third grade we had Mrs. Osborn and something happened in third grade. Everything just seemed to come even more easily, I don't know why; maybe it was because I was put in too stupid a class, but it just came so easily. It's not that I had the feeling the teacher really liked me at that point, but suddenly school was a place of success and it was a pleasure, you know, because all of a sudden it became easy. I didn't mind going to school because anything they could throw at me, I could take one, two, three, fill it out, give it back—take a test, one, two, three, give it back.

And from grade three-five I went into four-one, and then I stayed in the one classes. That was a big jump, from five to one; it surprised me. I couldn't imagine why. Maybe they had placed me in the wrong class at the beginning, but whatever happened, what I did in third grade placed me in the first class in fourth grade.

I didn't realize that the teacher had noticed me, but when that move had come in, I said to my friends, "Hey, man, guess where I'm going, to four-one. Don't even touch me, man!" It was a big ego thing, but it was only slightly more difficult. Like I said, something must have happened in third grade because it wasn't that difficult. I just know I kept on passing and here I am. I know I had to pass, I didn't repeat any grades. I remember someone by the name of Gail, she was a Jewish girl. She was not on welfare, also dressed nicely, and also very intelligent, so I always felt, even though she was my classmate, I always felt very cautious when I was with her, nervous, because you know, you were supposed to be a dummy and this chick was bright.

I think the teachers in the one classes were a little more demanding. I kind of got that from their personal lifestyles. These teachers were a little more strict with certain things, whereas the other teachers were a little bit more loose, a little bit more relaxed. I don't know how much my family appreciated what I was doing in school. I thought my mother never really cared. As long as I didn't have to repeat a grade, if I didn't miss any classes, didn't play hookey, and stayed out of trouble, that was it. I was told that you had to get a good education but it was a momentary kind of thing, you know. Like a report card was there, she'd have to sign it: "Hey, I don't like this grade," or something. You would think to yourself, "So what, you don't like the grade, big deal," you know, what does that mean to me? Nothing, you know, it just seemed like a traditional thing, that you had to put up with the mouth for at least five minutes and then it was just forgotten. She couldn't even remember what she told me, so it was just nonsense.

I had one older brother, one younger sister and two younger brothers. My older brother, he didn't relate to school at all. When I was about eight, we had both gotten into drugs, and I was able to stop it and he never really could.

It started with, you know, you get into some beer. My brother and I were drinking some beer and then, I remember, at 509 East 5th Street, right behind there, they were just beginning to build up the back a little. Right inside it a brick was missing, and I put my hand in there for some odd reason, and you know I found a junkie's kit, found an eyedropper, a bulb, you know, I found the whole thing. That's when I started, like I didn't know what it was, and I wanted to throw it away, and the other guy says, "No, don't do that—the guys, you know, they have to have that little thing, otherwise they'll kill you." So I was interested in finding out how it was used and what it was used for and what did you put inside, and I found out.

I was eight years old, or maybe even younger, and my older brother was about ten or so. And he just stayed with it. And I continued but the frequency increased up to a certain point and then I just stopped, you know. His just kept on building up and increasing, whereas mine was every now and then, things like that, you know, like I would screw around or something like that. It was very much part of the whole scene. It was an accepted thing, you know, like your mother's boyfriend. It was a commonly done thing, you know, you walk in, and you shoot it up.

I wasn't really aware of the dangers of it. It was so accepted that they taught you, like you go to school to learn how to do something, it was a taught thing. They taught you exactly what to do, when to stop, what to watch out for. And also with sex, you know, like they taught you certain things that you knew what to do.

By "they" I mean fellow students, my brother. My brother was the one who always sort of added color to the whole thing, you know, filled in the holes, you know, little spots I was missing. I would ask, "Yeah, but what about this, I don't understand," and he would just straighten it out, give you reasons why, things like that. So naturally you would gain experience from your friends. Then doing the things so many times, after awhile *you* were considered one of the teachers. Like this guy doesn't know, and he'd ask, "Hey, you know, what happens, do you have to let the blood come up first, or do you shoot it in right away?" "No, no, you got to let the blood come in easy as it goes, otherwise, whoosh, you're gonna be as cold as that wood."

You felt it was like a step of advancement and you were booming along, but it was no big deal. Maybe at first, it was almost like a sacred thing. You just don't laugh about it, you don't brag about it, you don't joke about it, you don't talk about it, unless you were in with certain people, and it was something that you didn't question either. It was just an accepted thing.

It was just like this. You get up in the morning, you brush your teeth, and when certain friends wanted to do it, "Okay, come on, why don't we go down, why don't we do it?" It wasn't that I needed it or anything like that. It was just, "Yeah, okay, come on, why don't we do it." But when I think of the risk of it now, it frightens me to look back at it. Now when I even prick my finger, I break into a cold sweat!

I guess I'm laughing now, but when they try to get a blood type out of me, I have to go through pure hell, practically, just to get the needle into my arm. It's just like I want to say, "Don't get next to me! Just stay away from me with that thing." Even when I went to a medical center last year and they had to take some blood, just to prick my finger, I was in a cold sweat. And then when I finally felt it, the nurse says, "Come on. Kids don't even notice I prick them. Kids I can understand." At this age, believe me, that bothers me.

I guess as you get older, you realize the dangers. But what they were teaching me when I was a kid was so automatic that even though there was a danger, I guess it was just something that you accepted. Now maybe when you got older you might say, "Now what would happen if this were to go on?" But at that age, I just didn't question it.

I have a younger sister and two younger brothers. And I suppose they're using me now as a model, at least one of them is. I think my sister is making an effort now, cause she messed it up a little for herself, but the oldest of the two younger brothers, he goes to Poly, which is right next to Fordham, and he's receiving very good grades, and he says, "Man, you know, I got to do it, look at all the attention Ramon gets and everything like that, you know, I got to do it, man."

It is a satisfaction for me to have him look up to me. I listen to him, and I say, wow, that's really good. He's in his sophomore year, I'm not even certain. You know, we never were really like that close, and I don't really know ages very well. Like I'm lucky I even know my older brother's age— I'm pretty sure he's two years older. The younger kids, they look up to me. They always used to look up to him, and it's only been recently that they've been looking up to me now, you see, and now I guess some of them have both the influences now. My older brother now looks to me, you see, I guess that's when he started trying to go back and start all over again, but it's a hard road. He kind of figures it's too late. He doesn't really have enough motivation or belief. He has some, but it's too buried, I think. I can see it, but it's so small that I'm not sure he'll ever do it.

I don't know how to account for the difference between me and my older brother. Maybe he was under greater pressure, or maybe there was stronger peer group influence on him. I think that would have had to be it, because, you know, he was older, so that type of effect would be much stronger on him than it was on me, because the younger you are, the less you care what the group wants to do, you know. It's always what *you* want to do that interests you, and if you do it all by yourself, I felt even better. Even today if I do things by myself, I feel a lot better. I feel more relaxed, and I enjoy doing things on my own. For example, I really enjoy just being in a library and just studying, studying, studying.

Of course there's other possibilities. You can be in the school building and look outside there and see all the streets and feel a tremendous pull to go out there where you can be what you feel is natural. There can be a big gap between the school and the social existence, so that you finally simply drop out of school. There have been times when the pull of the street has been very strong in me. Every time I'm working in the drugstore and I look outside, I just go crazy. Sometimes the owner of the store gets to the point, no matter how well I work, where he wants to fire me because, especially during the warm weather, I've got to step out.

When he sends me on a delivery, no matter how cold it is, as long as I'm warm and comfortable, I don't mind going outside. I say, "Fine." I put on a warm coat, my scarf, gloves, hat, and I'm out.

Sometimes I sit in class and I look outside and I say to myself, "I'd most rather be out there!" even though it's an interesting class. Up until recently that pull was very strong to go down East 5th Street. Every summer I would have to go down, or every chance I got during the warmer weather. Soon as spring came, you know, like high school, and more recently in college, down to the Village, down to East 5th Street. I don't know why, but I always go down there. That was sort of home base. It was something I had to do, and you would see the changes, sometimes you would see the people. It wasn't until about two or three years after I had gotten out of there that everything had changed to the extent where I didn't recognize people, or people didn't recognize me any more. One boy, Louis, he and I were like the closest friends you could find in sixth grade. But I went down once, and my sister knew him and he remembered her, but he just didn't recognize me; he didn't know me. He said, "You, I don't know you." I said, "Don't you remember Ramon, the kid who always used to be around with you, who used to do everything?" He says, "Man, not you, I don't remember." So I kind of figured that there definitely had been a break, you know, that something has happened here, but I didn't think much about it after that.

I was talking about my family. I don't quite know how to describe my relationship to my father, and the influence he had on me. As far as I can tell he had none. He was never around. He left when I was one year of age, maybe before that. He left for Puerto Rico and he stayed there, and that was it. I didn't see him again until I was 19 years of age. I didn't know too much about him. I had only heard that he and I were like twins, practically. I mean identical twins, and that was it, and he never wrote to me.

It was hard after a while because some people, even though their fathers were junkies and drug addicts, they still knew them, you know, but I could never say that. The men that were there were either boyfriends or else another husband, you know, nobody about whom I could say, "That's *my* father."

But from what *I* had heard about my father, I would not only be able to *say* that, I mean people would be able to *see* it, you know. People who came over to my mother's house and were friends from way back, they used to stand there and they used to say, "God, that kid, it's like looking at his father, like *looking* at him." I used to say to myself, "Wow, you know, imagine if I could be walking around, holding my dad's hand, people looking at us, and thinking, whose kid is that? Do I need to ask, even?"

I never knew what my father was doing. The only time I heard spoken of him was when my mother would make references like, "Okay, you look like your father," or something like that, sometimes in a good sense, or else in a bad sense, you know, like, "You're just like your damn father, you know. You're a son of a gun." She was projecting on me the things that she felt about my father. In a way it was threatening, because she wasn't saying it to compliment me, she was saying it to get at me.

They talk a lot about role models, and how young people learn to cope with things by modeling themselves on people they admire and so forth. And it may seem like I sort of did this on my own. But this isn't the case. I saw certain people to admire, and I guess at a young age, I started getting a little bit interested in science, and from that I used to think when I watched, that person exemplifies the scientist. And I would watch him on TV, and I would say to myself, "Oh, they always do things systematically." I didn't use that word systematically, but I noticed that they do things in a type of ordered way. And I did enjoy that, to live like that, in an ordered way, because I couldn't do it.

But then I said to myself, "Okay," and started looking at people I admired. You could see the good and bad, and I decided that from different people I'm going to take different things, only the good things, and see if I can make that a part of me. Even in cases like my boss at the drugstore, he has his good points and his bad points. So I'd look at the good points and I'd say, "Can I take something like that and make it part of me?" Or else I'd see somebody on TV, playing like a father role or something like that, and I'd see that one of the reasons people liked this guy so much is because he was this way, he reacts this way to this type of thing. I said, "I wonder if *I* can be the same way." So my idea was that little by little I would take different things from different people and see if I could incorporate them in myself, and, you know, make them part of me, until finally I developed *the* perfect image that I should follow. But as you get older, you find out you can't go out for that perfect image, because you'll never fit into it.

I did read some books that influenced me in this way. The one that I remember most vividly was something about Lincoln that I read when I was very, very young. I read that on my own. And there was some things in it that hit me. When I finished reading, I said, "The kid's got guts, you know, he's the type of guy that, if you smack him, he comes right back fighting." I said, "Look what he turned out to be, he didn't do too bad for himself. I mean the kid had it."

Then I developed a belief which is still a part of me now. I said to myself, "Okay, mister, maybe you can kick my butt now, but you're gonna remember me, you're gonna remember how hard you had to fight to do it." So that there was something in that book that told me that Lincoln was tough, he was tough. Not physically, it's just that it took a lot to pull him down, to get him out, and I said, "Yeah, you know, I'd like to be able to do that; I wonder if I can do it too, you know, so that no matter what they do, I still will come back for more." Before you know it I was getting into fights with guys that were really big. I just leaned back, and I had to reach up to hit him. I remember in third grade—I did it, man and I knocked him—I *knocked* him. He was a bully and I hit him so hard that, big as he was, he never bothered me. He never bothered me, and a lot of other people in school, they just learned to be careful with me.

I went to that school down on East 5th up through the sixth grade, then I transferred into the Village to P.S. 41, during the middle of the sixth grade. We moved, and I felt kind of bad about it because during the sixth grade, after school they had like a book club where you would go and you would read or else they would teach you how to read. And so I had joined it, and if you did well enough and stayed there long enough, you would be given an award, a little card; but just before I got mine I had to move, so that award stayed there, you know, and God, I was so mad, I said, "Hell, the first time I do something, and look what happens." I said, "Forget it, I'm never gonna do anything like that again." I really busted my humps to get that card, and we were leaving on a Monday or a Tuesday, and the award was going to be given out on a Wednesday, and still I didn't get it. I figured, "Man, why should I go back, you know, just to pick that up?" They may say, "What?" Who, you? Get out of here, kid."

The new school was very big, impersonal and difficult to cope with, but at the same time you liked the halls that were so huge that you could get lost practically if you knew places where to go. You could do a lot of different things. But coping with the administrating or knowing how to, you wouldn't know how to go about it; it was just a huge guy standing up being the principal. Like God. There was no sense of personal relationship at all.

Still I enjoyed it because it was a huge thing; it was like a jungle or like a huge park. I stayed in that school for one month in the sixth grade, and then in seventh grade, I moved up to live with my uncle. My mother's most recent husband convinced her to get rid of my older brother, for a while anyway, to throw him out, and then he convinced her that I should go too.

When that man came home one day, if it wasn't for a lady, or somebody that got in the way, my brother could have shot him right in the head. The only reason why that guy is alive today is because somebody got in the way. My brother was that angry and I was rooting for him too, you know. If it wasn't for that bastard, you know, we would have stayed together. He pushed both me and my older brother out.

So then I lived with my uncle and aunt, but it's just a place to be. Since then, my life personally, you know, has just been one big hell. I'd have been happier even if I came out a drug addict or something, you know, which I wouldn't have, because I'd already cut that nonsense out, but I'd have been much happier staying down there with my family. Even if I would have made nothing out of my life, I would have been much happier.

I would have been satisfied with anything, so long as I didn't have to stay up here with my aunt and uncle. When this semester finishes, I hope the medical school lets me start at least a course or two during the summer. I'll tell them, "Look, I'm a Mongolian idiot, I'm stupid, I won't be able to take the full course, let me take a couple of courses now, even if I have to pay extra." I'll take out loans, that doesn't bother me, I'll come out with about $50,000 debt after four years from now, but it won't bother me. If I live to be seventy, I have all those years to pay it back, but let me move into a dormitory this summer. I'll move out of there. That'll only be for the first year. But I'm definitely not going to go back to live with my uncle and aunt. I wouldn't go back there for anything in the world. The only thing that's kept me there has been study.

I guess I have had to learn to sort of put things in their proper places, to put things into separate compartments, because even when I was working at the grocery store, I wouldn't take it out on a customer, unless I saw there was an advantage to it, and then I *would* take it out on a customer. Most of the customers don't usually want to have the younger people there wait on them, but people knew right away that I was not only as good but might be better than the older clerks.

The son of the owner of the grocery store would tell me that when a customer asked, "Is this fresh?" I was to say, "Yes, it's fresh." But I would think, "No, no wait a minute. You know what this is. They're going to use me like that. Then a customer goes home, and then he's going to find out that I lied to him, and when he comes back, he's not going to want me." I said to myself, "I'm going to make it a point that when I tell them something, it's the truth." Now, if I know it's not fresh, I won't tell him it's fresh, I just won't tell him, and if they ask me I say to them, "What can I tell you? Like, I work here only part time, what can I tell you?" But whenever I did tell somebody this is it, I want them to know that this is the truth, so that when they came back they could say, "I can rely on this kid," and I worked for that. I said to myself, "I've got to make them think they can rely on me, and I've got to learn all about this business. I've got to learn how to do this, I've got to learn all these things so that people will no longer say, "I'll wait for Larry, or one of the other older people."'

The other young people who have worked there have never behaved that way. They just want to get paid. They're putting in time, but I wanted to learn something, because I knew that if I learned something there, it could carry throughout the rest of my life. But then I began to understand the market. I said, "Man, unless you understand these things you're dead, man, they'll take you for anything. You walk out and you may not even notice your underwear are missing." I said, "I've got to learn certain things, the price of certain things, the value of things." I realized that this could be an advantage to me. This is a way of coping. So that's why I went down after things.

That's why in the pharmacy right where I work now, if I get a prescription, I walk to the back, I whip out a label, I give it numbers, everything that a registered pharmacist will do, I even know what the heck it's used for. I can fill practically any prescription that doesn't need composition. And when I've done it, the boss doublechecks me to make sure, but you know, nobody else has done it. I said to the cosmetician and the pharmacist, "You people remember guys that used to work here only because you remember their faces. Me, I am going to be in this store for as long as it exists because *my* handwriting and my initials are in the legal records of this place. So ten years from now I can come back and I can open up the book and I can say, 'You see all of these things? That's me.' And you people are going to remember me, not just from working outside with the people, but because I worked in back in the prescription department, and the owner, whenever he needed an extra hand back there, it was Ramon, whoosh, and he pulled me back. None of the other younger people have ever done that. But I've been doing it because he knows he can trust me."

I got the job at the grocery store through the choirmaster at Corpus Christi. He had been buying there and he called me up one day, it was in January, I remember I had just come down with a cold, and he said, "Do you need a job?" I said, "Do I need life, man, of course I need a job." He says, "It's at a grocery store." Before that I just didn't like the situation with my aunt and uncle, and I was very unhappy there. This was for pocket money, so I wouldn't have to go to them.

A lot of times I would go without certain things just so I wouldn't have to ask for money from my aunt and uncle. Oh, they'd give it to me, but it's what you had to go through for it. I don't know, but children, you just can't fool them. They just know. They can't say, "This guy doesn't like me," they just know it. So I went there to work two days later and I had a terrible cold. My head was clogged, and I had deliveries, and oh, I was sick as a dog. The first two days I worked, then the rest of the week I couldn't come in, so I called up every day to tell them to hold the job, and then after that, two of the clerks started making fun of me.

I was being paid $1.60 an hour for this, plus tips. But a couple of days after they hired me, they had taken on a delivery boy, so I was just making the $1.60, and they took out tax. I said, "For a guy who makes so little, there's a lot of tax going out, man." Every day I worked from 4:00 P.M. to 7:00 P.M., and then on Saturdays I came in at 12:00 or 1:00, and I would stay until 7:00 P.M., so that was about 15, about 20 hours a week. It was almost like a half-time job.

But I developed and adapted. I remember when a man said, "Bring me a pint of milk." I didn't even know what a pint was, so I brought him a quart, and then he says, "I said a pint," and I said, "Okay," so I brought him a half gallon, and he was looking at me like he was saying to himself, "Oh, you poor slob," and he walks back and he brings down a tiny little thing which I had seen at the beginning, and I said to myself, "Oh, I'm going to make sure nothing like that happens again."

But right after that, Larry said, "Can I have some strawberry jam?" and I brought out preserves, and Larry said, "What's the matter with you, don't you know the difference between jam and preserves?" And right in front of everybody. And I said, "No, what is the difference?" And he told me. I said, "Oh." They were constantly putting me down. But I got to be so good that when Larry went on vacation I took care of his department, frozen things. I didn't do much with the real frozen stuff where the meats were, I had all the orders down pat. Then I started muscling in on Jim's territory. I would say, "Well, Jim, we need some pears over here," or something like that, and he'd say, "That's none of your business, you don't need to know that." I got to be so good that I'd come from school, go home, wash my face, zip down to the store, take out all the deliveries. I was so good that I could take care of customers and still zap out those deliveries and *not* make them suffer through any extra hardships. I made sure everything ran smoothly as if it was two guys there, and the boss loved it. He didn't always show his appreciation because meanwhile he also would say nasty things to me. One day he walked past me and he pushed me to the side, and he said, "Come on, get out of the way," and I was really angry, but yet I felt, "Ramon, this is a prime opportunity to show him something," and I said, "Oh, you like to play rough, huh? I can play rough too. I'm going to show you how rough I can play." He said to me, "Come on! Don't talk like that." That said to me, "Okay, he's not going to do any more pushing around." But I remember when he turned around, and he goes, "Come on, no rough stuff, don't talk like that." But at that time, his wife was always getting sick, so depending on how bad off she had started the day, that's how he would react.

To tell you the truth, a lot of these employers, like the owner of the grocery store and the pharmacists, I used them like father images. I could admire the owner of the grocery store. A lot of people just don't understand him, and sometimes I feel the same way too, and yet I also feel that there are certain things about him that are admirable. He's a useful person. He does his work conscientiously. That's what I like about him. He's thorough; I mean, he's the type of man who understands that there's a time for playing and there's a time for work. When there's a time for work, don't play, because then you're going to lose your time when you play. When it's time to play, don't work; you have plenty of time to work. He's efficient. One of the reasons why I became so good and quick at making deliveries was because it also got me out of the store. I was so quick at making deliveries that I could sit down for 15 minutes and talk to a guy, and walk back in and nothing was ever said. Sometimes I would just sit down and think about something that happened during the day. I would use that working time as recreational time. I would also use school time too. You had to study but there was always 10 minutes between the classes, and then there was that lunch hour, and gym was maybe once a week, or maybe something would happen and you would have time off. You were with friends, and there were good feelings. To me, it was balanced, and everything worked out.

I usually worked between 20 and 25 hours a week, and it worked out to be about $1.00 an hour. So I would make about $20 to $25 a week. I always put money into the bank. I gave money to my aunt and uncle, and then I kept money for myself to cover my expenses: carfare, lunch. Then they had a drive for the poor at school, so I used to make it a point to give something. I started giving $.50 a week and worked myself up to a dollar, sometimes even $2.00.

My aunt and uncle said that when I was earning money, it would be proper for me to contribute something to the household. For my mother, I would have definitely done it, but for them I didn't want to do it, but for them I had to do it to keep them off my rear end. I'd put $5 in the bank, give $5 to them, and then the rest I'd keep for myself. To them it was just $5, but to me that was five hours of *work,* which was saying a *lot!* I put it in the bank so that, in case I would need anything, I'd have something there.

And it worked out, because this year, I have had to spend a lot of money applying to medical schools. I had to go into my savings for this. I had $300, now I only have $17. I'm going to try to see if I can get some extra time working at the drugstore so I can start putting some money again into the bank, because I'm pretty sure I'll need it. When I'm in medical school I'm going to try to take out as many loans as possible to keep myself as free as possible. That is why I want to have some money in the bank before I go.

It was not easy to decide to go to college. Just before I graduated from high school, the owner of the grocery store asked me, "What are you going to do once you graduate from high school?" I said, "Possibly go to college; I'm pretty sure I will be going to college." He said that once I graduated from high school I could work full time with him. But when I thought about it, I saw it was a dead-end job. So I said, "No, I'm sorry, I have to go to college." I don't remember when it became clear to me that I was going to go to college. I realized that I wasn't mature enough to work a nine-to-five routine, and that it was a cold, cold world out there. I just didn't think I was prepared for it, so college became not only a place to learn but also a place to become more mature. All of these things just added together. I said, "No, there's a hell of a lot I still don't know, and there's a hell of a lot I want to know." So college became an educational center, but also something like a playpen. Working in an office or factory in a nine-to-five routine would be one of the most frightening things you could do to me. I guess I wouldn't mind a nine-to-five routine if I weren't stuck in one place, and I could move around and maybe see new things and hear new things, but an executive, you know, is just too confined to one place, as I see it. Life in an American corporation, in a large bureaucracy, does seem to me to be sterile, and you can even see that the business outlook is carried over into the American culture. For example, take those fashion shows in France. Now they're not going to sit down right away and just price things. Sure, they do that eventually, but then there's always either a wine party or a meal before and after. There's always something like that where you get to mingle around and you get a chance to talk, and that's true of a lot of business in Puerto Rico.

Sure, maybe at certain levels it's just cut and dried, and the people who are caught up in it do accept that. But when you walk into a Spanish store and you say, "Where's my spaghetti?" then you hear somebody else talking. Maybe that person happens to be a good friend of the store owner. You don't even know them, but you say, "Ah yes, but if that person would have done this, it would have been much better," and before you know it, the three of you are there just as if you knew each other for all of your lives. In addition, there is a hate for the nine-to-five routine, if you feel the pull of the street, that pull to the unknown, to the freedom, to the wild even, if you want that. The sort of career which in American terms might be a very successful career where you may end up with a good bit of status, and a good bit of income, means joining up with this sort of routine. A career in business, even becoming a corporate president, that's a career that might not be attractive to a young Puerto Rican unless he could add his own flair to it.

I've thought about a career in business, and personally I know that I wouldn't be able to do it. I would be able to be successful, but it wouldn't be as rewarding to me as other things. I wouldn't be happy with it, because it would mean usually that nine-to-five routine and I'd be stuck inside. When I go downtown, I can spot a lawyer any time. Even at the University, I'll spot any law student. And they're not attractive to me. I thought of teaching, but there was something about it that was limiting. Maybe I can see it at the college level, but even there there's something missing. There's freedom to it, but somehow I just sense there's an easiness about it, a lack of challenge. There's just something about it that just makes it seem too routine, too regimented, too uncomfortable for me.

You would think that going into medicine would mean the same thing. How regimented can you be? Doctors are people that just have to do things in a certain way, especially in a large hospital. This is what I believed until I started really getting into it. Then I saw that some doctors had quite a flair for certain things. In Puerto Rico I saw the same thing. I said, "Hm, it's the type of profession that does allow you, if you seriously want it, the opportunity to maybe go off on little tangents when you want to." Where you'll be able to say, "Okay, I'll start working three days a week, because I've already made enough money. I'm going to go out to the country and do this." I've been finding that you don't even have to do that any more.

If I *do* get to become a doctor, I think I will be an extremely important asset to any hospital I decide to apply to, especially for a residency. I'm pretty sure I'll have little or no difficulty, because I'm not only bilingual, I'm bicultural, and they recognize that's a big difference. Even as a volunteer worker in hospitals, I've found that to be the case. The patient, all of a sudden he moves closer to me, starts talking to me, and everything is oriented towards me. Even the doctors use me as an intermediary, and if I knew what the doctor knew, he wouldn't have to be there. I would be able to communicate perfectly well because I *know* what people with a Spanish background mean by certain things.

When I went to college I really didn't quite know what I was going to do. I had thought about a pre-med course, but the pre-med idea became something real to me only in my third year. I hadn't started in the pre-med program in my freshman year. In my freshman year I started taking social sciences, humanities, because you would have to get them out of the way. I think that you had to have a year of English to graduate, so I figured I would get these things out of the way. Medicine was always on my mind, but not in a clear-cut sense.

A lot of my childhood was spent in the hospital. I was in the hospital for a tonsillectomy, appendectomy. Once it was malnutrition. I liked it. The doctors were always nice to me. The hospital was clean. It was nice, you know. There were no problems, it was all there. This was in contrast to everything else in my life. You knew things were going to get better, you were going to get meals, there was nobody looking at you to say, "Hey, don't do that," and even if they were there to do something, you knew they had to.

But then, you know, the thing I didn't like about it was that every time I was there I always got stuck with a needle. And actually that fear of the needle was what kept me from seriously thinking about medicine in the first few years. But there was another thing too. Everybody, teachers, fellow students, doctors, they all said, "Oh, you have to put in a lot of years," and I said, "I don't want to spend that many years, I don't want to be 27 when I come out. What, are you kidding me? I'll be ready for social security by then."

But then, well gradually, I just started thinking about it. I'd always think about it, but never really seriously. I'd think, "Mm hm, wait a minute, I don't want to get into anything like that. As a professional you have to be mature, you have to be really serious about your work, and you have to be extremely knowledgeable, that's just the way it is. And I don't think I'm built for those types of things." At that time my image of myself was such that I didn't think I could be a doctor.

My freshman year of college was rather routine. I wasn't bucking for good grades, and if I could get a B in everything, I was happy. But then sophomore year was a very confusing year for me. I didn't know what was going on, and I was seriously thinking about dropping out. I was working at the drugstore and my boss had screwed me up. Because the other part-time worker had quit, he made it *my* responsibility to make up for any deficiencies for the six-to-ten shift. I told him finally, "Hey, your son's a pre-med, I'm a pre-med, can't you understand how difficult it is?" and he says, "Well, what am I going to do?"

So I was just overwhelmed with work. There was a terrible conflict between my job and staying in school. I had labs to write up, I had experiments to do. There was basic chemistry, organic chemistry, and then calculus, and physics, and biology, a tremendous amount of work, and yet I had to work every evening from six to ten, and I had to work every other Saturday all day. My grades were really slipping, and I just said, "Forget it, it's impossible."

But one night I was injured. It was in Central Park. Remember where John Kennedy, Jr., had his bicycle stolen? At that very exact same spot I had my bicycle stolen, and my collarbone was fractured. I was unconscious for awhile, and I suffered something like a temporary amnesia. This affected my studies after that for awhile too, because I couldn't remember things. You could tell me, "Ramon, would you get me those books over there." And I'd say, "Sure," and I'd be looking for them, and all of a sudden I would forget what it was that I was supposed to be doing.

I became very interested in medicine because of that experience. I had a run-in with this young doctor who seemed knowledgeable with the books, but not too bright, or at least lacking in experience when it came to actual patient care and dealing with me. Now I was not even a doctor, but I knew that anybody who has been unconscious, even for a short amount of time, should be under 24 hours' observation. He should be questioned at intervals. But this young doctor tells me, "Oh, well, you take that up with the other department when you get a chance."

I just didn't like the way the doctor was doing his job. He violated my idea of doctor. I said to myself, "Something's wrong here, definitely. This shouldn't be the way it is." I had always liked doctors; they were always good to me and it was always nice to see them in their nice white jackets, walking around like mysterious men, but they always knew what they were doing. When they said they wanted something, they *wanted* that; they *knew* why they wanted it, and when they got it, you saw the way they worked with those tools and the strange equipment that they would use.

But I was still a little unsure about deciding to try to be a doctor, still afraid. Practically every doctor that you see is an intelligent, mature, sincere person. And I was worried about whether I could be something like that. I'm always goofing around, always joking around, if there's something there to enjoy that you can make fun or a joke out of, why not? How could I be a doctor?

There was nobody to give me any positive advice about what you had to go through to become a doctor, nobody to go to and say, "Look, I'm thinking about being a doctor; what do I do to become a doctor?" I just had to figure it out by myself. No, there wasn't even a family doctor, and the pharmacist for whom I worked was concerned with his own family and the store. He really couldn't be bothered with anybody else. There were no teachers at that time that I could turn to.

I said to myself, "I'm thinking about becoming a doctor, but boy, there are some big obstacles that stand in my way. First of all, how am I going to finance this?" But I figured it this way; if I have to, I'll take out loans. If I have to work, okay, I'll do it. I'll make it somehow, even if I don't quite know how. As long as I can borrow money and pay for it, I don't care. I still don't know if I'll be able to borrow money, but I'm fairly certain there's got to be a bank out there that is willing to lend medical students money. Once you are admitted, I said to myself, the banks will figure, "Okay, if he's been accepted, what more do we want?"

But that's one of the obstacles. We're talking about forty, fifty, sixty thousand dollars in debt; that's before you can get to see your first paycheck. I think the medical schools provide some money, but they're kind of limited also. I don't know about things like the Ford Foundation. I've heard about Ford Foundation giving Columbia a lot of money, but that was for things like urban affairs. I had never heard of Ford giving money directly to graduate students. Someone just now told me that they have a program for professional training of minorities, but I had never heard anything about it.

Nobody in my family would be able to help me; they're barely making it now as it is. My family's attitude toward my going to medical school is mixed. My aunt and uncle got rid of their only kid four years ago when he got married, so that's no problem and he's doing okay. I try to keep the costs for them down at a minimum. Even when I was short for tuition in college, if the dean couldn't fix it up, I'd work it up myself. Even then I'd get hassled by them. They would say, "We know you made a lot of money because you were working hard and everything like that; what did you do with it? You never gave us any of it, you never put it into the bank or anything like that."

Little did they know that I had to help make up the difference for tuition; because I can tell you, at the bursar's office, either it all comes together at the right time or it doesn't come together at all. You have to get that tuition card so you can go to classes. My aunt and uncle just don't understand. But with my mother, it was different. When she heard that I was accepted at the medical school, oh, wow, she went crazy! It was a real satisfaction. She even bought me a watch. Two hundred dollars for a watch! I couldn't believe it.

It was clear that she did that because she felt that it was wonderful for me to get in. I really appreciate what she did. But there was another thing; I don't know, maybe it's mercenary, but I was thinking, if I ever need money when I am at medical school, I can always borrow a little on that watch.

There were some moments of unsureness before I got admitted to medical school. The whole process of application was grueling. That was really something because people just couldn't understand why I was so upset. They would say, "Look! Even if you don't make it in, you still have four years of college." But what's that going to get you today? Nothing, absolutely nothing. In addition, I'm taking courses that are preparing me in one specific field, not in many. It's a bachelor of arts degree, all right, in *natural science*. Now, if I go to a bank, they'll say, "Yeah, yeah, go grow your petunias or your genes somewhere else; if we need you, we'll call you; if there's a profit in the gene market, we'll let you know." That's what I was thinking.

Now if somebody's willing to train people, and the economy's healthy enough, he might say to me, "All right, obviously you were intelligent enough to take all these courses and pass them satisfactorily, so that means your mind is well trained enough so that you can still be taught something new. All right, we'll take you." But if the economy is sick, they're going to take somebody who's got the training already rather than train somebody from the beginning.

Some people said to me that a pre-med background, with the sort of science background I had, there are a lot of sort of health-related careers. There are public health programs, there are environmental science programs. I might not get to be an M.D., but I would still get a professional job; these jobs would probably be well paying, and a lot of them would be government jobs. But at the present time the government is not hiring, it's firing; the economy is lagging and what am I going to do with this specific training?

That was really scaring the hell out of me, you know. I also figured that it would mean that the end of my education had come. I figured that once I graduate, I was not going to try to get any master's degree or anything like that, because that's just not what I'm interested in. I said to myself, "It is medicine, or else." I said, "That's it, man, unless it's for an M.D., no more education, no more learning, that's where I stop." I started thinking again, the way I had in high school. Am I reading the right things, am I developing in the right way, am I getting all I should get, receiving a variety of stimuli rather than one specific kind of stimulus?

When I had to think specifically about medical schools, go through applications, I didn't know too many people to go to for advice. There was one Spanish kid who had made it into medical school the year before. He said to me, "I don't care *what* you do. You have to have gotten good grades, but above all, make sure you apply early, especially if it's a school that you want to go to. Make sure that they get what they want; you keep a file on them." And I kept a file on every single school. Yesterday, since I've already been accepted, I took the medical schools' recent catalogs, '74—'75 medical catalogs that I would not need, and I took them over to the science department office. I know when a lot of students are going to start preparing their applications, and I want them to have the most recent catalogs.

I had a friend here at the college and one thing he said stuck in my mind. It must have been his junior year. He came to me one day and he said, "You know, I've always been sure I wanted to be a doctor, but suddenly I'm troubled; I'm upset." He was very much involved in a clinic on the Lower East Side. He said, "I don't know whether becoming a doctor will put me on a path which will remove me from my community and my friends." He said that it worried him, and he almost felt if becoming a doctor did mean that, he wouldn't want to be a doctor, that he could only be a doctor if he could also keep his sense of himself as a Puerto Rican, as a person involved in his community. When I talked to him after he got admitted to medical school last year, this problem was the last thing he was thinking about. I know him well enough to know that he's going to make a marvelous community doctor.

The first interview I had was at Mount Sinai. That was an odd coincidence. That's the hospital that got me seriously interested in becoming a doctor. You remember the accident that I had and how a young doctor treated me. That's when I said to myself, "Oh, I definitely have to change this, man. I want to become a doctor, and I'm going to show them what a doctor should be like." After the interview at Mount Sinai came one at the school that I'll be attending. Several other schools asked me to come for an interview, but I had decided to accept the offer I had already received. It was all amazing to me because I didn't think any school would touch me!

I think I had two weeks' notice on the interview at Mount Sinai, which was hell. I got the letter from them and I nearly wet my pants right away. I said to myself, "Oh, my God! This may be the only interview I get, but this is a biggie, man! This is not one to fool around with! This is one of the big babies here."

Even getting the interview was a big deal. You go to school and tell your friends, "Hey, I got an interview." And they say, "Where? Where?" Everybody is excited. Some poor fellows don't get any interviews. And if you don't even get an interview, then you know you're not going to be accepted. You've got to have an interview. If you get twelve interviews, even if you apply to one hundred schools, you know that seriously you're only dealing with twelve schools. If you only get one interview, you're only dealing with one school.

Well, I have to admit that I kind of plugged for an interview because I would make myself available. I would just walk around the medical school. I would say, "Hi, I'm a premedical student. This is my year, you know, this is the year that I have to apply, and I'd like to get some information." After I had done that I tried to get close enough to some one person in that place so that if they heard my name, they would say, "Oh, yes, I know that person."

I was lucky at Mount Sinai. One of the important doctors there came down to the college the year before to give a lecture on cancer and his research work. I tried to muster up as much as I could possibly remember of his talk, and then I went down there. I said, "Hey, can I speak to Dr. Monroe; I'd like to set up an appointment." Then he walked in, and he said it was okay. I walked into his office and he says, "Well, what's troubling you, lad?" And I said, "Oh, nothing. You gave that lecture at my school, didn't you?" And that showed him that I was really interested in the work, which I really was, at least academically. Then I said to him that what was bothering me was, why did he want to do this research, what was so interesting about it? What did he notice? What happened to make him enter this field? And those were enough questions to keep him going.

It took some courage to go into his office. Those large medical institutions are the epitome of efficiency; everything is just one, two, three, and that's it. And there I was, just standing there. I had just these everyday pants on, this shirt. I didn't think about getting into a suit or anything like that. I guess I should have. But I got into his office and then I got him to pull out my application. I said, "Oh, by the way, could you check my application? I know I sent it to you, but there is a little thing in the back of my mind that says perhaps you haven't got all the letters of reference; could you check my application just to make sure?" And that is the trick. You get him to look, and he'll become involved.

I wrote a lot on my application about extracurricular activities. I was always involved in a lot, and he opened the application up. I knew this is what must have happened. He must have looked at it and said, "Wow, this guy is really involved." We checked it over, and in the process of looking for what I had told him to look for, he must have seen a lot of things. Then I said, "Did I have the letter in there?" and he said, "Oh, yeah, yeah, yeah, your application is complete." This gave me an idea that he had checked it over. Then I said, "Oh, by the way, do you think I'll ever get an interview?" And he said, "Yeah, I was just thinking about that." He must have taken to me right away. He said, "I think you'll definitely get one. Maybe later this year, you know." I figured right away that means I'm not that good, and yet in October, only a couple of weeks later, there was a request from Mount Sinai for an interview, and in those two weeks waiting for the actual interview I went through hell!

I was worried about what would come up in the interview. You have to think about things like euthanasia, abortion, some of the classical ethical problems in medicine. They didn't ask me too many questions about science. There was another premedical student who was asked a lot of scientific questions but not me. I think it was because I was taking advantage of the minority program that they had.

Some of these doctors feel about us something like this: These kids, they're not too bright, but we think they can make it. I sensed this attitude in them, whether they try to deny it or not. Only I made a point of showing them that if I want a 3.5 grade index, I can get it, and I got it. And the subjects I took weren't easy subjects. It was my way of proving to them that if they accepted me under this minority program, they should not think they are accepting an idiot. "Here's my proof. Two A's and two B's."

In this interview, I did think about questions of dress and behavior. The other pre-meds were vicious to me, the pre-meds who were waiting to be interviewed. They were from other schools. They were trying to cut me down. Even in our own school we have that type of nonsense. That's one thing that I have prided myself about in my success—and I call it a success because I have been a success—because I was able to avoid being vicious and cruel to other pre-med students. I didn't have a suit, so I had to make the best of what I had. It was a colored shirt, too, and I figured that might be the kind of thing that might lead them to an adverse impression.

But the actual interviews were rough. I felt like I was dragged through the gutter. When I was taking that interview, I was trying to defeat the other applicants. There are, you know, ten people interviewed for every one position in the school. I was trying to outsell the others, so you know you really have to sweat, you have to think about what to say, and you have to come at least with some idea of how you're going to behave. You have to be very astute; you have to try to analyze a question as quickly as possible but not hesitate too long before answering them, because then they'll know that you're analyzing them. You have to take it in and quickly respond. It has to seem natural, but it's really very calculated.

Once you have your interview, it's just a waiting process. But I don't have to wait anymore; I've been accepted; I have already sent in the money, and I have my seat secured. I'm considered a student down there; they said to me, "Walk around any time you want to; you're a student here." It's a great feeling.

Once I got the acceptance, it was a kind of watershed. That's my "before" and "after" point right there. There are some good things that come from my success, and also there are bad things in getting into medical school. Now I can concentrate upon learning again, rather than on memorizing. Last semester I did nothing but memorize. If I learned something, well, that was good, but I was primarily memorizing. Now I don't have anything to worry about.

I'm thinking in terms of my eventual profession. Before I got admitted, I had nothing to work for except admission. Now I do. Now I know that everything I study is going to be for that profession. The Church plays some role in all this. I still serve Mass every Sunday. I've been doing it since 1966. Religion came late in my life, but it definitely took hold. I'm not the most religious person; from my language alone, you can tell that. But still my religious beliefs make sense to me.

Obviously it still is an unusual thing for someone who started where I had to start to end up in medical school. Now being Puerto Rican in New York City has, I think, affected all of these things—school, work, choice of career, and so forth. It's had its effect; I mean, it's been more difficult because of it, to tell you the truth.

I felt as though there really was a system out there designed to set obstacles and to obstruct me, or to demean me, or to lower my confidence in myself. There was a system. It's the everyday system. It affects you whether you're Italian, or whatever. This means specifically that certain people would just make things a hell of a lot tougher to negotiate or tolerate or deal with than would ordinarily be so. And in some cases, people I like or respect, like even the owner of the market and the pharmacists at the drugstore—as soon as they hear a Puerto Rican kid has certain expectations, they feel that the fact that he is Puerto Rican precludes anything. Anything and everything. But it's curious. In a way, these same people have helped me because I made damn sure that I was going to show them. I would make them know that they were wrong, and that they were wrong all the way about me.

Pedro Rivera

I've lived in the same place all my life, in the same building at 110th Street and Madison Avenue. I guess that is unusual. Puerto Ricans move around quite a bit, you know. We stayed always in the same place. I never really thought we had it that bad. I really had a nice childhood in a way. The apartment was like big, tremendous. It was eight big, big rooms. My father even knocked down a wall in one of them to make the living room bigger.

When I began to get conscious of what was happening around me, my mother was studying to be a nurse. She was also working. She worked for the city for 11 years. She graduated, I think, in '58 or something, as a practical nurse. My father was different. He first worked at some odd jobs here. Then he finally settled down and he worked with this chain of hotels. My father was way older than my mother. My father was about maybe 33 when he came here. My mother was 18, 19, somewhere around there. Then my grandmother came over. Then they got married and they lived over in the South Bronx, and then they moved over to where we live now. When my mother had me they brought me right over there so I never lived in any place else. And they wouldn't move. My mother knew some English. My mother had studied English in school in Puerto Rico. And my father picked up English while he was here. And he used some English down there also.

My father told me at first he had some trouble getting a job. But once he began to work with the hotel chain, he never left that chain. He still works in a building that was once one of the hotels and was just recently taken over by another company two years ago. He didn't do this kind of work in Puerto Rico. In Puerto Rico he used to go and measure how much you owed for electricity. He was very well known around his town.

My father came from a very big family. They originated from Siales and from that area around there. It is a town in the interior where there's more light-skinned people. And they also tend to have more racist attitudes than, say, on the coast. Now my mother's from the coast where there's more of a mixed population than in the interior.

My grandfather, he owned two gas stations, and he made a bundle during the war. But he never helped his children in anything. My father always told me this. He said, "My father never helped me in anything. He took me out of school; he didn't help me to continue, and the only reason I picked up electricity was that I hitched on a truck to San Juan on my own." And he did that until he finally achieved some knowledge in electricity so that he could work for the Puerto Rico Con Ed.

And his dream was to be an engineer. But he had no one to push him. His father was making money but he would not help my father. My father had the desire but he didn't have the money. And his father did have the money which would have opened up a lot of doors for him, but he didn't give him any help at all.

My grandfather is a sort of legendary character in the family. We call him the Cowboy. In those days the cars were a little bit higher, you know, and he'd punch this guy so hard that he went right under the car and hit the sidewalk on the other side. That's how strong he was. He was known for his strength. And my father was something like him, you know, short, stocky, very well built, and that was the way my grandfather was. I never knew my grandfather. This is what they told me. I never knew my grandmother either. They died before I was born.

My father brought my mother up to the place where his family lived. Oh, that's deep. My father, he's up there in the truck, you know, going around to towns, checking the electricity. So one time he took my mother, who was his fiancee at the time, and another friend, both very dark, up to the mountains where he came from. He left the two of them there alone while he attended to some business. So my mother and his friend stayed in the car talking, and then they looked up and it was like a scene out of the cowboy pictures. They looked around and all these people were gathering around slowly, looking at them with curiosity, milling around. My mother is beginning to wonder what's going on. And the people, they acted as if they had never seen a dark person. And they were filled with curiosity. They're looking and looking. This is in Puerto Rico. This explodes some myths that people have about Puerto Rico. They even asked my father, "Why did you bring those two monkeys up here for?" My father, I don't know what he did. I never heard the ending, what succeeded *that*. Mountain people, they were very violent in their attitudes, like the way my grandfather treated his daughters. Fathers, they were like lords.

That's exactly the way my grandfather ran his house, too, like he was a little lord. And my father, after the death of several of my aunts, he really took the lead in the house. He had to take the responsibility, since he was a young boy, for maintaining the house. My aunt was telling me when I went to Puerto Rico recently how my father practically raised them since he was young. My father has a very keen sense of family. He raised his entire family, he became the stronghold. And it was my father who built the two-story house that we live in. He built it with his own two hands. And he was the one who supported the family.

He has told me many times, "I'm going to give you what my father never gave me. My father never helped me. My father never did this, my father never gave me that. But you're going to get everything that I can give you."

My father became clearly the exact opposite of his father. My father never wanted to run around. He wasn't the type to go around fighting. Neither was he a big drinker. He might take a drink, but nothing like my grandfather. He was in a different category altogether. And he was a pillar of strength for the rest of my uncles and aunts. And then he fell in love with my mother. He wanted to marry her because he loved her. My father's always been like that. He doesn't care what anybody thinks. And I guess you had to be like that when you're living under those conditions. Either you do it on your own or it never gets done. That was his attitude. So he took it upon himself. He really never had to work in the cane fields, because he had that job. Now that was a rough job. He had to learn driving when he was 10 years old. He learned how to drive standing up, driving trucks up in the mountains. But he wasn't working in the cane fields. My uncles, yes, they had to work in the cane fields, and that's because their father was not really giving them the kind of support they should have received.

My grandfather was a ridiculous man. Thousands of dollars he made during the war, thousands, and he's hardly given them a cent. My uncles aren't very educated either. They had to work in the cane fields, and that's back-breaking work, you know. And on top of that, my father had to make money at that time. Not only that, he was helping out my mother and her mother.

My mother was born in a community in the northeastern part of Puerto Rico. But my grandmother and my grandfather on my mother's side, they were not married. It was just a one-time thing, you know. So, anyway, when my mother was born—you see, these are really deep stories they tell me—my grandmother, she was suffering very much because she didn't have a real steady man. She was left with the children all the time. Now the area she was from is San Turse, around there, and San Turse, it's a terrible mess. It's like a real bad ghetto-type of scene. You have the real culture of poverty down there. There are hardly any permanent marriages or anything like that.

Then my grandmother caught a bad sickness and she thought she was going to die. Her body was filling up with water. She didn't want to give her children away. But she had a couple of sisters who were telling her, "Look, if you're going to die you might as well give your children to someone who will take care of them. At least put them in a home where they get taken care of." So my grandmother started to give her children away. They were put in different places. There are many people that have been raised like that who don't know who their mothers or fathers are.

In a sense the whole community would take children. Even if she's well, a mother might say, "I can't hack this. You want it?" They take the child graciously, and the children would get raised up. You're a "child of raising," that's the literal meaning, but it means that you've been raised up by someone other than your real mother. It's not a formal adoption. It is something like a foster child, but stronger. You just say, "This is my son whom I raised. He's like my son because I took him into my household under those conditions. I raised him in my house. Therefore he's my son." That's what it means. Otherwise you are not distinguishing between your blood sons and "the son you raised" that's just like your son. Everybody considers him a brother and everything else, even though the natural mother could be living. But in my mother's case, this lady wanted my mother with papers, that's the difference, because my mother looked like a daughter that she once had whom she had lost, and she was childless. So she wanted my mother. So at first my mother's real mother says, "No, not that," because she was thinking, "What if I recover and want to get my child back?" But it didn't look like she would get better, so she finally agreed and said, "I'm going to have to provide for them somehow. Okay, fine. I'll do whatever you ask. But on the condition that you tell them who I am eventually." So that was agreed and my mother's real mother recovered. So she went and got back all her children, as it is natural for a mother to do, except that she wanted my mother back and she couldn't have her because she had been legally adopted. And the lady who had taken my mother started bouncing from place to place until she finally left San Turse, and my grandmother couldn't find her. That's when they moved to the city where my mother was raised and where my father met her, a city more towards the northwest. And my real grandmother and my mother were separated until 1963.

My mother didn't even know that the person who raised her was not her real mother. They didn't tell her what was going on. And so my mother was raised and I was raised up until 1963 thinking my cousins were my foster grandmother's family. And so everybody was under that big illusion until 1963 when the shock of the world came down, and a lady showed up at the house saying that she was my mother's real mother. When they opened up the door, the woman resembled my mother so much that it was obvious she was the real mother. At first it was a happy reunion. But it turned very tragic, because my foster grandmother never got over it until she died. She got the feeling that she would never be loved now. She was old at the time already, and this really affected my mother. You know, it was a big shock. My grandmother took that to the grave. And my mother is still suffering the repercussions of it.

It upset the house a great deal and it was connected to another thing. When my father settled here he got a night job right away, and after that he always had steady work. My mother was always keen on becoming a nurse because she was very bright and she had graduated from high school with good marks. And when she came over to New York City, right away she got into a nursing school, and then she got a job with the city. She was doing fine. She worked at that job as long as our foster grandmother could take care of the children, but after my foster grandmother could no longer take care of us, my mother had to. For all that time up until about 1964 or 1962, my grandmother had been raising us.

So during that time with my father working and my mother working, the economic conditions were pretty good. There was a double income and so forth. I had the attitude when I was a kid I could have anything I wanted. My father would always ask us when we went to school, "Do you have any money?" And he'd go into his pocket to get something to give us. And you know, it reached the point where we actually said, "We don't want anything. We don't need any more. We have enough, Pop." This feeling is still carried over into the present because my father was the kind of person you could rely upon. My father always liked to drive a car. We'd go places and then we had that big apartment, and we were paying only $29 a month for all that. When my father was working steady and my mother was working steady, we were going fine. So then I thought things were okay. They had fixed up the apartment nice. I thought the place was the most beautiful place there ever was. You know I could ride a bike up and down the hallway, it was so large. And my grandmother lived there.

My grandmother, she raised us Puerto Rican style. We weren't given prepared baby food. She didn't know what that was. She raised us on plantains and things like that and rice with milk and things that she was used to making, like corn meal. That's the way we got raised. And she raised us on all kinds of traditions and it was very different, not like later on when my mother took over and we'd have TV dinners and that kind of stuff. Before that it was like completely different, almost like that Old World atmosphere. And then everything was okay.

My mother worked. Now some families have a feeling that the mother should not work. But my mother always felt that she wanted a career and wanted to do something with her life, and my father did not prohibit that, and I think I came out suffering because of that. There is a problem when women assert themselves by going out to work. It produces a problem within the home. That problem arises when you degrade one position, that of the housewife, and you exaggerate the position of a woman who has a career.

Part of this is not just because society is doing it. But things have actually changed in the position of women in terms of what they actually do in the household. To give you an example, my mother had several of children and she sewed clothes, she did the laundry, all these things we knew had to be done. And we valued these things. We liked clean clothing. We liked socks darned. We liked good food. Partly because of the changes in technology, these things are just not done in the home. And so one of the problems for young mothers is that instead of having a home which is really an active place, where all sorts of things are taking place and children grow up in it, unfortunately the mother sits there staring at one or two children with four walls around her in an apartment with nothing to do except to mess in their lives. And it isn't healthy for the children, even if you try conscientiously to be a good mother. There is a profound change taking place today. The sisters that I'm going to be particularly talking about later on are making their own clothes in the house, and cooking their own food, and getting away from the canned stuff, and doing these things that women would be doing, and taking pride in it, which makes it very different from that poor woman who's sitting there watching *Days of Our Lives* reruns, you know, and having nothing to do, yet feeding her children junk and buying them cheap clothes or whatever the case might be. I don't particularly think that that's progress. It could be the opposite of it.

I was given a lot of responsibility in running the household when I was young. I had to manage that household. My father had a great deal of trust in me, and he knew where I was coming from because I was doing well in school. If there's one thing that at least I was blessed with, it was in my academic work. I did very well in grammar school. I started in public school but I was only there for kindergarten and first grade. Then I got transferred to a Catholic school where for the first time I had to wear a uniform. My family put me in a Catholic school because they believed that the public school was an awful place. You go to a private school and not only are you taught well, but you're better disciplined in there. You'll be a better person. You stay in a public school, you come out an animal. So therefore you go to a Catholic school.

I think I went to the cheapest Catholic school there was. We only paid something like $2 a month. Of course sometimes that'd be too much for some people. It really wasn't that much, $2 a month. You could dig it up, but if you had four or five kids, then it was different. And I didn't see too many big families in there. Usually two brothers was the most you'd ever see in there, unless they were well spaced. But usually about two was the limit. Anybody in Catholic school felt they were special. You always felt superior to a public school kid. The thing is you really were superior—in terms of academics anyway.

We were right across the street from a public school. Our teacher would say, "Look over there and see what you see." I can remember clearly seeing public school teachers sitting at the desk with their feet on the desk reading a newspaper while the classroom resembled a total war game. These kids were throwing desks out the window. We weren't doing that kind of stuff. I mean we would sometimes get out of hand, but we would get punished for it. It's like the Marines. They'd beat it into you. You felt better than the children in the public school. You said to yourself, "I'd rather be here than there any day," because you felt you were going somewhere. You were getting educated and learning how to read. We felt that our parents cared more for us by putting us in the Catholic school. Of course that's what we felt.

They wanted me to make it. They had heard about the public schools from their friends, and they had seen them and they said, that's not for our children. Even now people have that attitude except they have no out. If they had a choice they wouldn't have their kids go to public school.

It's a mad-house scene. You can't possibly get educated unless you're in a college-bound program. You might be lucky, but that's such a small group.

Anyway, I did very well in school from the first grade. I don't know how the teachers really noticed it—but they noticed something. So they started taking me to the side and asking me to read. And they saw that I could read a second-grade reader. I was in the first grade at the time. I remember one time they asked me to read a third-grade reader and I read that, so I never went to second grade.

I don't know why I did so well in school. First of all I was always reading. I liked it. You were always learning things, and my parents got me an encyclopedia, and that was a big thing for me. When they saw me take a liking to education, they began to provide for me anything that I wanted that was related. They went to a lot of trouble for a lot of time to get $200 or more to get me this encyclopedia set. In the encyclopedia I was reading at a very young age about different kinds of animals, and what the prehistoric age was, and trying to figure out those names. I would see Tyrannosaurus Rex and I was already reading that. And I was reading about different cats and how they evolved. And I was reading about different horses, monkeys, how time started. What about the planet. What's an eclipse. But I couldn't share this with other children. I was always by myself reading and reading and reading. And I used to spend time reading about ballet.

This did affect my relations with other children. Ever since public school my parents used to say that I didn't hang around with anybody. And they used to bring people to my house and I wouldn't even play with them. But I didn't miss playmates at the time. I had acquaintances that used to come by the house, and I remember at times playing with them. Most of the people in my class used to have groups that they used to hang out with together, whereas I used to only during school itself.

They were telling me to become a doctor. I would say, "I'm going to be a doctor." Not because I had a great interest in it but because my mother said, "You're going to be a doctor," because she was into medicine. I had just a deep interest in science, and still I like to look through science books.

But I developed a block about mathematics which I didn't have when I was younger. And I still don't understand it. And I got that when I was in high school. I always had 90s except for one time that I had an 86 in math. I had 92 on the Regents in algebra when I was in high school, and then I completely collapsed. I got something like a 66 in geometry. I failed trigonometry. The class I had in trigonometry was absurd. There were 45 in the class. It was the sixth period and that means it was close to one o'clock, and we didn't have any lunch. And you could forget about personalized attention. And the funny thing about it is that when I took trigonometry in the summer—which I had to do—I think I had the second or the third highest mark in the class—the course that I completely failed with a 47 on the Regents.

But this experience seemed to destroy my interest in mathematics. But I still loved science. I don't know whether this experience kept me out of the sciences. There were times when I thought of being an engineer or being an architect. And I ducked physics when I was in high school. I said to myself, "If you keep on going into the sciences, you're going to have to take a lot of math, and you can't do math, so..."

None of my counselors said this to me but little things were telling me so. Then I took another test, a test to find out what I was good in, and I did well in verbal and not too well in math. So I said, "I must be verbally oriented. I guess it must be where my tendencies are." I like all those types of things which helped me to analyze. I loved composition writing. So maybe it has all turned out right. But that interest in and love for science helped me out in a way, 'cause I don't feel that I'm purely verbal. If, for example, you tell me this is effective but also scientifically concise, it attracts me. And I always try to use that kind of structure when I am writing or when I am talking. If I could find some kind of pattern in it, it's almost like putting it in its place. There's a certain law. You obey this law, you get a desired effect.

I don't like to feel that things are absurd or that I can't understand them. In the past I used to find a lot of things absurd. But a lot of things lately are becoming very clear to me even though I don't expect to know every little intricacy of everything. If you see an effect and you see no cause, you call it absurd. But once you pinpoint the cause, then it means something. And there were a lot of things which I used to consider absurd because I couldn't see what was behind them. They don't look so absurd to me now.

I have friends even now who say, "Why is man in such a mess? Why is he going through so many changes?" It looks to me obvious. Of course a person may not accept my conclusions. I don't really care. But my answer seems more logical to me than his because it fits into the pattern. The way my whole mentality has changed over the years is something even for me to wonder about. When I was in high school I read a very important book. The book was to change my life. It's called *Down These Mean Streets* by Piri Thomas. It pinpointed my family. I don't know how many young Puerto Ricans read that book. I was affected by it not because I lived everything he lived through, but because one thing that he went through related to me, and that was his racial situation at home. In my case the roles of the mother and father were reversed. The attitude was almost identical. My mother was what his father was: black wanting to be white. My father is like his mother: white but he didn't care what he was.

I feel my mother has suffered from what you call blackness. That she really wanted me to be white. I remember a time when she had a couple of drinks or something and she came up to me and said, "I messed up your mouth and I messed up your brother's nose." That means that my lips are not my father's lips. And my brother's nose is more flat. She used to tell me many times in her secret ways, although she doesn't do it anymore, "I know you wish you had come out another way," or something like that.

There are inner feelings which I began to see, things which were in the Puerto Rican culture. I was beginning to pick them out. And I began to reject those attitudes. Who are you to tell me my hair is bad? What do you mean my hair is bad and your hair is good? Where did that come from? And I started saying, "What do you mean I have to accept that? I don't have to accept that." I said, "What are you talking about, ma? Your ancestors could've been right next door to his ancestors. It's just that you wound up here and they wound up there." And, "How dare you?" And people looked at me like, "Where you get these ideas?" I began to see how arbitrary the whole thing was. And I began to question. And I began to look at myself in the mirror. My experiences in high school were another thing. I began to see that people were treating me differently because I was a black-skinned Puerto Rican. I noticed that Manny and Tony had a lot of friends whereas not too many people were hanging around with me. And I was beginning to wonder why. I had read the book by Piri Thomas already during the summertime. I had always been in an all-Puerto Rican school until then. It was the first time I had been in a school where the majority were what I call Europeans.

Then one time we had a biology class and this biology teacher started talking about the black foot. He started talking about biology and anatomy and he started talking about the black foot. In other words, he was saying that there's something over here in the heel—it's genetic. And that's why they can jump so high. Right then during lunch period, I went downstairs and this guy behind me, he just came over to me. I was just standing around in the lunch line. I wasn't particularly thinking about anything. But he came up to me smiling and said, "So you can jump higher than me, Pedro." To myself I said, "Oh now I know what it is. I'm not just Puerto Rican." Now I was not only Puerto Rican but I was being differentiated right inside the school because I was darker. And I had obvious Negroid features and they didn't. They wouldn't jump so high. I would jump high.

Then I became very socially conscious. By junior year I was very preoccupied with oppression. "Wait a minute, we're having a horrible time over here. Everything is not so rosy." Before that I really hadn't had that feeling. There was a thing about white against Puerto Ricans. But that was more like a gang thing. But I hadn't seen the white as dominating. But now I saw that we were having a really bad time of it. But things that I was reading in Piri Thomas's book gave such a description. I felt it because he was saying things that I had been experiencing. And he was very critical. He was pointing out racism and discrimination. I said, "Holy God, look at this." Before this I hadn't noticed it and suddenly I just caught the light. Not everybody lived that way, but we lived that way.

I saw people's attitudes towards us and I said, "This guy's against all races, man." And then I began to feel black 'cause I knew that when he said black he meant anybody that didn't look like him. And then the students at high school used to write things on the wall and people used to draw spears. And I said to myself, "These guys are sick." Then I began to think they're not all good. A lot of these people can't stand me and then I started thinking of hypocrisy. And I said, "This guy really can't stand my guts. He is going to laugh and joke with me and a few minutes later makes racial slurs about me to other people." I said, "Wait a minute, man." I began to look around, to choose my friends because they were like me.

I really didn't start working till I was 15 years old, because up to that time I never really had to have a job. I didn't go out like my brother to shoe shine. I wasn't too interested in going out. I had everything I needed. And when I did go out to find work for the first time, it was because I had never worked, and I wanted to go through the experience of going to work and making my own money. It was part of growing up to get a job. I didn't really have to go out to get a job. I went out because I wanted to and it was time. I had spent every summer playing games in the street, and it was about time that I got a job. The important thing was that at this time my mother was working as a community worker. She had some connections with the Puerto Rican Community Development Project. I think it was my mother who brought up that there were summer jobs. It was at the start, the beginning of the Youth Corps—this was 1968. So she mentioned it to me, and I just fell right into it 'cause I wasn't doing anything.

Up to that time I had just been hanging around during the summer, reading, playing sports. I was about 15 and it was getting time for something new. I remember when I had made my decision. I found out that I had to go down to West 4th Street to get working papers. That was a day that will stand in my mind for the rest of my life.

I remember that I went down there early in the morning with my birth certificate and everything. I don't think I was late, but I think I was number ninety something, maybe even higher than that. The place was a madhouse, filled mainly with blacks and Puerto Ricans, although there were some Europeans there too. This was all new to me, taking a number and having to stand in line. And you had a physical and you got an eye test. It was like going into the army. You had to stand in a big line, and you had to get a physical. There were long hours of waiting. I went there something like eight o'clock in the morning and I came back something like five o'clock in the afternoon.

It was a trip—going through that whole scene, from one seat to the next seat, and it looked like it took ages. After we finished with all the physical exams, I guess we had everything except our working papers. Then there was a whole bunch of chairs and we had to go sit over there and wait until our number was called. I just felt that I was there for the longest time. There were a couple of people up front, and what they did was process you. We went up there and they would stamp some things. I was looking at the whole thing from back there. I was looking at people going up, people who had been there like me all day. I spent the whole day just in that routine. Finally they did call my number and I went up to the front desk.

I can't remember exactly what they said. I guess it was very simply bureaucratic detail, stamping things for office use, and things like that. And finally I got my working papers. It was an experience for me, but that was just a premonition of things to come. There were scenes that were more wild than that in the Youth Corps. But I had to go through a similar experience at Hunts Point, in the grand ballroom. It was packed, I mean really packed, with only blacks and Puerto Ricans. It gave me the sense that the whole Youth Corps program was a black-Puerto Rican thing. Everybody on that line was black and Puerto Rican. Only when I went to get my working papers did I see people who weren't.

You had to get enrolled. There had to be something to identify you as part of the job. I just know that I wound up there and I got what I needed for the job. All I had to do was report for work on July 5th. Everything was taken care of.

I really didn't stop to figure what was going on. They said, "Go here," and I went. Why was I there? It had to be for something. I just remember the enormous scene. The place was packed. The line was steadily going up to the stage. I remember going up to the stage. I remember going up some stairs. The stage looked so high to me and up there were the machines that processed identification cards.

Finally everything was taken care of. I didn't have anything to worry about. Then I went to *La Sultana del Oeste. La Sultana del Oeste* was the name of a day camp. It was part of the summer program. And I just happened to be caught up in it. *La Sultana del Oeste* meant the sultan of the west, and I guess they just took that name and attached it to the day camp.

We would take care of children and take them on rides and things like that, and I was a junior counselor. I really had things to do, but it was so easy and we had so much fun. You didn't learn anything. You had some kind of responsibility. You felt responsible for the children, but at the same time we were having a ball. I was going places I would never be allowed to go during the summertime. For the first time I went to Pelham Bay Park.

It was a deep thing for me because I needed that type of thing. It was something like a breaking out. I was developing a kind of social life, more than I had before. I really did enjoy it. It lasted from July to August. That would take us to my freshman and my sophomore years in high school. I got a job in sophomore year, too. I wanted to work again, but this time I went through a bad experience.

Summer was over. Around October there was an opportunity for after-school work. At my high school there was a place where you could go and inquire about work. They gave me an address, and I said I'll go check this out. I remember it was in the garment district, and I went down there. The job was carrying boxes. When I first went down there the boss interviewed me. He took out a box and he said, "All you gotta do is carry this." And I looked at him and said, "Is that all I gotta deliver?" He told me something about the salary, and I could've sworn he gave me a set salary.

He gave me a list of addresses where I had to make deliveries. And then the boss said, "And this is what you gotta deliver, and this, and this, and this . . ." I said, "Wait a minute. What is this?" There were so many boxes that he had to tie them up with a rope. This was on 38th Street. And the farthest place that I had to go was 67th Street and Madison. This was on 38th Street and Broadway. I had to walk from there all the way to 67th Street and Madison for my first delivery. And then I had to walk back. I had to make one delivery here, another delivery there, picking up things and dropping off things.

Sometimes the boss would give me carfare for only one way because he expected me to walk back. And there were times when I was so loaded with boxes they wouldn't even let me on the bus and I had to just walk it all the way. I felt absurd as I walked along because, first of all, I'm flat-footed. I can walk a lot but it hurts my feet after awhile. I didn't like this. I felt conspicuous carrying this load through the city streets. Anybody could tell you were making deliveries. You felt and looked kind of funny. I had to deliver things to Bergdorf Goodman. I never forgot their name. It was October and it still wasn't that cold yet. But I was saying to myself, "It's gonna get cold. And I gotta be carrying these things. I don't think I'm gonna like this job."

Most of the time I was away from the shop. I only came there to pick up what I had to deliver and to bring back whatever I was going to bring back. Then one day I was very depressed by it all and the boss noticed my face. He looked at me and he said, "You don't like this job, do you?" And I said, "No, well, not really." The person who had the job before me wanted to come back. What he really wanted to do was to get me out. And I don't know if that was what he had in mind from the beginning or if he just thought about it along the way. It was very smooth. He said, "Okay, finish off." And I said, "Fine." I quit and got fired at the same time. So I left. I just went back to get my check. When I got my check and I saw it was a real meager amount, I said, "What the hell is this?" I was mad. I think I got something in the teens for five days work, chicken feed for doing all that.

I said to myself, "This wasn't worth it, man." And then I didn't work for a long time. I didn't work all through 1970. When 1971 came around I had graduated from high school. After that things changed radically. I had five jobs in one summer. Up to that time I hadn't felt a need for a job either. I wasn't that pressed. Now I was coming up to a whole new world. Up to that time I always made it a policy not to work during the school time, except for that job in the garment industry. My parents didn't want me working and going to school at the same time. They didn't mind me working during the summers. That was fine, but their main interest was my studies. They said, "So don't try to overburden yourself. Stick to your studies." At that time my mother hadn't been working for a while, and my father was bringing home most of the bread, but there was no crisis in the house.

When I got out of high school I wanted to start a new life. I was 17. I decided to go look for work. That was a very bad experience. I always knew I was going to go to college. My parents had ingrained in me the idea that I was going to college. I never had any doubts that my parents would support me or that they would back me up. The major influences on me were pro-college, pro-education, pro-advancement. Things like work for me were only looked upon by my parents as a distraction, as a burden. Even when I made the decision to work in the summer of 1971, it was purely my own decision 'cause I wanted to work. I wanted to do something. I was having trouble during the summer of '71 getting a job. It was more or less an accident that I got one.

I had to go to the employment service because I was trying everything. I had to find something. I looked at want ads and all that kind of stuff. I was looking everywhere. I was having a little bit of difficulty. I went to the State Employment Office. And I got hooked up with a job, making very little money. I was making something like $40, but the job was a very good experience for me in that I was there as a recruiter. That's what it turned out to be. I was supposed to be just there to help. I was just part of a group of other people who didn't have anything else to do and they didn't want to be in the streets. Basically what I was supposed to do was to give help to those people who needed it, in terms of information about universities, tuition, and so forth, really doing a big favor to those who were trying to get into college. It was really good service to the community. I was assigned to five guys. That's all. And we didn't do much when we were there. The important thing was I got stuck with a person who became a very close friend of mine. We talked for many hours. And he introduced me to many facets of life that I had never seen before.

The experience I had was a real awakening in many ways. Part of the mission of the agency was to inform people. I had to prepare to speak before groups. I had spoken in high school. I got a kick out of it in high school. I remember how nervous I was the first time I had to speak. But then I caught the knack. And I didn't mind doing it in front of people. But my friend was awakening me to a whole new side of life that I hadn't seen, the adult world. Particularly, he introduced me to a little bit of the intricacies of what was going on with the Puerto Rican middle class.

He was only making something like $8,000 a year. He was on the staff, working as a recruiter. He had been a gangbuster. He had been in the streets. Now he was in a position where he has seen the other end of the stick. He knew the little things going on in the heads of these community action corporations. He knew was was going on—little deals and things. He was hip to all the corruption—hip to the political scene, where Puerto Rican politics was really coming from, who was controlling the power, who was the puppet of whom, things like that. This was a whole new field for me. He would say, "Look, so and so did this. So and so did that."

It was enlightening. I wasn't shocked, but I was interested. Also, he was a very cynical person himself. He felt disgust towards middle-class values, and middle-class Puerto Ricans with their bourgeois attitude. We used to have very deep talks. And he would emphasize to me honesty and truth and not superficiality and artificiality. He saw those middle-class values as artificial. These political figures and bureaucrats would lie to get their positions. They would put false images in front of people. My friend pointed out that this is what the whole game was all about. These people are childish, immature. But the thing about it is that they have the power and the money. We don't have the power and the money. It all looked sick to me. It all looked like it was a game. You could go to a party and think, "Look at all these people. They're all phonies. That's not acting for real. You don't have to act like that." But I've seen the whole scene. People were actually acting. And I'd say, "Oh, man, I don't want to have nothing to do with this. I'm not into this. I'm not from here." Tony, the brother, related to me because he was from the streets, and he was telling me, "Don't be like those phonies. Be yourself."

My friend showed me the little power games that people were playing—blacks against Puerto Ricans. I mean people were fighting over money and petty things when the essence of the thing should have been, "Let's get together." And I saw very clearly the power struggles.

My friend and I, we saw eye to eye. I don't like acting. At the time I used to say to myself, "If I had a million dollars, what would I possibly do with it?" I saw the mad dash for power and I saw that inside these people were rotten. Just the attitude of my friend was a present to me. He was honest and faithful. He was telling me, "Don't be arrogant. Be honest and truthful to yourself and to other people. Try to help other people not because of any personal advantage you want for yourself but just because you want to help them out, not for a motive or because you want to use them." That was a very common thing, people using other people, people wanting to rip off other people. And I said to myself, "I don't want to have anything to do with that. That's not real." I was glad I went to work there. The attitude that I developed was sort of a hostility towards all kinds of artificiality. The only thing you saw was power. The people in charge of these programs were the Puerto Rican middle class. And these were their values. They were imitating what they saw on TV—the style and talk, the attitude. It's the hypocrisy. I went to middle-class schools. If you acted like them, you're a hypocrite too.

I remember when I was very young, I was invited to my friend's house. They had published a paper in the public school and an article said, "Kill rats, starve a rat to death." And my friend said to me, "Come over to my house. We're going to start doing in the rats today." But when I got over there, he took a couple of sticks and he said, "This is dynamite." And he went, "boom," faking. I was about six years old. I thought we were there to really kill rats. I didn't think we were there to make believe we were killing rats. And I never got over that. And the young people in these community programs were pretending to be doing something, and they weren't sincere. And the people who were really sincere were squashed. And that's what told me that these people were hypocrites. "Don't inquire about what I am doing with the money," or, "We must hang it up in parliamentary procedure."

My friend emphasized that I should continue to go to school. It didn't change my views toward getting anything in school. It changed what I'm going to do with what I get. I couldn't picture myself getting a house, working for an agency, and not doing anything constructive. All those goals about having a house sometime, about status, were gone, I think forever. I just couldn't picture doing what was not constructive. First of all, there was our plight, the plight of the Puerto Rican. We didn't have assets, we were going through poverty, people were suffering. And these people were doing all these phony things, and I was going to consent to that, be part of it? My experience that summer completely demolished all those concepts. And I was at conflict with my family because of that too.

My father was saying, "You should get money and you should get a good job." I was saying, "Yeah, Pop." But at the same time I didn't really want those things. I felt there must be a better way. I felt that this system is corrupt, that there must be a way to hit it, to strike it. I began to become aware of oppression. I began to be aware of who's really controlling things. Here I was 18 going into college. My mind was wide open. I was seeing all this and I was saying to myself, "My mission is different." My whole train of thought from then on took a radical turn.

I don't knock anybody who wants to go out and become a doctor or a lawyer. I'm not saying that's bad. I'm saying what people are doing with it is bad. There's nothing wrong with being a doctor. If you become well-to-do while being a doctor, fine. You can impart that knowledge.

My friend that summer imparted to me the point that with that knowledge came power. He encouraged me to continue to go to school. Getting up in the world can increase your influence. Power is not bad, but it can be corrupted. When I came to college I started wearing dungarees, whereas before it was silk pants, and patent leather shoes, knits—all that went out. And I started saying, "No, there's a different way of doing things. What's wrong with dungarees? It's simple. It's practical. Let's just be ourselves—a whole different attitude compared to when I was growing up in high school." I was never much of a conformist. But I did conform, not so much in the high school environment, but to the street environment. You had to have your silk and shoes. I had to reject two things—the middle class culture and also the street culture. When I went to college I wasn't the only one who was thinking like that.

Actually it started out with our freshman year in college and along with it a certain repugnance towards drugs. This was in 1971 and times were changing. The real drug addicts, the freaks, they were slowly going off. That was beginning to be looked at as kind of silly. The only thing that stayed around was marijuana, because it was considered mild. But heavy stuff was seen as oppressive to the community. It could cause a lot of disruption. Also, a whole new political attitude developed, something that had begun in the 60s with mass movements like the Puerto Rican socialist party. They were offering an alternative. They were providing explanations at the time. They were providing an outlet for those of us who had come to these conclusions and were looking for a way out. There must be some other alternative, an alternative to voting or revolution.

Even my mother and my uncles were all getting into that. We would go to a ball game and everybody would stand up for the national anthem, and we would stay sitting down. They warned us not to do that during football games, because one time a guy didn't take off his hat for the national anthem and they just took it off his head and threw it on the field. But we wouldn't stand up, because colonialism, imperialism, all these things were being articulated. The nature of oppression, why prices were high, why we were going through changes in the school system, the unequal relationship there, why we were really here in New York—all these things were becoming clear to us. The factors that lie behind them, Operation Bootstrap, industrialization, American interests, these began to be evident to us. People began to see that it started with the declaration of Puerto Rico as a commonwealth of the United States. It got to the point where public opinion was strong enough to finally define Puerto Rico. We began to understand what was really happening in the community. And this was affecting the young people, especially those who were getting to see things for what they were. You could go to school and now you're being taught Puerto Rican studies and black studies.

We were awakening to ourselves and to the culture. As a result you look at TV and you see John Wayne shooting Indians, and you see where that's coming from. You're no longer happy when you see Tarzan riding through and knocking down natives, or the British great white fathers walking around and making the black people look like fools. You begin to see it for what it is. You've crossed a bridge and you can never be the same again. And you can never just sit there and laugh at that kind of stuff any more. You're sensitive to every little thing now. You begin to see how you've been stereotyped. What Frito Bandito and all that means. And it becomes clear. Then we start learning. That's not all of it. There's another reality. Freedom? What happens if you talk and somebody shoots at you? The police attack Puerto Ricans just because they're standing in the street, just because they're another color. Or the cops go around knocking old men. I saw that, brutal stuff. When they broke up the Puerto Rican parade, when the Young Lords wanted to march, I saw that. I saw it from a distance, but the people in the march told me the rest later.

I'm trying to reconstruct the puzzle. I am speaking like a person who saw it at that time several years ago, and it is, of course, still part of my conception of reality. But other things were to take place in my life which were going to change my way of looking at things. College was a different scene. In college I was learning a lot. I was being exposed to new things. And my desire to learn was greatly increased. I became critical. Many of these teachers, they knew more than I did. But I would see little things about that teacher and what he would be saying and I'd say, "No, it's not like that."

I had lived it. I was beginning to read; I was beginning to study; I was beginning to investigate. That was a big change for me, you know, not sitting down and just taking in stuff. I was looking at the thing as a member of an oppressed minority. I was aware of the Spanish coming to Puerto Rico and ripping us off. And then America. I was aware of that, and nobody was going to turn me around. I'd be a hypocrite if I turned my back on this.

Look at the experience of those Puerto Ricans who went before us. Haven't we seen what our educated Puerto Rican leaders look like? Shouldn't we be suspicious? People were transformed into middle class monsters. I'm trying to look at it from our perspective, the behind-the-scenes machinations, the arrogant attitude of the administration in the schools, the blatant racism. What else can you possible think about it? All it could do was reinforce our new convictions and understanding. I'm not coming out with any answers. I'm just trying to let you see it from our point of view so that you can understand what was contributing to the formation of our minds.

José Ramirez

From the beginning work has meant a lot to me. I couldn't wait until I received my working papers when I was 13. I wanted to work because I wanted to earn some money on my own. I was sort of driven by this idea: going out and getting a job and having some money of my own, basically to be independent. And to be grown up, that too. That was one of the main things that my father tried to teach me, to be independent and to have things done ahead of time.

My father is pretty experienced in terms of the United States. He's been here since 1929 and held the same job. My father will be 65 this coming March 2nd and I'm twenty, so he was relatively old when he had me as a child. I actually grew up with one sister in the household, although I have three others who are much older. So I got a lot of attention from my father. My father, he came from the mountains of Puerto Rico. And at the age of 19 he came to New York City on a cattle boat. His family were farmers, tropical fruits mostly. Out in the hills there you don't grow much except what grows naturally. He was born on the top of a little mountain and grew up in a little town—you could call it a town because it had one street and there were houses on both sides and a couple of little businesses, and that's the way I saw it first in 1964. He said it had changed tremendously because of the erosion of the land.

He went into Ponce which is now the second largest city on the island. My parents met and married here in New York City although they knew each other in Ponce. The odd thing is that my mother was born and raised in New York City. He wasn't, so he says when he first saw Ponce as a kid it was the first time he saw any kind of vehicles, any kind of shoes, or radios.

My father only went as far as the eighth grade in school. That was up in the mountains. He used to walk five miles to school and back. He never talked much about the reasons why he left. I think he left because of money, trying to better himself, realizing that there was something up there to be had— some sort of opportunity. He lived as a bachelor for quite a while—then married and with his first wife first came here. He stayed here. But she went back and the children of his first marriage were raised over there away from him.

My father had the same job until 1970. It's a factory job. He worked for Horn and Hardart, where he loaded bread into the machines that would put it through an automatic slicer, wrapper and label. And once he put it in by hand, he just had to make sure it would be cut right and packaged right and sent out. He did that from the beginning to the end, and I think he got one raise. His salary never changed much. I think on an average he used to take home less in the later years than he did before. The union didn't come into where he was until 1967 or 1968. I think he brought home anywhere between $85 and $150.

He didn't talk about the factory work too much. When I was getting into my later teens, I used to question him and ask him about the unfair practices, but I was coming from a very critical point of view and sort of attacking him. I started to see injustice in his working conditions. I couldn't understand why he was still earning the same, why, no matter how bad he felt, he had to go to work. My father was a chronic asthmatic. He had severe health problems in old age. But he always went to work—every day. And he was on his feet all day so he ended up with calcium deposits. But he went every day. I don't know how he did it but he was really afraid that if he didn't show he would lose his job, even after 20, 30, 40, 43 years. It is the only kind of work he knows, and his brothers ended working there too.

He never would think of charity or any kind of charity benefits. It seems that he had too much respect for himself to even think of things like that. Once I asked him, "Dad, all these kids are getting allowances on TV. Can I have an allowance?" And he says, "Food in your stomach, and clothes on your back. You just received your allowance." And that's the way it was.

I admire him now because he's taught me a lot that I only appreciate now, now that I'm on my own. But living at home when I was younger, I couldn't understand it. He was very, very disciplined, and very different from other people that I knew, at least in my family. He took risks very, very rarely. He was very safe. Always took precautions, extra precautions. Almost too many.

But back in 1954, when we moved out of El Barrio and I was just born, he took a large risk—family loans and loans from friends—to put a down-payment on a house. I don't really know why he did it except for the fact that maybe he realized that this was one way out. He knew somehow that the neighborhood in El Barrio would definitely change for the worse.

He moved into a neighborhood where there weren't many Puerto Rican families. But the actual row of houses that we had was very strange because it was sort of two houses together—they were joined. And the families ranged from Irish policeman families with about eight children to black families from the South to Greek immigrants to Jamaicans. So we all grew up together, black and white and Puerto Rican. This is in what is now called the Soundview section of the Bronx—by the Bronx River. It has changed drastically recently. It used to be largely white, but recently more and more Spanish families, more than black families, have been buying houses because they're built on every piece of available land. The composition has changed. There's transition. I'd say it's from lower-middle to middle-class. Some of these houses are now very expensive, and people who bought them a few years ago have made a profit. My father sold our house after 18 years.

I went off to college and so I'm pretty much by myself now. I have other family—three sisters and a couple of uncles and aunts are still in New York City, and I'm very close to them. It's strange how it turned about, because my father was the only member of the family who had a house in the city. The other relatives lived in apartments, and on weekends they would show up to my house to wash their cars, to have big dinners. Every Saturday was sort of an occasion. That's where they grouped, because it was not exactly centrally located but easy to get to. And the neighborhood was pleasant. Now that they've moved and sold the house, there is no focal point any more. So myself and my younger sisters end up making rounds on weekends and Christmas holidays. Christmas with an aunt here, New Year's with a sister there. Every weekend you sort of have dinner at different places. But family relations are still very important.

The word for lazy is *vago*. There's a whole lot of meaning to it. It's something that you are taught not to be. I remember I was called lazy if my chores weren't done on time. And I used to hear it every day. There was always plenty to do while we had the house. It was full of chores for me because I was the only male. Upstairs were my parents, my sister who is six years older than myself. Downstairs was just my mother's sister and her husband. And that was it. They had no children, so my father was the one who'd have to take care of the household chores. There was a back garden and some cement yard, and a garage that went inside the house, plus a front garden and a porch. So they did need some taking care of because my father used to plant corn, tomatoes and everything. He loved to grow things.

My chores included sweeping up the yard, sweeping up in front of the house, cleaning up my room and some heavier chores, too—taking out the garbage. Me and he would paint summertimes. As old as I could remember, I was doing these things. I guess he just wanted me to help, so that I always had something to do. My mother would say, "If you have nothing to do, just let me know." So as soon as my chores were finished, I'd sort of disappear because there was always more to do.

Usually, it was very hard to find jobs, but I was very lucky because this was back in '67 or '68, at the time of Johnson's program, and my first job was a Youth Corps job. Thirteen or fourteen was when you started. And it was through a connection my mother had in one of the poverty agencies. She was very active in community work.

My mother worked first as a seamstress, but my father didn't consider it. He never used her income. It was for whatever she felt she wanted to buy for the house—little things here and there—clothes for me. But any time she gave him any money, he had a series of wallets for different things and he would put it in a wallet. And whenever she wanted it back, she'd have it.

My father took care of all the bills. My mother's income was really for nice things, and, you know, for the children. She made $30 to $50 a week at the dress shop, doing piecework. This was in the South Bronx. She's about to retire now. Right now she's not working because she is taking care of my father. But she doesn't want to lose her pension, and she has been there for so many years.

She never told me much about working in the garment industry, but I used to visit. Most of the people who worked in the plant were Puerto Rican women, but there were many Italian women. Mostly immigrants, if not all. She only worked for unions and later worked for the union, picketing places.

She was interested in the Community Action Agency. It started with the Liberal Party. My father was very distant from it all, but he always voted. My mother was the one who really played an active role. She was around when Herman Badillo, our Congressman, started to run for office.

My father was very clear about his values, even if it worked to his disadvantage. Our house was a two-family, but it had a small basement with pretty much apartment-like facilities—a bathroom, a small kitchen, a couple of rooms. And everybody on the block had a couple of boarders downstairs to help with the mortgage expense. One time a housing inspector came by and said that the basement was two feet too small in terms of legal restrictions, so you'd have to move the boarders out. My father did, on a two-foot technicality. He probably could have gone and gotten what they call a variance, or something like that, or he could have just said to pretend to move out. He could have had a lot of alternatives and kept the income, but he believed that if that's what the law said, then that's what you had to do. So he lost money on account of his principles. My mother used to hate that.

My father wasn't a religious man in practice, but deep down inside, very much so. In terms of discipline, he never laid a finger on me and my sister. He didn't have to. My mother did it for both of them. When I was quite young, my father wasn't a positive image for me because he symbolized something that was very harsh and very stern. If I had trouble in school, I had to take care of the trouble because my father could not and would not leave work, and he made that very clear. So I just had to stay out of trouble, because if he ever left work it was suicidal for me. My mother was different.

She was a lot more open about viewing the circumstances of her life. My father believed that things are the way they are and this is your fate. You took what opportunities arrived and made the best out of the opportunities that were there. However, he believed firmly in education.

When I was in first grade I was already told by my parents that I would go to college. And they were never satisfied with my marks—no matter how good. They constantly emphasized that if you wanted to get ahead, you have to make some money. That was my father's only concern, for me to get a decent job, because he knew what it was to be without money. He tried to show me that his suffering was an example of not having an education. He says, "If you get the education, you won't have to get up and go to work at six o'clock in the morning. You won't have to suffer the factory conditions and always have a constant supervisor."

He saw his life as a life of suffering, but for a purpose—for his children. He was very sick and still is very sick, and both sides of his heart are permanently damaged. And he's a chronic asthmatic. His job did it to him. And he didn't have any benefits. I think he gets $40 a week. His job was a means for my advancement. It gave him the opportunity to have a house.

My father was in business on the side because his salary just about made the expenses. For example, he would spend the same amount every week on food, and the entire week's meals would be pretty much planned out. He didn't believe in snacking. Food was for three solid meals and you had to eat a solid meal. And that's the way it was budgeted. Everything was budgeted. But trips to Puerto Rico and any kind of family recreation, barbecues, buying extra food for anything like that, would not be covered by his regular salary. So he used to go down to the wholesalers, and he'd buy anything from ties to toothpaste to soap and sell retail at the factory. So at the end of the year he made $3,500 extra.

He never talked about the barriers to Puerto Ricans. He never mentioned anything about how far he could have gone with an education, but I realize and I think he realizes that he could have gone far, because technically he's been the most successful of all his brothers. He had ten brothers, and he's the one that now, in his old age, has fared better.

When I got that job with the Youth Corps, I was investigating violations in housing. I was only 13 or 14. There was a lot of housing in the South Bronx. Some of it was being torn down. Most of it was in pretty bad shape as usual. And the job of this agency was to go out and knock on doors, and talk to tenants in Spanish or English, whichever. I had a check list to look for complaints.

There was a big difference between my neighborhood and what I saw down in the South Bronx, although it wasn't all that surprising or shocking or really new because my brother lived in similar conditions in a different part of the city. But at 13 or 14 I started to become aware of what people were actually suffering through. I worked a whole summer there. The rate of pay was $45 a week.

Nothing was ever said to me about contributing to the household. It was a natural thing to do. I contributed and I wanted to, and I felt a bigger part of the family, so to speak. But I also knew my father's policy with my mother. I gave him some money; it went into a wallet. And he said, "When you need it, you'll have it. The only difference will be that when you ask me for money, it won't be mine, it'll be yours." And being that the family budget was very tight, there wasn't room for extras, so any extras that I wanted was paid for from my salary. That was the main thing.

And I've worked every year since then during the summer. The first two were basically the same kind of jobs. I went from the Youth Corps to the South Bronx Community Corporation as a counselor. That was through my mother again, but it was only in the mornings. I worked from 9:00 to 12:30. And I found a messenger job in the afternoons, and I worked from 1:00 till about 10:00 at night.

The messenger job was at 43rd Street and 3rd Avenue. A friend of mine, his sister was working there, and he had a job and said they might be looking for someone else. It was a big company and they had accounts with advertising agencies, and so they needed messengers to go back and forth. I was a sophomore in high school then. I was 15. The job was pleasant enough—I like walking around the city, and the packages were basically just print-out sheets, so they might have been big but thin. I earned a good salary because I had both jobs. And I had a second motivation. Once I turned 13 to 14 and entered into a Catholic high school, I would have to buy my own clothes for school. The school demanded businessman's dress, so if I was going to buy a suit that was going to cost me $80 or two suits for the year, I would have to be sure to save at least $300. That meant working from 9:00 until 10:00 at night, five days a week. I never considered that I was giving up summer vacation. Each summer I had to find a job.

There were about half a dozen messengers employed. They were under a senior dispatcher and a junior dispatcher. The dispatcher was a friendly enough guy, but rather abrupt. He just had a job to do. Advertising depends on deadlines. So you had to get there on time and call in, get back on time, and pick up your next job. But I was lucky in a sense that his son was the junior dispatcher. He worked part-time summers and full-time during the year as a school teacher. And the son was a likable sort of person, and the senior dispatcher went on vacation for about a month or so, and that took up most of the summer. So we had a good relationship with his son, the junior dispatcher.

Basically the messengers were young minorities and very old men who worked part-time, enough to buy booze. I took it for granted that this was the way it was. I sort of had a realization that I couldn't get a decent job. I thought it was a great job for me because it was the best one I had had since the Youth Corps. I was earning $1.85 and was overjoyed about making that much. But I realized later through my friends in school that others made more. My high school was such that there were students from Westchester, from well-to-do families who had earned tremendous amounts of money, and they would say, "Oh well, I had connections through a friend, and I worked as a waiter at this fancy restaurant and made a lot of money."

I kept the messenger job just for that summer. The next summer was with the New York City Parks Department, cleaning up the parks. I realized then how government work is different from private industry. Our foreman, for example, would come by at 9:30 a. m. every morning to check the time sheets. And I found out from the older workers that after he did his rounds he was finished by 11:30, and he did whatever he felt like doing. The man who worked regular in the park was 72 years old and was receiving two paychecks, one from Macy's and one from United Parcel, and he was going to receive a third from this job. There was another man who was there who was close to retirement age, but he was a very wise and old guy, a lot of fun and knew the system so well that he went home by three o'clock every day. And so did everybody else, except the seasonals. They had to wait. This was a city job. It wasn't like a youth program.

It was better paying than the Youth Corps job, and I had to hunt this one down myself. Somebody said, "A friend of mine said that they were taking people out at Orchard Beach," and I said, "How do you get to work at Orchard Beach?" And he said, "The Parks Department." And I went down, but didn't go for Orchard Beach. I went for a park three blocks down from my home.

I was putting in time there. It wasn't too enjoyable. It was close to home. That was nice. I could walk so I'd cut on transportation fares. It was tedious, boring, it gave me a lot of time to think, some time to read. Basically, all I had to do was to keep the park clean. You'd start off in the mornings cleaning and sweeping away everything that was around, and once you took care of the cleaning, that was it. After that, you had to just keep out of sight. Once in a while, you'd have a foreman come by, so you pretty much hid out.

You basically worked hard in the morning if only because the morning was cool, and after the park was in good shape and safe for children to play in, your job was completed. It was just to keep it that way, so that you could feel you did your job even if you weren't spending eight hours a day. You had to make sure there wasn't glass or things like that around, and you'd fix the swings or repair some of the equipment you used to clean the park. Again, like the other jobs, I worked for the Parks Department for just that one summer.

I never had time for part-time work. You see I was very involved in community activities then, and I would volunteer 25 to 30 hours in community volunteer work. Eventually I sort of went on my own into local anti-poverty agencies, without my mother's connections. That work was a part of developing a feeling for the community. Also, my mother worked for a political party for a while, and I went to meetings or to a party with her, and she knew people. So I was conscious of politics. My nickname in my family was Perry. And the connection with Perry Mason was made early. So I was seen from first grade as a lawyer.

After my junior year in high school, I became part of a four-man team that ran a busing program for local children. I had been experienced in handling money for public programs for the past couple of years, and this program ran about $90,000 or so; and we four high school seniors were in charge of everything from getting permits to having community groups go to the park, to getting the buses, to scheduling everything for the entire summer, to making sure that everything went through. It was a big job, scheduling buses to state parks, Rockaway, Bear Mountain.

It was a Model Cities program. I came in contact with Model Cities through Aspira because I was the president of the high school Aspira club, and they had connections with Model Cities. So I had picked up the word that they were looking for someone, so we all went. We were all friends. We all went asking for jobs. They said no jobs for high school students. You have to be a college student. And we pleaded our case to the supervisor and agreed to get $2 an hour as a community service aide, but we would take the responsibility for the program. Not the ultimate responsibility. That was hers—the supervisor's—but we would have to take care of the day-to-day running.

We scheduled as many as 500 buses. The public announcements were made by the agency in the Model Cities areas, which may have been twenty or thirty agencies of different types who were under the supervision of the Model Cities Community Corporation, and word had gone out before we were even hired that they were establishing for the first time a recreational bus program. So we were the ones that initiated the whole program. I don't know how successful it was, but I suspect that it was very successful because it was brought back the second year. But it was very hard work. We sometimes put in 16 hours. Buses were available—chartered by a central office that would take Model Cities orders from around the city. These were ordinary school buses. And we would have to take care of our area. We would have to take care of the Bronx—the South Bronx area, so that I got to know the whole operation.

I guess Model Cities serves a purpose now in the sense that at least it is helping a little bit, but I don't think it was designed for any long-run goal. I think it was just another way for people to survive for a certain number of years. When people reach the end of their rope and there is an uproar, there is a little bit of a concession. And that's the way it would be, and we used to call it "chump change." You see, a chump is a person who's pretty gullible and rather stupid and could be easily fooled. And if you had $10 or so, you could always give the chump just ten cents. He'd never know the difference anyway. So chump change was what eventually trickled down through federal program bureaucracy. There was a feeling it didn't benefit too much the person at the end of the line. Like band-aids for cancer—that sort of thing.

But Model Cities was supposed to help the people in those communities. I was involved in a different way with a youth program which used basically anti-riot monies, because that's when it was developed—after the riots of the sixties. They developed community corporations in poverty areas. And they had what you call youth boards, who would not only have control of money, but would also have control of programming, which was a pretty new idea—allowing teenagers to do what they wanted to, or to do what they felt was right in their own community. And we would be trained as officers in some kind of agency. And the result in our group is that we financed a teenager counseling center for $60,000. We were trained to write federal proposals and to run meetings. It was sort of a community service center, catering to young people. It was a combination teen canteen program, tutoring program, and counseling center.

Supposedly they were there helping change things, but basically they were just trying to keep things from getting any worse. So I guess there's some positive things there too. It was also an avenue for certain leaders in the Puerto Rican community to jump up the ladder. One of the main results of poverty programs was that they offered an avenue for black people and Puerto Ricans to jump into the middle class. I think it accomplished its purpose of keeping things from getting worse.

If there was really some honest effort to change things for the better, there would have been a lot more pre-planning, a lot more training, because you shouldn't give people, who think that ten thousand dollars a year salary is a whole lot of money, two hundred thousand or two million dollars to play with.

People with a narrow scope were totally confused about handling large amounts of money. So you developed your fat cats, your poverty pimps. Everybody is lining their pockets because this is almost free money, and eventually those who get hurt were those who should have received those services. It also demoralized a lot of people too. I used to come home from community corporation meetings at one in the morning and cry, because I saw people, Puerto Rican people, literally cutting each other's throats for the money.

That was senior year. Then I went out of town to school. I had been very active since my sophomore year in high school in various kinds of community programs that took up the time a part-time job would take, plus school, so I was constantly busy. And as a result, I built up a pretty extensive record for college in terms of extracurricular activities which helped my admissions. So as a result of all that work, I got so disgusted at what I saw that I could not take New York City any more. I was disillusioned with the whole poverty program, because it was designed for failure. I was so involved in the day-to-day meetings that I could not gain any kind of perspective. My face was up against the mirror. This is the effect

Model Cities has on a lot of young people. What hurt the most, though, was that they saw parents, community people, taking money for their own benefit. There was no sense of collective responsibility, which young people did have.

I can sympathize with why the parents behaved the way they did, but I can't condone the self-gratification. It's my conflict with minority professionals. Somehow you have to reconcile the responsibility to duty and work it out.

Choice of college was not easy. Tufts had a beautiful campus and still does. I had been accepted to Amherst and was all set to go there. I had been accepted at Georgetown and at St. John's University—all pretty good schools—because my high school record was good. I had visited Amherst but was turned off by the atmosphere there and by the people I met. It was all-male then and I had just come out of an all-male high school. It was a big thing for my family, though. They were very excited about the possibility of going to Amherst or Tufts.

And my high school, though, wanted me to go of course to Amherst. But I didn't like the campus or the Latin people I met. I met two guys there who were supposedly going to show me around and give me some insight as to how life was there. They might have been Puerto Rican New Yorkers, but they didn't look it—not in terms of style, dress, mannerisms, speech. I was sure if I went there I'd be very lonely, so I turned Amherst down, financial aid package and all.

At Tufts I found a friend. I had worked on a political campaign for an assemblyman up here in New York, and one of the persons who ran the campaign with me was going to Tufts. And I found out by surprise, because she was the Latin student who directed me when I went to tour the campus.

A large majority of the Puerto Ricans that are at Tufts are from the private prep schools or elite schools of Puerto Rico. The status of the Puerto Rican community in Boston is different from the status of the Puerto Rican community in New York City. They're two generations behind. But at least Tufts offered the possibility that there'd be people with whom I had some common interests. It turned out badly, though.

I was shocked. I went up after having received a letter from one of the juniors there who was from New York City, right from Tremont in the Bronx. I found out later he had gone to a private prep school through a special program. The letter said that they had 25 Puerto Rican students, 15 other Latin students from South America—that they were a very cohesive group, a very solid group, they were intent on starting community programs and keeping a lot of interaction. It was totally untrue. I guess he was lonely, or that he hoped it would influence me.

Tufts wasn't all bad. It was good in the sense that I got away from New York, and I had some time to think. The bad parts, however, were very bad. I don't understand how I could have gone through all of that and have come out in one piece. I guess the worst part was not being able to identify with other Puerto Ricans there. For the first time it actually hit me that there were middle-class Puerto Ricans, there were wealthy Puerto Ricans. And I had no conception of Puerto Ricans with immense wealth, but yet here they were, the very, very elite among the Puerto Ricans. They were cliquish. They all knew each other, all went to the same private academy, were fluent in at least two or three languages. There was no accent. They had been back and forth to Europe. And so I come on campus with my Afro haircut and I don't look very white at all, and when you're away from New York City, away from large numbers of Puerto Ricans, basically things work out in terms of black and white. And this upset me very much.

Of course, they didn't want to include me in anything. I went up and said hello and got the coldest stares. And I said, "What's going on?" I had thought, after working a lot in Puerto Rican communities, that basically all Puerto Ricans had the common experience of being Puerto Rican, of growing up Puerto Rican. It was not true. There was a class difference and this was something that I had to accept. They just didn't even want to deal with me and two others who came in the same year—one from Brooklyn, another one from Hartford. It was an amazing situation because Tufts was basically for two kinds of people. Tufts is either for the very rich or for the very poor. And that's the way it was for most people there. You were either very rich or in total financial need. So you paid your way many times over or just barely made it.

I had been alienated from what you might call my peer group here in the city, because of my good grades and because of good credentials. My friends did not see me as the same as themselves. I was what you might call white-ified because I talked differently—did not use as much slang. I was very much into academics. I'm talking about people I knew here in New York. They saw me as very hostile and against them, which wasn't true. Eventually we worked out a good understanding, because I became head of the local Puerto Rican student group and they realized that I was working for their interests as well as mine.

In high school my problem had been to keep a relation with a group who were working class. They might think because of my language that I was sort of betraying them. Now at Tufts, I found that I was automatically lumped together with the drug fiend, ghetto Puerto Rican that everybody sees and hears about in newspaper accounts. And this is what was believed by not just the white students and the black students, but also by the Puerto Rican students at Tufts.

In my freshman year I wasn't in touch with all that much faculty, but the ones that I was in touch with were pretty receptive, except for a couple of bad instances. That doesn't mean it was easier to have contact with the faculty than it was with the students. That wouldn't be true. The faculty were pretty much good people and as such they were devoted to teaching; and if your background hampered it some, because they really couldn't talk to you or understand you, they tried to just show you that this was their job. They tried to teach, but didn't make any effort to bring into classes material which would be relevant to us, because we New York Puerto Ricans were too small a number. I was at Tufts for two years. I was driven from there basically because they didn't have a program for me. I realized early that I wanted an Urban Studies Program. And they didn't have it.

For as long as I remember the idea of law has appealed to me. I guess I was in first grade when I knew that law was something to think about, but it wasn't my choice. It was my relatives who had already made the connection with me and Perry Mason. There wasn't much talk about careers until high school. And once I was in high school I was already into public speaking, I had gone into junior achievement. And things like law and public speaking were connected. As a senior in high school I considered business, but only for a short while.

My parents wanted me to have a Catholic education. They felt that it was better. And it was better than most public schools at the time. Classes averaged about fifty students. That's awful big, but very tightly disciplined. You know, very straight rows, very fierce nuns and a lot of memorizing. And that went on for basically eight years. Doing good in school made things a lot easier for me at home. If my marks were always 95, then I wouldn't get any kind of pressure from my mother or father. And that was the idea. My father said, "Don't have people on your back all the time. Get your job done. Get it done right and you won't receive any kind of pressure."

And for the most part if I did good class work, I didn't get it. I had to do good work or else I'd go home and get beaten. Mother and father both checked the report card and my aunts and uncles downstairs, since they didn't have any children, naturally looked after me too. They were there whenever I asked them to help with school work, but they just couldn't help me as much as they'd like to. As the school work got harder, I was pretty able to handle it pretty much on my own.

I remember I couldn't lean on anyone, except I had an uncle who had a decent job driving a truck. He was making it as far as I was concerned. The only other person who might have been a help was the Jamaican who lived next door. We grew up together since we were a year old. So we talked about things we'd like to do, but we didn't talk a lot about school, because it wasn't his favorite thing.

I don't remember a political or public figure who impressed me or who I wanted to be like. I remember when I was about nine, or maybe eleven, looking for some sort of a figure. My mother's figure was John F. Kennedy. She would comb my hair to the side with the part. Puerto Ricans in general have this love for John F. Kennedy and this whole thing about any child can become president. Even that went to my family for a while. They really had high ambitions for me then. Strangely enough, I wrote a poem once—a very short poem. It was about lack of leadership. Martin Luther King was very prominent at the time, and it went like, where is our King, where is our Martin Luther, where is our JFK, in terms of a Puerto Rican symbol.

The New York Puerto Rican community has been here for many decades, and there is just the beginnings of leadership. The most prominent is Herman Badillo. There are now four state senators, a couple of assemblymen. Badillo doesn't seem to have the capacity to be a leader in the sense of a symbol. He was just not directing himself to the Puerto Rican community. Again, it probably wasn't expedient for him to do that and to reach the level where he is now. But he's still criticized by Puerto Ricans for not doing what he should have done on a lower level when he first started.

Herman Badillo had a positive sort of function, though, when I was very young, in the sense that this was a man who was on his way up the proverbial ladder of success. He came from Caguas, Puerto Rico, an agricultural place, and he came as a teenager here to the city not knowing much English. The story goes that he worked his way through college, setting up pins in bowling alleys.

He used to identify himself more with workers because that was his early basis for success. That's what got him up the ladder. The Liberal Party, thousands of Spanish workers, the International Ladies Garment Workers Union, they all strongly supported him, because he was good looking, he was handsome, a positive political figure.

I don't think it's hard to find common denominators among Puerto Ricans in terms of political issues. I think the issues are pretty clear-cut. You could start off, I guess, with jobs, jobs and housing, unemployment and welfare and all the problems that welfare brings, the various psychological problems and adjustments that have to be made. If they're not made you are apt to end up in some state hospital or prison. Also, there is the question of schools, health care. All of them are linked together.

For a long time I've been hung up on color, although I'm starting to change now. But I used to have a lot of problems just among me and my family, because Latin or Spanish views of color are very different from other western views. In Puerto Rico, even today, if you have one drop of white blood in you, whatever your background is, you are considered white. Over here if you have one drop of black, no matter your heritage, you're still considered black. My parents are very light-skinned. Obviously, I'm not. And I had to come to terms with my own blackness, if only because I was seen by others as black, no matter what kind of color consciousness or value system they had. So I began to examine the history of black people in this country to see what exactly went on. Puerto Ricans have a very heavy African heritage. My blackness is a sort of distinct and unique thing. Nevertheless, I'm seen as black with all other blacks by others in this country.

All of a sudden it struck me: Puerto Ricans are the rainbow people because we come in all different shades and colors. And so if they're going to segregate in terms of black and white, what happens to the various mixtures of Puerto Rican students? Recently I met someone from the admissions office at Boston University, and he said that the Spanish students were pretty much mixed in with the black students. But as a result of the desegregation of schools in Boston, they eliminated 270 classes of the recently enacted bilingual education law. So the Puerto Ricans came out losing.

In New York City, people are pretty much aware of what Puerto Ricans look like, and of course you can pretty much tell a Puerto Rican young man from a black young man and vice versa. That's not true for the Boston area, and I realized that in Boston nobody had any idea that I am a Puerto Rican. I was immediately classified as black. I was walking down the street and little kids were saying, "Oh, look at the Afro-American." The calculus teacher confronted me when I asked her about some help in the class, she said, "Oh, well, you're black and there is money available, so why don't you go down to the office?" I was shocked. A very nice sweet old lady saying this to me.

Although Puerto Rico may be a rainbow people, and used to be heralded as the showcase of democracy, it's not true. If you go to San Juan today and walk into the bank, any bank, behind it the teller will be usually white, very fair skin. Look at the peasant in the street hauling a cart and nine times out of ten he'll be dark. But Puerto Ricans still go through this whole self-hatred thing of denying any kind of African heritage. My mother practices certain African practices in her religion, yet she is a devout Catholic. She is like most Puerto Ricans. It is not a contradiction. Historically, it evolved that the Spaniards catholicized an African religion. That would be things like bread above the water, water on the window, certain tokens on babies' wrists to ward off evil spirits.

After I graduate from law school, and include a year or two in urban planning, I'll have the credentials that will make me a lawyer and an urban planner. What that may lead to I really don't know as well as I'd like to. I have certain ideas, but as I've seen happen with college, opportunities present themselves once you're in the situation. Once you head in the direction, all of a sudden there will be sign posts on the road saying, "Stop at Joe's Diner," or "Here's a community agency that will help you in getting into law school while you're in college."

Grammar school was for me a kind of childhood. That is where everyone was my friend. There were very few Puerto Ricans in the class. There were about three or four in my class. We knew each other. We knew we were different. But it was a subconscious thing—that we all had Latin-sounding last names—that we were all shades darker than the others. We ate different foods, did different things, but I don't remember any incident in terms of our being singled out. But the white friends I had at school were friends only at school.

Friends at home were a different group who went to mostly public schools; they were kids from the immediate neighborhood. I lived in a private home, but it was across from a city housing project. Outside the area I lived was an all-white section. It had been all white and still was until recently. The barrier was very clearly defined. You just didn't go down there unless you were looking for trouble with the white people who lived down there. You'd get into a fight. They'd say things and they had their dogs come after us. I remember this from when I was really a little kid, as early as I could ride a bicycle, because I wouldn't walk down there. You'd have to be careful because there were gangs of white students—Italian or Irish. You knew which territory was which.

High school was different, because I spent most of my time away from my neighborhood, except when I was in the community program that was based in my neighborhood. When I was older, I discovered that there were certain areas of the city where I didn't feel safe. The bicycle gave me a great mobility, but most of the pleasant areas that had parks, nice scenery, enjoyable places to ride in were places where I knew there was always the possibility of my being attacked by some white students or just any white people in general. You know you'd be looking for trouble just by being there alone. Even Pelham Bay was restricted and still is. If you rode up to Pelham Bay Park or to Westchester, you'd be looking for trouble, because you could be sure a dog would chase you. It's not that people set dogs on you, but that they wouldn't stop them from coming after you. But there were gangs up there too, and they stayed up there and sort of protected their area, just to be sure you stay out. They did that in any area that didn't have Puerto Ricans or blacks or any minorities living there.

I still have an inner consciousness or awareness. There is something about me where people may eventually say, "I don't know. There is something about you. You are just not the typical American. There's something there that isn't for real, something that isn't founded in generations of being in the United States." I've had friends of mine come to me and say about themselves, "Well, here I'm in a responsible position, supposedly successful, and as black people might say, 'You're still a nigger.' In a sense I can say about myself, 'I am still a spic.'"

Most people my age will feel this. A little story will tell you how early you get taught this. One day I was riding my bicycle in Parkchester in the Bronx through one of the parking lots, and I was stopped by a guard, threatened with a gun, and almost had my bike taken away. He just said that I wasn't supposed to be there. I didn't know I wasn't supposed to be there. There weren't any signs. There were other kids riding their bicycles through there, but I guess the guard knew they lived there or looked like they belong there, and I didn't.

Outside our own neighborhood we were always aware. We have a common awareness of what we are, of the difference between us and them, even just sitting across from someone on the bus. People often don't recognize other individuals as Puerto Rican. They feel free to air what they honestly feel about Puerto Ricans. It doesn't happen to me very often. But it's happened to my sisters, because my sisters are all very fair—they are easily taken to be Italian, and they are often in situations where a taxi driver, bus driver, people talking on the train, say derogatory things about Puerto Ricans.

In New York City, people are familiar with the Puerto Rican face. This is not true outside the city, something which I learned rather harshly. Outside New York City they classify you as either black or white. Just recently, I've been dating this girl who is very fair—almost lightish brown hair, also Puerto Rican, but we would get the looks that I've seen before when I've dated Jewish girls. From certain people it would be sort of a look up and then a stern and serious look down, disapproving. Black people, especially women, are often sympathetic. They look me in the eye saying I understand. I'll get that look from black men too—like they can sort of sympathize with me in dealing with a white person as opposed to someone more or less like myself. It's all done through the eyes. With my present girl friend we'd laugh because she never noticed it before. But I'm sensitive to it because it's happened to me for so long.

I used to go and ask for Spanish periodicals and Spanish papers on some of the newsstands around town as I rode by, just to see what kind of a response I'd get. I would ask, "Do you have a copy of *Latin New York* magazine?" And I'd get this, "Latin what?" and "You've gotta be kidding" kind of looks.

When I worked as a messenger, it was pretty much recognized that most messengers were either black or Puerto Rican. If you saw somebody dressed in stylish clothes, but in sneakers and carrying a couple of envelopes, you knew what his job was. After I'd walk into an artist's studio to hand him some printing materials that I had had to deliver, the doorman would give me such a scrutiny. The only reason blacks and Puerto Ricans are in those neighborhoods is because they're messenger boys or things like that. You can be sure they don't live there.

If I can show people that somehow they have something that I admire in them, they'll sort of be easy on me. I guess they feel more at ease that way. Many times they just feel threatened by looking at me because I look like the stereotype. As soon as I'm not part of the stereotype, then things are all right. The first thing is my voice. They calm down a bit, because I'm not saying, "Hey, man, like I need some money." Language has gotten me more connections than anything. I used to be able to get into libraries in Boston to do research where non-white students could not get in. My voice on the telephone was in my favor. They were shocked when I'd show up in the office.

I'm sure my parents noticed because I spoke a lot differently from my cousins. But my parents wanted me to be different from everyone else. My mother did not believe in dressing with the style, or going with the prevailing trend. If I said, "Wow, gee, I'd like to have this jacket because my friends have this jacket," she'd say, "Well, you're not your friends." My mother was independent.

I think I've got more than my parents wanted for me. They want to avoid what they suffered. My father wanted me to have a good job, money, and freedom to do whatever I had to do without anybody being on top of me. My father was convinced that education would eventually lead to financial security. I accepted that, although I didn't have many examples in my family.

What was constantly drummed into me was the fact that if you didn't get the education, you'd wind up trapped. You were trying to stay in education to avoid getting into drugs, getting into crime. It was always a matter of caution and sometimes overcaution, to keep to a straight and narrow path that would eventually lead to some sort of freedom, freedom from being like father—from being trapped in a job that was physical pain. School and my mother provided the positive influences, although I only realize it now.

The priests of my parish were mostly Irish priests. I never came to know them much. I felt they were prejudiced against Puerto Ricans, as I got older, because I then realized that the area I had lived in was in transition—that there were more and more Puerto Rican families moving into it—that they were causing factions within the Church. They wanted a Spanish Mass started. They wanted a Spanish priest there, and they wanted to have facilities open to them so they could celebrate their religious festivals in their way. And my mother was active in this. She would be bitter at the obstacles presented by the other people in the Church who were Irish and Italian, and by some priests also.

Spanish Mass in my neighborhood was held in the basement. They had to fight to bring it up into the Church, but they eventually got it. The parish there was anti-Spanish. They wanted Puerto Rican parents to stop teaching their children Spanish because it confused the children in the early grades. I was the proof that it wasn't true because I was bilingual as a child—more so than I am now. And I was going very well. So I was resented by the whole parish.

But there were signposts to a career. The early signpost was school activities—all kinds of school clubs. Initially, I didn't realize the benefit I would gain later by the extracurricular activities on my record that colleges would favor. And after I participated in different kinds of activities, teachers, guidance counselors, friends would say, "Hey, stick with it." I really got positive input from the one senior guidance counselor.

Then there was the whole anti-good marks thing. If you had good marks, you were white-ified. You were sort of betraying the rest of the Puerto Ricans. They'd say it right to my face. They'd say, "Oh, Jose, you even talk white. What's the matter with you?" And that would hurt me. But it was like my friends saying to me, "Don't do well in school. You'd be better off. You'd be more like us then. Things'll be nice." As it turned out we became friends, because they realized I wasn't out to show them that the white way was the right way, and what they were going through was their own fault. They realized that I was out to help them as well as myself.

We were 10 to 15 percent of the total population, and there weren't many Puerto Ricans in the honors program. There was a sort of tracking system. If you could track into the honor classes you wouldn't see the rest of the Puerto Ricans, except maybe at lunch. But I made it a point to always have lunch with them, because they were my friends. I could get friendship and warmth from them that I couldn't get from anybody else, because as much as I excelled academically and associated with the white students, they felt that I was just another Puerto Rican.

The whites didn't think much of us. They'd let you know that you're a spic. There were fights in the train, curses through subway windows, that kind of thing. The school was a Catholic school, and the teachers always tried to foster the idea we're all brothers here. The outside world does not exist. Over here we're a Christian community. And we laughed. What else could we do?

With some white students I felt close, but that was because we had gone to grammar school together. Their friendship ended once we started getting any kind of awareness, because the differences automatically made us separate. We could only handle things that were common, like our attitudes towards teachers, school work, sports, and things like that.

School activities and later community agencies were the signposts, and I realized that I was learning much more from them than I was learning in school. School gave me a lot of academic things, but I learned more from the community corporation board about dealings with people, especially older people.

I never found myself challenged by school. My challenges came outside. My challenges came in fighting for money, or a certain program, in trying to hold together a couple of advisers we had hired. I competed with white students and did well. The fact that I knew I could do it also made me realize that I knew that all of my other friends, who weren't doing so well, could too.

I learned that there are a lot more intelligent people on the street than there are in the classroom. People on the street have a keener insight, because they're with it every day. They don't become desensitized. They have a true sense of how people act and react, especially towards people like themselves.

School may weaken you in the sense that it tries to promote "You're all the same." Especially in my school. The more they tried to do that, the more it made the difference that much clearer. We're not Christian brothers. You hate my guts. I hate your guts. That's what you felt because there were always the gangs.

The children of white immigrant groups, the groups that I've met and dealt with in the city, we could understand each other. Because there was a struggle in the family. There's just no link at all with the other group, the middle-class children. They seem to have no concept of struggle. That's what used to amaze me. Life was like applesauce for them, smooth and tasty. I couldn't understand their looking for a sense of purpose, even in high school, whereas I always had a sense of purpose.

In one English class, the teacher asked each one, "What is your goal for college or later on in life?" More than half of them said, "Make money, make money . . ." They gave sort of the shrug of the shoulders, as if to say, "I guess that's what we were supposed to do and that looks good anyway." I believe I said, "Become a lawyer," because I knew there was something behind that. I wasn't becoming a lawyer because lawyers made a whole lot of money, because I never saw Perry Mason as being very rich anyway.

I believed that there was a direct connection between knowledge of the law and politics and poverty programs. I realized that I had to learn about economics. I knew that, as soon as you got down to the final decision-making, there was the Board of Estimate. I said to myself, "Well, it looks like you have to have a knowledge of money matters," because the existence of our programs depended on money matters. I had to justify the program in terms of its costs and the benefits it would bring.

I kept seeing more and more political figures who showed that one way to change things is through legislation, through making changes in present laws. What I can do with the law, though, is still unclear. I want to talk to law students and to lawyers about the possibilities of law. I've looked through law school catalogs and seen the various different kinds of law that you can specialize in. If my career as a lawyer didn't permit me to be community-oriented, influential in terms of policy changes and business practices and government practices that I thought were basically unfair and unjust, I would be discontented.

Looking into the future, if I got into politics, there's a possibility I might become a state senator, a congressman, or become a commissioner or this or that in the city. It might be the kind of thing I'd like to do if only because those positions turn real power in your favor.

I've had friends who have left school and have joined Communist parties and militant leftist parties and who do actual community work, working with workers and lawyers who go out to Puerto Rico and work for independence—a direct sort of struggle and political social movement. I feel that politics works. And I feel it's one way that I can work for the best interests of not just Puerto Ricans but of everyone. If I was into a total Puerto Rican bag, I guess I'd become warped, I'd start hating people and there's been enough race hatred and conflicts throughout the history of this country. The way I've seen Puerto Ricans get any kind of political action is through massive organizing and strengthening whatever positive things they have on their side. In a sense a political battle is necessary to get their piece of the pie, their piece of the allocation. It is ruthless because everybody's fighting for the same so-called piece of the pie.

I wish I knew why the Puerto Rican community is fragmented, why it doesn't have solidarity or organization. I know it has nothing to do with island politics. Politics on the island is different from here. Politics on the island is like down-home rallying and partying. Here, it's a different kind of thing.

COMMENTARY

Before we identify and explicate some of the themes of Puerto Rican adjustment to life and work on the mainland, it is well to recall that the three men whose life histories we have just reviewed represent a substantial variation from the norm. Each is a college student; one has been admitted to medical school. One need not be an expert on Puerto Rican occupational adjustment and career mobility to recognize that the three young men are in the phalanx of a group, most of whose members are still close to the bottom of the educational and career ladder.

But in every generation, and among people of different racial and ethnic backgrounds, some individuals succeed in moving up the ladder and often advance two steps at a time. While the stories of these three young Puerto Rican males report interim successes far beyond the average for their fellow countrymen, one must not overlook the fact that their progress has roots deep in American experience.

A second important generalization to be extracted from this small group of three also has its counterpart in the earlier experience of the United States: the importance of family background. While the body of social evidence overwhelmingly demonstrates that the offspring of stable families with adequate resources are likely to undergo development experiences that will favor their future achievement in work and life, there are always a few with disadvantaged backgrounds who have been able to pull themselves up by some combination of personal strength and fortuitous circumstances. Such a person is Ramon Gonzales.

It is difficult to imagine a worse beginning: not knowing one's father; having a brother who became addicted to drugs, having a mother who lived with different men, being ejected from her household in early adolescence; and moving in with relatives who resented making room for the outsider.

171

Yet Ramon studied and worked, worked and studied, completing high school and college, and finally, because of the changed attitude toward minorities, gaining admission to medical school.

Another lesson to be learned from these three case histories is the caution needed in generalizing about the labor force participation of Puerto Rican women. While it is true that their participation rates are considerably lower than those of whites and blacks, we find that Rivera and Ramirez come from families where the mother worked, one full time, the other as a supplemental earner. Their earnings made a significant contribution to the total family income and to the quality of life that their families were able to enjoy.

An interesting sidelight on parental work experience is offered by Ramirez who notes that his father held down not one but two jobs in order to care better for his family. That he was a careful planner with his eyes fixed on upward mobility is demonstrated by his willingness to move out of a Puerto Rican neighborhood and buy a house in a more congenial area in which to rear his children.

The early life histories of these young men shed an interesting light on the education of minority children which has proved so frustrating in most large cities. Despite the annual expenditure of $2500 per child or more, a high proportion of them is seriously retarded by early adolescence; many drop out before high school graduation and many who graduate are barely able to read, write, or calculate. Their poor educational achievement is a burden that they will have to carry all the days of their lives.

There is little to be gained by seeking to assess blame among their families, the pupils themselves, or their teachers and school administrators. What our life histories record are three young men who take to their studies, gain the attention and encouragement of their teachers, and who, at least in two instances, receive encouragement at home. They were imbued with the notion that if they wanted a good job they must get a good education.

Each of the respondents reports that he early became interested in reading, devoted much time to books, and derived much pleasure from them. Since the inability to read, particularly to read easily, and to cope with complex materials is a major educational hurdle which confronts many young people from low-income homes, the desire to read and the facility for this skill set these young men apart. They won the approval and support of their teachers; they were able to get on the fast track in school; and they acquired the one basic skill they needed to take command of the speed and scope of their own learning.

One of the additional burdens that members of minorities face is coming to grips with their inferior status in the larger culture. However, the individual who is able to work out a satisfactory answer to the question, "Who am I and what do I want to become?" frequently matures into a better-integrated adult than the members of the majority who slide from adolescence into adulthood preoccupied with their sexual maturation and little else. Ramon, with his early inclinations towards medicine, had more than enough to do to gain admission to medical school. He apparently gave little thought to the more perplexing issue of how to build a bridge from his Puerto Rican background to the dominant American culture.

The adolescence and young adulthood of the other two young men are dominated by their search for identity. As with many adolescents, there was a "friend" who enabled Pedro to see the class differences among Puerto Ricans and to recognize the power brokers who got rich by burdening the poor. Pedro's maturation is speeded by his encounters with employers who demand much and pay a pittance, with the oppressive bureaucracy that treats people as numbers, and with a growing awareness of the rising nationalism of embryonic Puerto Rican political movements. All of these helped him to find a new center, at least for the time being, outside and different from the values that dominate his parental home.

José's story parallels that of Pedro, except that his mother helped in his emancipation by being interested and involved in community action groups and in the political rise of Herman Badillo. His political maturation began early through his active involvement in various poverty programs from the Youth Corps to Model Cities. As a high school senior he had the opportunity to run a large busing program, but he recognized the difference between what he called the "poverty pimps" who learned to skim large sums of federal money and the "good" bureaucrats who provided services to the poor for whom the money had been appropriated.

Members of minority groups suffer not only the handicaps inflicted on them by the ruling majority but also the wide-ranging prejudices and hostilities pervasive among members of their own group. No one who has spent time in Puerto Rico will question that color is a sensitive issue, and the people of means look down on those who have less. The man who breaks out of his group is likely to be scorned by the less successful. These sources of tension are revealed in the stories of our respondents.

These three young men are not typical of the many thousands growing up either in El Barrio or on the fringes of New York City, for they clearly had special strengths which got them into and out of college and into professional school. If they are not typical one must also not see them as exceptional. They come from modest homes, attended indifferent schools, started working for money by the time they entered high school, had little career counseling or advice from their parents, and had to work out their identities for themselves. The fact that they were able to do so should be encouragement to many more to do the same.

PUERTO RICAN WOMEN

Maria Diaz

Even before I started working, I had a sense of the place of work in people's lives. I felt that work was basically something you *had* to do because you had no choice. I remember when I was about six or seven, my father used to bring home some little electrical sockets that you could plug into another socket and you would just screw it onto the wall. He would bring those home and we would put the screws on. This was something that he did to make extra money. It was by the gross or something. And the more you did, the more money you made. So he would bring home boxes of these things, and we would assemble them. It was sort of like an assembly line, putting it in the little parts. My six brothers and sisters and my mother, we were like a little factory. But my brothers and myself—the rest were too young—we thought it was fun, and we couldn't wait until our father got home with the boxes of things. It didn't last too long, a few months or something. That was my first experience with work. I knew even then that this would help with the family income.

My mother was not working at that time. It was kind of understood that she wouldn't work because there were so many of us to take care of at home. Around that time, I must have been about seven, my sister was born and she was just a baby when this was going on. And then right after that my father lost his job. It was awful because my father used to drink. He was working as a mechanic for a sewing machine company. I don't know how he got that job. He was trained as a mechanic, and he used to work for the Morse Sewing Machine Company.

My mother came from Thurianto. She was born in Thurianto, Puerto Rico. That's very close to the metropolitan area, San Juan. I've been there.

174

It's beautiful. It was a farming area. They were very close to the main artery of transportation. Her parents had a farm but it was not a successful farm, because there were too many family people involved. There were 13 brothers and sisters trying to cultivate a moderate amount of land. They were all beginning to marry and have children so by the 1900s, there were just too many so they couldn't all stay on the farm.

When my grandmother died, my grandfather became very sick, so my mother's older sister took my mother and another of the younger children home with her. She was already married. And they went to live closer to the city. They went to live in San Turce, near San Juan. There was a very strong sense of family among all of them, a responsibility for each other. No question about that.

My father was from Ponce, on the other side of the island. He was orphaned around the age of seven or eight and put in a Catholic orphanage. His family tried to take care of him, but the problem with that family was that they weren't all from the same mother and father. The only two that were from the same mother and father were my father and his sister, and she couldn't take care of him because she was just married and was having a lot of trouble with her husband. Another brother from another father was the one that decided that my father should go to the orphanage, because there he would get an education and he would be better off. He was very young, and they really couldn't take care of him, but, anyway, my father didn't stay in the orphanage. Around the age of 13 he escaped, he literally escaped, roamed around the island, got a job, did odds and ends, and when World War II came, he was old enough to enlist in the army. He went to Germany and France and every place else. He got training as a mechanic while he was in the army. My father was one of those telegraph operators, Morse code. He knew how to fix things and welding and things like that. He was very handy.

After he lost his job, there was hard times, and he died in 1964. I was very close to him, close in the sense that we were constantly in each other's hair. I can't describe the kind of relationship we had. We felt helpless with his drinking. Even while my father was alive, I guess maybe I was 10 or 11 years old, I remember that my brother had a shoeshine kit that my father built for him. This shoeshine kit was a means for my brother to make extra money, to go to the movies, or buy a basketball. He was younger than I, a year younger. This shoeshine kit was a terrible thing for me. I wanted to borrow the shoeshine kit so that I could go and make some money too. My brother was willing, and he showed me how to do the spit shine, as they call it, and the whole thing. I went over to 6th Street and Avenue C and stood on the corner on a Sunday morning while there was a lot of hustle and bustle on that street, and I started to shine shoes. I had been shining shoes for several hours when my father came along and sent me screaming home because I had no business being on the corner of Avenue C. It was all right for my brothers, but it was not all right for me. And he beat the hell out of me.

That was my first attempt to make money for myself. It was just unbelievable. So after that I was able to compromise with my father and I said, "I won't do it again. I won't want to make money if you will buy me a bike." And he bought me the bike, but then, because he was drinking one night he came home without it and and I said, "What happened to the bike?" And he had sold the bike. It was just awful. But this didn't affect my school work. To the contrary, it made me feel more independent, because I felt that I could do things for myself. And I did. I did my work in school, and was able to do well, through the eighth grade.

I was pretty sure what was going to happen at home. I knew that either my father would be drunk or he would be sober and very strict. He felt guilty about being drunk all the time, so when he was sober, he had to be very strict and everything had to be very orderly. It was a terrible contradiction, but I managed to adapt to that kind of situation.

School was a lot different for me. It was like being free, a place where I would have fun. That was after I went on into fifth and sixth grade where we were doing music and I was playing the tuba and we were doing all kinds of exciting things. Music meant a lot to me, but I don't know whether I would have liked to have become a musician. In any case, I did not have any opportunity. I resent the fact that they didn't track me into music in the seventh and eighth grade, or at least offer the opportunity to do it.

There were plenty of students in my classes who had ballet lessons and music lessons. The Third Street Music School was right down the block from us. I knew that all these things existed. But because, you see, I didn't experience them, I really didn't miss them, because I didn't know what they were all about.

I never had odd jobs. It was either working at home, although I didn't get paid for that kind of activity, or full-time work outside. You see, I had a lot to do at home, even when I was quite young. My job was to iron everybody's clothing and to prepare breakfast in the morning. By the time I was seven years old, I had to go shopping. If my mother had to go some place where she couldn't take all of us, I had to stay home and take care of everybody. At that time, I thought it was wonderful, because I thought I was my own person and I thought that was just grand. I was the mother. And I literally behaved like the mother of the whole family until I was almost twenty. Everything had to be together, and I had to make sure that this one was not wet and that that one was fed and the diapers were done, and that kind of thing, and make sure that the milk was in the ice box, or I would have to go to the store and get it. I was like a mother hen.

When I was around seven years old, I remember making what we call rice milk, a kind of soup. I have four brothers, three brothers in between, then a sister, then another brother. So it was mostly boys that I had to contend with, and there was no companionship from my sister. Instead she was my responsibility. She couldn't give me any assistance. I had to do practically everything for her. And I feel resentful because I really didn't have what I would call a childhood. I wasn't able to do certain things that normal kids do. I was always busy taking care of everybody.

I make friends easily, but always with older people. I always want to know that I am the youngest, to avoid having to be mother hen. And that bothers me because I would like to make friends with people my own age, but then I always have a tendency to overexert myself and to overwhelm them, so I have to kind of shy away from those relationships. My mother was working part of the time. She worked after my youngest brother was born. She was a seamstress, a very good seamstress. She made all our clothing. She learned that after she finished the eighth grade. She went to work with this woman who had a small shop in Puerto Rico, and she taught my mother to do smocking and all kinds of fancy work by hand. She never made gloves or anything, and never crocheted or knitted, but she did detail work on clothing. She worked for a high fashion company at that time. She did sample work. She didn't design dresses, she would only make them.

She could have had her own business, of course. Her life has been kind of oppressed because of all the children and because of the whole cultural thing, the belief that the mother had to stay home. You don't go out to work when you have kids, you don't abandon them. Her sisters saw that as abandonment, and because of the close family ties, unless she left the kids with a sister or an aunt or a cousin, or with me when I got old enough to take care of them, it was scandalous.

My mother was an interesting and admirable person. I said "was," but she is not dead. I said "She was" because she has become so bitter, with all the problems she has had and the problems with myself and with my brothers, that she has become a vacant smile. She has a beautiful smile. She doesn't say that it was all for nothing, but she acts that way. I have been trying recently to see if she would wake up. She lives with my brother Eddie and my brother Felix and with my sister, who is still in high school.

I guess I would have to attribute it all to the fact that my mother was very dependent upon my father. Even though he was an alcoholic, he just did everything for her. She never had to go shopping. He would wash the windows and wash the floors, if she wasn't feeling well. When he died, she didn't know where to turn. Of course the family all offered help, but she knew from previous experience with her family that it would be all very restrictive help. I think that they prohibited her from remarrying. And I am sure that that hurt my mother, and she has never remarried. She fears that her sisters will come down on her like a ton of bricks.

When I decided that I wanted to get married, the first person she called was her sister, instead of calling the priest. Her sisters live nearby but they hardly ever visit. In some ways her sisters had easier lives because they had no children. Both husband and wives worked. They didn't make fantastic amounts of money—they all worked at unskilled jobs—but they worked steadily, and they didn't have children, and they didn't take vacations, so their circumstances were very different. And of course they did help their families, my own family and the family of my other aunt who has a lot of children. They brought us clothing every once in a while and took us out to activities and took us to parades and so forth. They did the cultural things. But we had a feeling of dependency upon them. We liked to have the things they brought, but we hated the idea.

So my mother went out to work, but she did not work regularly, just on and off, usually in the summer. She would go out and get a job, because just before September she would have to get us clothes and books and everything. You see, we were on welfare all this time, because my father was an alcoholic. And welfare gave money for clothing and so forth, but it was minimal, and when you have six children and all of them are growing up, there is no ending—shoes, clothing, everything would be gone in a matter of months. Welfare gave us money every six months, but it was just not enough, so she would go out and work during the summer, make extra money, and get everything we needed, and sometimes when she would have a little extra, she would buy a lamp, you know, buy a secondhand TV, or something.

I thought welfare was the worst thing in the world. I remember just at the beginning, when my father lost his job because of his drinking, something happened to his leg—he sprained an ankle or something—and he was very sick, so they put him in the hospital for a week or two. Anyway, my mother didn't have any money, and she didn't even know that she could go to welfare to get money. So she went to see her sister to get money for food and whatever, but when we got home, the lights had been turned off and so had the gas. So we didn't have any place to cook and we didn't have any lights. We stayed in the apartment for about three days, burning candles and cooking in the neighbor's house. My mother got so frustrated, she packed all five of us and took us down to the Welfare Department on 2nd Street, and she said, "I'm going to leave you here because I can't take care of you. The Welfare is going to have to take care of you." So she put my little sister in my lap and she left. And my little sister was about two or three months old.

I didn't know anything. All I knew was that we didn't have any light and we didn't have any gas. And that my mother was out, going to see my father at the hospital. And that my cousins were coming to stay over and would bring food. And we would stay up until all hours of the night and play games in the bed. It was fun, but I didn't have any idea. I knew that the lights didn't work because we didn't have any money, but that was all. So when she took us to the Welfare and she put this baby in my hands, I started to scream.

I thought she was *never* going to come back, and I knew that she had had conversations with the people who were there in that office, but I don't remember what they were about. I wasn't listening. All I knew was that she was going to walk out. So when I started screaming, all my brothers and my sister, they started screaming too. And there we were, all five of us children screaming away. And the Welfare people ran to get us because my mother had gone out of the door. And so they brought her back in and they convinced her that they were going to give her some money.

My mother didn't know a thing about welfare, because when she first came to New York, she was working, her sisters were working, their husbands were working, so they didn't need to know about welfare. They didn't need to know that they could get money some place if in fact they lost their jobs. Nobody in the family had been on welfare. But apparently somebody told her that if you leave your kids at the Welfare Department, they'll get taken care of. So that's what she did. Anyway, she got money, the lights got turned back on again. I was about eight years old when this happened.

Welfare was our means of livelihood from when I was eight years old until I got married. The case worker was around, the investigators, the social workers, all kinds of people would come around the house to ask questions of my mother. Only once in a while would they ask me something. I didn't resent it, because I knew that it was going to help us, that we were going to get money, that they would ask questions about the bed, do you need another bed? I remember things like that. At that point they were helpful. They would, at that time, practically give you a full household of things. You would get money for utensils, for laundry, and for other things.

We felt dependent upon them, of course. But it was worse if we didn't have it. My mother was very bitter about it; she resented it. And that was basically why there was a lot of bickering between my mother and father. She nearly killed him one day. She picked up a can of beer and threw it at him, hit him on the head and knocked him out cold, and she had to call the police and everything, and she thought she had killed him. She had reached the end of her rope. She couldn't stand it any more because he had bought beer. "Where the hell did you get money to buy beer and meanwhile we are starving and waiting on welfare to feed us and you're bringing in beer!"

How did this affect my school? I really don't know. I remember having to tell the teachers that I would be absent on a particular day because I had to go on with my mother to the Welfare Department. And I did feel that the teachers treated us differently. They would require certain things to be brought to school, like Scotch Tape or colored chalk or crayons, stuff that I couldn't afford, so the teacher would say, "Well, you can't participate in this group that is going to do this special activity because you don't have the material." My mother was very good about trips, but she couldn't give us money to buy things. She couldn't give us money to buy cards and stuff at the museums, so I remember having one teacher who bought stuff for me. She took us down to the Stock Exchange and to another place where there was a statue of Washington. Anyway I remember the teacher buying me some cards and a little pin because I started to cry. I wanted one and I couldn't have it and she said, "Don't worry, honey, I'll get one for you." And she did.

School was pretty good up until the eighth grade. Trouble really started in the seventh grade. I started to hang around with my "peers" as they call them, and I started to drink wine, and I did all kinds of weird things at that age and in that grade. Of course the students that were older were friends who lived in the same neighborhood. And since I associated all the time with older children, I got introduced to everything that they knew and were doing. And by the eighth grade I was a full-fledged wino, as they say.

I remember seeing older teenagers or men—I'm not sure which—shooting up in the building where my aunt lived. That was a terrifying experience for me. I just stood on the stairway and screamed. I knew it was not a good thing to do 'cause I had heard my father talking about it. He was totally opposed to drugs. That experience of the drugs was unbelievable. It was so gruesome. I think because of that experience—it stayed with me—I never experimented with hard drugs. But, nevertheless, the wine thing had developed and a lot of kids were doing it.

I had tasted wine at home from my father's wine bottle. And during that time I was smoking. I've been smoking since I was eleven. I was hanging around with boys, too. It was thrilling, it was doing things behind people's backs. But, looking back in retrospect, it was awful because I could've been doing so many other things.

This sort of thing did not take me away from school because it was in school that all these things were done, the wine and everything. Everything was done in school. The teachers must've known. They weren't blind. I mean if a kid walks in high as a kite into the classroom and stumbles all over everything, the teacher has to be aware of it. They wouldn't call the doctor. They wouldn't call anybody.

Where did the wine come from? The children would buy the wine for $.50 a bottle—$.35. They would go into the stores themselves and buy it. Usually we got ninth graders to go. Not only did they look older, they were older. Some of the ninth graders were 17. They were left back so many times. We were exposed to much older children on our grade level than would be the case in most schools. One of the problems was that if you came from Puerto Rico and you didn't know how to speak English, even if you were 17, you would go into the seventh grade. They would just dump these boys into the slowest section of the grade. So we knew that those were the 'dumb' kids.

They weren't dumb, but we thought they were dumb because they didn't know how to speak English. I knew how to speak English because I had been in the school system since kindergarten and because my father spoke English at home. There were children 11 years old mixed with those who were 17 years old. I think the older children, if you can call a person 17 years old a child, deliberately took pleasure in corrupting the younger ones. That happened to me and to a lot of other younger kids. They were simply preying on us; they would be fascinated to see an 11- or 12-year-old kid drunk.

And then you became their tool. This was the kind of thing that happened and continued, and then luckily we moved from that neighborhood. I went into another school where I didn't know too many people. So in the ninth grade it was different. And I had good grades in the ninth grade.

I dare say that if my mother had not moved, it would have been a disaster. She didn't move because of me or anything I was doing, because she didn't know. Till this very day she only knows what I've told her recently, because I wouldn't have dared tell her six or seven years ago, even though I was married. She would have killed me. I probably would not be here now talking to you if we had not moved.

The next stage would've been drugs. There was no way out of it. The neighborhood was just unbelievable. Where we went to live wasn't much better but it was some better. I think part of the reason why my brother went into drugs was because he couldn't break away from his friends. He would keep going back to the old neighborhood, and ultimately he got into drugs.

I got a full-time job when I was pretty young. I was only 14, that was when I got married. I thought that the normal thing to do was to go out and get a job as soon as you get married. You weren't going to stay home and live off the air or be dependent on your husband. My husband was 20. So I went out and I got a job sewing in a garment shop in the downtown area.

I had no working papers. I didn't even know that I needed working papers, but I got the job anyway. I had a Social Security card because I got that when I was in the ninth grade. The teachers would bring in the cards and everyone would write in the information and apply for a Social Security card. I was ready for work—literally because I had my Social Security number. They never asked me how old I was. They just assumed that I was old enough to work. I said I was experienced, and I was experienced because I used to sew at home. So I gave them the Social Security card which is all they asked me for, and they showed me to my machine and told what to bring.

It was a pretty large shop. In the section I worked in there must've been about 25 sewing machines. And then they had pressers, and the boss was right up there. As a matter of fact, he was behind me. His office was just behind my sewing machine.

There was a lot of pressuring from the floor lady. She was an Italian woman. I was setting in sleeves and, of course, I did that slowly. I didn't know how to do it fast. So they put me on piecework 'cause they saw that I wasn't fast. So I could come home with $25 after a week's work. Anyway, I got so sick of that job—putting a binding on the bottom of a dress for two cents.

It was a non-union job, but some of the people made good money. These were Italian women all dressed in black, who would put out dresses by the million, it seemed to me. Some of their paychecks were $75 and $80 for piecework, which wasn't bad at all. That was in 1964, and I was getting $25, $35, $40, working as hard as I could. But then, of course, I began to pick up speed after I had been there a month or so.

In the section I was working in, they were mostly Italian. There was another section that was all Puerto Rican where they would be pinking the garment or pinking just the sleeve. That was less skillful work. The Puerto Rican women were put on the less skillful work, and I was working on a finished garment. They put me there because I spoke English and nobody else in that section spoke English.

I had a sense of the division between the Puerto Rican and the Italian women, but the Italian women were friendly. They would talk to me, and they'd bring me candy and everything. I was pregnant so they were falling all over me. They were generally in their 40s, late 50s, and dressed in a very austere manner. I thought they must be widows, most of them. They wore dark stockings, and black shoes, and black dresses, and black veils, no make-up. They spoke only Italian, except for a very little English they would use with me. And some of the words they would say in Italian I understood because it's similar to Spanish.

The only one who wasn't friendly was the floor lady. But they had this other black woman that came in who was a floor lady who was really very good to me. She taught me how to set in zippers, and do a whole host of things. There weren't many other blacks in the shop. The person that pressed was a black man. Some of the more skilled work was done by blacks. At that time I was very conscious of discrimination against blacks.

I chose this particular job because it was the only thing I knew how to do, that I was sure that I could get a job doing. I didn't know anything about clerical work. I knew nothing about sales work. I worked there for about six months and I quit because the baby was going to come. I started getting sick and my mother was getting upset, and she said, "Don't work any more." Also my mother began to work at the same place. There was an opening and I said, "Mommy, you should come and work there. Besides, Felix is in school all day. You should come," and she said, "Fine, I'll go." And she worked with me in the same place, longer than I did. Then in the winter she decided she would quit, too.

I never thought of going into business with my mother, and I don't know whether we could have at some later time. At that time I didn't know the first thing about setting up a business. I had no concept whatsoever about it. Some Puerto Rican women who had the skills did set up businesses which were successful. But usually the women would get tired, or they would get lazy help, or all kinds of problems would come up. Then they would have to leave their businesses. But there were a lot of shops where Puerto Rican women would do special custom-made clothes on the lower East Side. They had been taught by their mothers how to work on garments, and weaving.

I left school at the ninth grade. I had graduated. I went to graduation, and that was it. I didn't want to leave school. I was prepared to go back to school in September, but when I went to Mabel Dean Bacon, the first week of school they wouldn't take me because I was pregnant. And I was only 14. They didn't tell me to come back after the baby was born. All they said was, "We can't accept you here if you're pregnant. Sorry, you have to get your mother to come in and sign a discharge." And that was that. I stayed home. After that I had the baby, and then I stayed home for about another four or five months.

And then I went to Seward Park High School. I decided I was going to go back to school. I wasn't going to stay around and do nothing. My mother was going to help with the baby, and so I went to register at Seward Park High School and I was accepted, although I was married and they knew about the baby. I had a French teacher who thought it was just marvelous that she could call me "Madame" in the class instead of Mademoiselle. She was just fascinated with that, and it was a wonderful experience. But then during the latter part of the semester the baby started to get sick and I was missing a lot of classes. It was too much to do both, so I never finished.

Then after that I went into so many other jobs, so many other things, so many other experiences. I finally got my high school diploma in 1971 by going to a special program. At that time I was secretary in an anti-poverty program. I would read all the mail that came in, and therefore I read that another anti-poverty program was offering instruction for high school equivalency. They had arranged with Pace College to have community people come in and take lessons and go for their GED. And so I applied, and they accepted me, and I went to Pace College. That was after several years of fumbling around. That was five years after I left high school. Then it took me another two years after I got the GED to decide to come to college. I always felt that education was what I really wanted. My husband was happy that I was going to school. And we had a lot of fun together because he would test me at home. My husband is not a high school graduate. My husband went to school up to the ninth grade, and has no interest in formal schooling whatsoever, but he cares about mine.

As soon as I dropped out of Seward Park, I went into a training program at Mobilization for Youth. It was right across the street from where I lived. I saw all these young people going in there, and they were being trained to do different things. I knew one of them and I asked her, "What's going on in there?" She said, "Oh, you can go too if you have someone to take care of the baby. And they will teach you how to do a number of things and they have sewing machines. They have typewriters, they test you in packing and in welding and all kinds of stuff, and then they get you a job." So I thought that was just great and I went into that program.

Even if I hadn't lived across the street, I think that I would have heard about the program because my sister-in-law at that time was working in an anti-poverty program and she was constantly asking me whether or not I was going to go back to school or whether or not I was going to do something. She's at least ten years older than I am, and she had not been working. Then she decided that she wanted to go to work. She started first as a teacher's aide. This was in 1967 and 1968 when the whole paraprofessional thing developed in the city, and she was accepted as a teacher's aide. Although she didn't have a high school diploma, she spoke English quite well. So there was no problem about her being a bilingual teacher's aide. Then she got a job in an anti-poverty program, and she suggested that there were all kinds of special programs for the teenagers and that I should take advantage of them. She encouraged me but she never told me which ones to go to. Obviously she didn't have the information at her fingertips, but she was aware that things existed, and she kept telling me that I should go find out.

The program people were very glad to get me, of course. The more Puerto Ricans and blacks they got into the program, the more money they would get. They would give you a test to find out whether you had some kind of basic reading skills and basic adding and subtracting skills, which most students did.

They had me wrapping, soldering, making jewelry. They put me on a typewriter. It was like a little shop with all these things in one place, and they would try you out and test you to see where you were the best. And I turned out to be good at the packing and at the sewing machine. And of course I had already worked in a garment factory.

Although they might have been pushing me in the direction of becoming a sort of packer or an operator of a sewing machine, there was one person there who was conscious of my intellectual capacities and interests. He was perceptive about everyone in there. At that time they had maybe fifteen people on the slate, but he could and would talk to us individually and he insisted that I go back to school. He said, "There is no reason in the world why you shouldn't finish high school and maybe even go on to college." But, you know, he just said it. There was no attempt to bring me to school. He was not Puerto Rican. He was a white man, and I am not even sure what his nationality was, but he was very encouraging. He was in his early forties. He was a kind person and conscientious, and he reached out to us, and of course that was the right place for him to be. These kinds of programs should have these kinds of people; if there are potentials in people, they can develop them and steer them somewhere.

I was there for six months, and I learned how to thread every single needle that you can find in a sewing machine. I learned how to make buttonholes, put buttons in, do pinking, everything, so that I could work in a garment shop in just about any given job. Six months later I went out and got a job of my own, because I didn't want them to get it for me.

While we were in training, there was a stipend of $40 a week. They would deduct taxes and you came home with $38 or $36 a week. It made it worthwhile. It was an incentive to go back. Of course there were expenses;

you had to have some clothing. You had to wear something decent so that you'd be prepared for just about anything. The program was relatively new. It was a pilot program and experimental. There were a lot of people doing research, taking pictures and asking questions, so you had to look your best at all times. I didn't feel that we were sort of guinea pigs. In fact, I thought it was wonderful. I was hoping that the program would work so that it would be continued and that more people could participate. But as far as I know, there are no programs just like this one today.

I would like to know why that program failed. Of course, it didn't fail with me. And it didn't fail with a lot of other people, but in terms of administration and of funding and what the program was accomplishing, you know, in terms of its relation to a community, it failed. It really made a tremendous difference in my life. I don't mean if there hadn't been such a program my present circumstances would have been different. I think that somewhere along the line I would have gone on to something else, as I eventually did.

Even if you didn't go out to work in the garment industry, the training it gave was valuable. If you know how to sew, you can get a rinky-dink sewing machine for $35 and you can make all your own clothing, and it was valuable just for that. The typing is valuable for me right now. I had some typing in the seventh grade. This reinforced it, and they had good machines to work on. They had fantastic equipment. I think that part of the reason the program collapsed was that it became politicized by the administration, you know, the people who ran the program. The program failed after I left. The federal funds were being cut every year, and there was no innovation and nothing new was happening.

The program became static. For something to continue to function and to function well, you have to do more things. The program just went down hill. It was because of that and also because of all the politics. And it is sad that that is what has to happen. And it makes me angry because that program could have offered a lot of help to a lot of others in that community. But it just fell into the wrong hands. So, as I said, I went out to get some jobs.

Some of the people in the garment shops, they were just miserable. For example, when we did piecework, if they were paying $.05 a garment to sew up the side seams or something, women would literally fight in the shop to get that specific job because it paid more. Since I had already learned how to do all the machines and was never laid off, I could go do anybody's job. The boss simply used me as a replacement for everybody else. Some women got very angry at that, because they felt that if they were out, the whole factory was supposed to shut down, and no one was supposed to do their jobs. When they found out that I was doing their job, they got angry and they would make snide remarks. They would say, "Look at that young punk," you know, things like that. I felt terrible and it became so vicious that I couldn't deal with it. Then in the street, there were all these young Puerto

Ricans, blacks, whites, pushing hand trucks down the street, and they were obscene and vulgar. They were just miserable, and I couldn't take it. It was like another world.

Later I got a job in a nice place, where they made fine clothing. It was all beads and all kinds of laces. They were paying $9 a garment which was fantastic. However, they used nylon zippers and I didn't know how to set those in properly. There is a whole art to setting zippers. So I worked there only three or four days, and then I was told they couldn't keep me unless I would learn how to put in the nylon zippers, because they were only using nylon zippers. It was when the nylon zippers first came out. I felt so bad because it was such a nice job, and I was making a lot of money. I would finish three garments in a day which was $27 a day, and that was fantastic. But I didn't know how to set the nylon zippers, so I lost the job and felt just awful.

So then I went back and I got another job on 36th Street between 6th and 5th Avenues. That was the last garment industry job I had. And of course I've worked in a lot of different places, but there wasn't any stability whatsoever in these jobs. For almost two years I did that, I roamed around from one place to another. I wasn't thinking of a career then. I just didn't want to be idle. But I had no notion that I was going to be sewing for the rest of my life. I was thinking that I would sew, and then eventually I would be doing something in the garment industry, but not necessarily working at a sewing machine. I could see myself doing other things, maybe floor lady, supervising. That was as far as I could see. But then when I started to see how people were treated and how I was treated and how everything was so vicious, I felt I had to get out of the industry. In the last place I worked, I had to have my own bobbins, my own shears, everything. You know, $9 for a pair of shears and $.15 a bobbin, and they would get stolen every week or so.

And then when I was 17, I stopped at Gimbel's just before the Christmas rush. I had to lie on the application, otherwise I wouldn't have been accepted. I remember that I said I was born in 1944, so that I could get away with being over 21. I really looked like I was 21. I was accepted and I was put at the special gift wrap desk. I knew how to pack and wrap so I got that job. There the salary was a lot better. I was making $75 a week in one of these garment places. At Gimbel's I would be making $2.75 per hour for 37 1/2 hours plus 25 percent discount on anything I purchased. It was really much better. I worked there for about a year. I made a lot of tips. I met a lot of people.

Being Puerto Rican did enter into the kinds of relationships that I had with the people that ran the shops, the people that were supervising, not directly with the bosses. The bosses would marvel that I could speak English so well. They expected that I would be just another one of those people that couldn't speak English—Puerto Rican, Italian, whatever. It wasn't only the Puerto Ricans that were treated in this way. Anybody that didn't speak English as the bosses spoke English was treated the same way.

It was surprising to them when they heard me speak. Also I understood some Yiddish, so if they were Jewish and spoke Yiddish, I'd understand what they were saying. Sometimes I'd retort back in English and then they would fall apart.

They knew I was Puerto Rican from my name and from my face. They would just wonder where did I learn how to speak English. And I would say I was born here and I learned to speak English in school. That would change their relation to me because they would ask me for special favors. But then that would make me feel so terrible, because the other workers would stare at me and say, "Look at her. She just came in and she's already in the bosss office." They would think it was favoritism. The boss of the garment factory would ask me to do office work sometimes, to write a letter or do this or do that. It was a small shop and this was resented by the other workers, and they would take it out on me.

They would say things—not overt insults—but subtle. They weren't really trying to hold me back. I think it was more resentment of their own position, resentment that they hadn't grasped the language. A lot of them spoke English, but they spoke it with an accent. They felt frustrated. Even though you knew how to speak English, some of the employers sometimes would say something in a nasty tone. If I answered them back, the workers would say, "Well, look at her. Now she's running the show here."

I worked hard at Gimbel's, and I had a strict supervisor. It's hard work to have to stand on your feet all day. You've got to be running up and down to get paper and ribbon and boxes. Especially during Christmas time, there is such a lot of people that you don't get a chance to stop and take a break. It was a job in which I could have got promotions. I could have become a supervisor, floor manager, just about anything there, provided that I had gone to school. Without a high school diploma or without some form of formal education, they wouldn't make you an assistant manager, even if you had ability. They just said these are the descriptions for such and such a job, and these are the qualifications. And that's that. It was a real bureaucracy. There were many workers who were pinned down just because they knew they were never going to get a high school diploma. These were mostly women who had been there for a long time when I came there. Some of them had been there for forty years, literally pinned in. Gimbel's would give them a little ruby pin for forty years, but they would have been in the same position in the same department for all that period of time unless they requested a transfer for some reason or other. And I knew that was not for me.

All this time my husband was working for the Institute for Crippled and Disabled, training crippled people how to do certain kinds of jobs. I think he fell into this job. Just before we got married he had been working for a place that made menus. He would go pick up the orders for the menus from the different restaurants, bring it back to the shop, give the instructions to the people who printed them up. And then he would deliver it back to these people. But that job was way out in Long Island, and he said that it was too much traveling and he was running all over the city. He didn't enjoy that job at all, even though the company had given him a car to do all this. He had fallen into that job too, through a friend. And then he went into the Institute for the Crippled and Disabled. He was really a shipping clerk there, but he had all these disabled people whom he had to show what to do in the shipping department, how to assemble things and put them into boxes. This was a training program for the crippled, but they had regular people working there, showing them what to do.

He had to go out and work when he was very young, because his mother was taken out of the place where she worked on a stretcher because she had a heart attack right on the job. Because she couldn't work any more, he had to. And that family never went on welfare. They were very work oriented. It was very hard for him to stay home and not have a job. Who was going to feed him?

He has contemplated going back to get a high school diploma. But that was about two or three years ago, before I decided to come to college. I suspect that he has decided now that he is not going to do too much right now. He doesn't feel that it stands in his way in terms of the kinds of jobs that he can do. For manual jobs you don't need a high school diploma, so that's not his problem at all. You see, right now he doesn't even have a job. He was getting trained and he finished the training and got his certificate, but he hasn't gotten a job. That's been for almost a year now. He hopes that something is going to open up in the longshoring. He has a friend who is a longshoreman, and he keeps promising him that he is going to get him a job there. Then there's the other possibility of the unemployment people getting him a job.

I don't think he's considered public service work at all. In 1968 my sister-in-law had started to work in the anti-poverty program. She said that there was an opening for a community worker if I would be willing to come. She said that I was good, aggressive, easy to talk to, easy to get along with, and that I should apply for that job. I knew what community work was because she had already been working there for seven or eight months. It was fascinating going to all these conferences and meeting all these commissioners and dealing with a city government. So I applied and the man who interviewed me was a priest whom I still know. He has been very kind and supportive.

He didn't know many Puerto Ricans before he worked in community work. He's Irish. He had been there like for three years when I came, and he had learned how to speak Spanish quite well. Now he speaks it better than I do. He was very positive in relation to Puerto Ricans and how he dealt with them. Initially we sometimes had some clashes because we're both aggressive. He was chairman of the board of directors of the anti-poverty program in that area. He interviewed me for the job and approved my application. Then I began to work as a community worker. It was just thrilling to me. I did all kinds of things that I had never done before. I would come in around

9:30. I would make sure that my time sheet was signed, and I would get an assignment sheet. Usually there were clients who had already participated in the program. The program was very active; it had a lot of resources. I would deal with those clients who had come in for help on welfare problems, education or whatever. On a normal day I had usually five or six clients. I had to go visit them and do a follow-up on something that had already taken place, or I would go to do out-reach. I knocked on doors in buildings to find out if people had any problems. I learned how to deal with the Welfare Department, and I learned how to deal with the Social Security Administration.

I would see conditions in the apartment, the furniture, how people were dressed, things that were inadequate. I would compile all this information and any complaints that the family had. I would suggest to the mother that we could try going down to the Welfare Department, making an appointment to see the caseworker or investigator, that I would be willing to go with them if they didn't know how to speak English, that I would present whatever complaints and whatever suggestions they had to their caseworker.

My task was to demand more services from the caseworker who was supposed to provide them. So I would go pick up the client at their house. I was given carfare at the agency, and sometimes I was given carfare for the client, if they couldn't afford to pay for their own, and we would go up to the Welfare Department. We would solicit the social worker, and I would go with the client and tell the social worker exactly what the client needed.

Most of the clients were Puerto Rican. In the area where I was working we had some black and some poor whites, frequently young people with large families. The caseworkers were mostly white, usually women. However, there were some men and they were of the hippie type. They tended to be very liberal. In some instances we didn't have any problem with the caseworkers. They would respond immediately to what we were saying, and they would recognize the community agency as an authority and things got done, and the people would be happy.

But when we started to get into the school system, that caused a lot of problems. That was because we were challenging professional authority. I'd go to the school with the parents and we would be prepared. We would either get a lawyer from the Civil Liberties Union, or we would bring the pamphlet with us that described the student's rights. There was one that was published by the Board of Education and we would use that sometimes. We would go in and demand explanations for suspensions or discharges. Some students were sent to psychiatrists or to psychologists, and we wanted to know why. These were mostly disciplinary issues and academic issues as well. We didn't stop just at the disciplinary issues, because there was a lot of academic reshuffling of students that was just arbitrary. The parents usually had no knowledge of what was going on, especially at the high school level.

One case, for instance, that I worked on was at the high school I had gone to. They had opened up an annex in a condemned elementary school. They repainted it, put in new windows, and that was that. And they just dumped all the 10th graders and some of the 11th graders into the condemned building. The place was literally falling apart, and there was an accident in the school where one kid was hit by a piece of ceiling and knocked out cold.

We went to see the principal because we wanted to make sure that the principal, along with whatever other officials he would get in touch with on the Board of Education, would come up with a plan for construction of a new building. But we also insisted that the building be put into reasonable shape for the students. Finally, the principal became irritated because the students decided that they were going to strike. And of course we, as a community agency providing a resource to the community, let them come in and make posters and organize and make phone calls and do whatever they had to do. The school officials called Senator Javits, they called Senator Buckley, they called everybody. And as a matter of fact, people came down to investigate our agency because they alleged that we were using public funds to attack another public institution. That was our job, to make sure that the rest of the public institutions were doing what they were supposed to do. We got attacked and finally I was banned from the school.

Then I became secretary-bookkeeper of the program. I was 19 or 20 years old and that's a lot of responsibility to have at that age, but I was fascinated and did it with no problem. At times there were obstacles in terms of what you could do. You couldn't get involved in political activity if you were working for the agency, but that's where I got my education in politics. I know pretty much the whole city structure. That's also where I really became oriented toward college and toward acquiring intellectual skills. I knew that I had the vocal skills.

This was my real growing up, a sensing of myself in relation to my family and my neighborhood, and my community and everything else. It was a sort of applied political science and sociology. I had learned bookkeeping from the secretary that was there before. She taught me how to do it, and I've been doing it ever since. You handle the thousands of dollars that are given to the agency. You disburse the money, you keep ledgers and journals, and you do monthly financial reports. You make sure that the money is in to make a payroll. I was doing all of that.

Most college students have no idea about things like that, but I was doing all that. There were all sorts of federal guidelines. I would have to make a written report that would be included with the directors' report. But then when I became director I would have to make the directors' report. I would hire and fire staff, and everything. I thought I was queen of the world.

The city, the Human Resources Administration, the local community administration, the community development agency, the Comptroller's Office, they all checked up on our report. We were responsible to all these other agencies. In anything as big as this, regardless of what it is, there will always be cases where things go wrong, but I wasn't worried at all because I knew what I was doing, and I had no interest in stealing money because the salary that I was making was fantastic. I was one of the lowest-paid directors in the whole poverty area, but I was getting $8,500 a year. Everybody else was getting $15,000 and $16,000 for doing the same job that I was doing. But at the same time I thought I was making a pretty good income. I was only twenty years old and I did not have a high school diploma.

That was in 1969-1970. The work was thrilling. It was during that time that I got the piece of paper in the mail offering this program at Pace College for the GED. I went to classes for 13 weeks, took the test for the GED and that was it. So I did in 13 weeks what would have taken me four years in school.

Sometimes I wonder if it pays to go to school. I wonder if it pays in terms of time, in terms of the other skills that you get. Getting the diploma this way was not the equivalent of actually going to school. I missed reading all kinds of Greek literature. I missed making book reports, I missed all the skills that you learn, the oral reports, and things like that. In the agency I had to write reports, and I had to give oral reports to the board meeting, but it wasn't the same. I had no sense of literary skills. In that sense I felt deficient when I came to college. I really felt deprived.

When I went to college, the first book I had to read was *Crime and Punishment*. And that is full of all kinds of complicated material. It would have been a hard thing to handle for me except that I had a friend who could help. He constantly asked me questions. If I didn't phrase it right, he would ask me again. It was an intense six months where I had to learn everything that I had missed in four years. If it hadn't been for the friend, it would have been hard. Although it was so difficult and I had to apply myself in such a strenuous fashion, I got an A in that course. It made all the difference in the world.

At this time an incident occurred which influenced me very much. It made clear to me what I wanted to do and why I should go to school. A housing project was being built in an urban renewal area where the former tenants of the area were supposed to get first priority to return to live in the apartments if they qualified under all the regulations of the housing authority. The housing authority had decided that a certain number of apartments in the building were to be reserved exclusively for the Jewish population. They were going to install Sabbath elevators in these buildings. The buildings were just beautiful and the construction was absolutely magnificent. While I was director at the agency we found out that people who had lived on the site were being called to the office. They were being asked to bring a certain amount of dollars in a money order for their apartments; then they would be turned away. The managers that were doing the renting would tell them that they had no more apartments.

We couldn't understand why. So we went in and stayed in the office and watched what they were doing. We saw that all the Jewish people were getting apartments, and the Puerto Ricans and the blacks weren't getting any. So I went and got this older woman who is committed to working for people who are poor. She said, "Let's go and get a lawyer." We had free legal services in the city, and these people would qualify because they were poor. We gathered all kinds of information. What we couldn't get from the tenants themselves we got from the offices, because we finally decided to occupy these offices and stop the renting until some kind of court decisions was begun.

This got in the newspapers, it got into everything. And we even got on Channel 13. They did a whole program on this. What finally happened was that we were able to get all the documentation we needed to start a lawsuit. We got a lawyer, a very good one, and we started a lawsuit. We won twice. We got our preliminary injunction, we got some judgment. The Jewish community then entered into the lawsuit as interveners and they appealed the court decision that was handed down between the plaintiffs, the tenants that were discriminated against and the housing authority.

What finally happened was that we had to sit down and work out a compromise, because otherwise we would have continued the battle in court for another two years. I think the compromise was a fairly good one, and I think that it set a precedent in that community for further compromises on different issues, for instance on the whole issue of appointing a Puerto Rican superintendent in School District One. In the case of the housing issue, seven of us were members of a joint planning council of which I was chairman—we were the ones that mediated with the rabbis. It was with rabbis because there were no gentiles on their side. We got the priest that I mentioned before to sit with us also and give us his good wisdom in this mediation. And we got the good services of the Institute for Mediation and Conflict Resolution. It was something that could have blossomed into a whole working relationship.

When I finally decided to go to college it did not seem to be a big decision. It seemed to follow from everything else. I knew the financial thing would be a big hurdle, but I said, "It'll be worth it for me to go to school and lose whatever I'll be losing in terms of money, rather than to continue in this kind of job which is really dead-end." Although I had gotten my school diploma, I knew that I wouldn't be able to go into an institutionalized social agency to do those kinds of things that I thought had to be done, just because I didn't have a BA.

I was thinking about security for myself, about a job where I wouldn't have to be worried about being fired or where the funds were going to run out or that kind of thing. In any activity that I did in the area of community action, the local community corporation or HRA or the federal government could say, "You're violating X,Y,Z guidelines," and I would be out of a job. You have to be free to express yourself, to say the kinds of things that you have to say, to fight the housing authority and city hall and everybody else. You have to be able to fight without the fear of losing your job.

I really wasn't afraid of losing my job in the anti-poverty program. I was prepared to resign the minute that they challenged something that I had done. But I didn't want to jeopardize the jobs of the other people. Since I was director, they would hold me responsible for the activities of the whole agency. That troubled me and I didn't know exactly what to do. Finally, I decided that this was not where I wanted to go.

A friend of mine got me to work in a political campaign for a woman who was running for State Assembly in our area. So I came in contact with people with whom I had never associated while I was doing community work. These were people from another side of our neighborhood who were mostly white. They demanded a kind of performance from the Puerto Ricans that I was willing to comply with when it came to organizing and getting people to vote. We had been doing that in the poverty program, but it wasn't with a specific goal in mind. We had had voter registration drives, but they had the broader goal of making sure that the federal government was going to undertake programs.

And I saw this long-range aim up there in the sky. The State Assembly seemed a lot closer. We could point to that as a specific goal for which we should go out and vote. I learned a great deal in that campaign. I did a lot of public speaking and I got people together at meetings. And I learned a lot about political tactics. This was a group of white radicals, but I felt myself militant rather than radical. There is a difference. To some degree, some of the people involved in the campaign were looking to use the Puerto Ricans, and there was a lot of bickering among them. They couldn't get together on who was going to control the Puerto Ricans.

When I started college it was going to lead to a BA, and from there I would go on to law school. And from there I wasn't quite as sure about where it was going to lead, but I thought I would probably go into free legal services and possibly into some kind of political organization. I just can't wait to go to law school, but I get chills down my spine every time I think of taking the LSAT, and I have had very little advice about how to get into law school. I graduate from college in the fall, and I want to go to law school the following year. That's a long time to think in the future. It means that I won't get through till 1980 if everything goes right.

And I started this all when I was 22 at the end of 1972. I have had this dream for eight years. I don't know of any programs that are going to help me get through law school. I have a certain expectation from friends of mine that are knowledgeable and that I admire very much. They wouldn't cheat me of the opportunity to do certain things if they had the resources in their hands. I don't mean the resources in terms of money, but in terms of contacts and people. So when I get my BA degree, I think I will get into law school, but that's another question. I'll worry about that when I come to it. I know that a few years ago the Ford Foundation said they were going to have a big program to increase the number of minorities in professional and graduate schools. I know that those programs exist, but I don't know the specific details of them.

I want to go to a really top-flight law school. If I went to schools like Columbia and Harvard, I know I'd be competing with some very able people. And I know they've had the advantage of really first-rate schools from the time they were little. I am concerned not about my capacity to understand, but rather about my capacity to demonstrate that in examinations. But I wouldn't say that it discourages me in any way. To the contrary, it's a challenge.

I have been thinking of going into criminal law, but I'm now thinking more about going into civil law if I get my law degree. I think I could have more effect on things through civil law. It would perhaps open up a political career. That's in the back of my mind. It would be a ladder toward some other thing, but I'm not sure what. If I do go into politics, my whole expectation is not to run on the basis that I'm Puerto Rican, but on the basis of what services I could provide. Puerto Ricans need spokesmen and spokeswomen, but I'm not sure that they need them in New York City.

The whole question of going back to Puerto Rico is very much in the mind of every Puerto Rican in the city. I'm not a native of Puerto Rico so I don't know what the life-style is. I have to see what happens within the next ten years and then make a decision of whether I'm going to go to Puerto Rico. One of the things that would make me decide to go to Puerto Rico is if I don't see that Puerto Ricans in the city make any kind of progress in terms of their economic, political, and social standing. I am looking not for equal opportunity but equal outcomes. Equal outcome would mean that the percentage of young Puerto Ricans going to college would be the same as for the other groups, that kind of equal outcome. I'm talking about the basic institutions of society—education, youth employment, what kinds of outcomes are going to result out of the opportunity that is offered to these people within the next ten years. That's what I'm going to be looking at, because I think that's what is going to determine my decision. If there's some progress, I will stay and work to make sure the progress continues.

I'm not saying that young Puerto Ricans have to become executives or the typical corporation man. If the idea of a nine-to-five job, where you have to dress up all the time, where you have to be formal, is contrary to their idea of self, then they should feel free to reject that career. Some people maintain that the best possibilities are in large corporations or in the professions, but that's not what I'm concerned with. I am concerned with equal outcome. If my son decides that he wants to go to George Washington High School to learn how to repair TVs instead of becoming a doctor, I want him to have as much opportunity to do that as anybody else, and I want there to be a market out there waiting for him so that he can do whatever he has learned in high school. That's what I'm talking about. I do not have a preconceived notion of where people should go. I think people should be able to make up their own minds. There's potential in everybody. If they want to be bums, well, fine.

This is my primary concern. It will determine whether or not America is a place where I feel that I belong. I have noticed that a number of people have a sense of "we" and "they". And when I ask "Who do you mean by 'they'?," sometimes they say the establishment, or white America. I too have that sense of the "we" and the "they", but I think I can delineate exactly who the "they" and the "we" are. The "they" are usually those people who succumb to the bureaucratic structure, procedure, mentality. Those are the "they"—where there is a traditional point of view and it is maintained and there is no room for other views. They could be anybody—black, white, green, purple, Puerto Rican—anybody. If that mentality is the rule of the day, those are the "theys". And the "wes" are the other people who have no power to buck the "theys," but constantly try amongst themselves to do whatever they can for each other and buck that system from underneath. My answer is very different from many of my friends. To many of them, "they" are simply white Americans, the "we" are all the rest. I account for the difference in our views partly because of character.

At this point I have to talk about the Puerto Ricans, because I do know something about my own culture. Part of the problem has been that many Puerto Ricans have always identified themselves with whoever has been ruling them. Spain was the mother country and some people had a ritualistic feeling about Spain. Anything that Spain did was right. Other Puerto Ricans would question this, but they would have to go along with it anyway because they had no power. In spite of that long experience of loyalty to Spain and to Spanish culture, we Puerto Ricans finally developed a culture of our own. We stem out of the Spanish culture, we stem out of the Indian culture, and the black culture. It's a very cohesive feeling.

The same thing happened when the Americans first came into Puerto Rico. I think that accounts for the fact that some Puerto Ricans are on the side of "they." I may be wrong, but I feel that for some reason a lot of Puerto Rican people are in this position. For instance, my mother will never question authority. And that attitude stems from things that went on in Puerto Rico even before the Americans came. There was *La Ley, La Autoridad,* the law and the authority. You keep quiet and you bow your head down and you don't say anything. You don't talk back. Many older people have that attitude. If you take a look at Puerto Ricans when they first come into the school system here, that's exactly how they behave. They will not answer a teacher back, they will not challenge the teacher. I can understand that because this is the way I was reared. But then again I learned something different from the American culture. This was to challenge and to talk back and to look people straight in the eye when you had something to say.

I had no choice but to learn this. I know both sides of the coin and I can deal with my people. I can talk with my people, I feel comfortable being Puerto Rican. Again I feel comfortable being Puerto Rican and speaking in English to anybody else, challenging anybody else and dealing in this system which is totally different and separate from what I learned at home.

Of course there are some characteristics about an immigrant group that the members want to preserve because they feel comfortable. In that sense the Puerto Rican culture is valuable to members of the Puerto Rican community in New York, just as other cultures are. All the other cultures are valuable. And whatever is valuable I would like to know about and have a feeling for. A lot of my peers are ethnocentric. They are not open to other cultures. It's what some people call a ghetto mentality, living all amongst yourselves. "You made us live in a ghetto and we're going to live in our ghettos and to hell with you."

Maybe this is something that young Puerto Rican men feel more strongly than young women. In some parts of New York Puerto Ricans feel comfortable, but there are other parts that are almost like enemy territories. Boys come to feel this sometimes when they are quite young. Maybe they are taught by their peers. But I didn't have that experience at all. I didn't have that feeling of not belonging in certain parts of the city. I could go just about any place and feel comfortable. And any chance I had to go to a museum, I went. I like the city and go where I want.

Of course you are never safe from hearing nasty remarks directed at Puerto Ricans or blacks, in the bus, in a taxicab, on the streets. I've experienced things like that, but it doesn't bother me. I take it for granted that it exists, and that it could happen just about any place, even in my neighborhood.

For instance, I had this experience at a Board of Estimate hearing when the question of the Forest Hills projects was being debated. I decided that I wanted to go down to the hearing. I was with another woman, Mrs. D., she's Puerto Rican but she's very light skinned, light hair, light eyes. She doesn't look Puerto Rican. They made room for her but when they saw me they wouldn't make room for me to sit down. A woman who was in charge of the seating arrangements said, "What are you doing here?" I said, "What do you mean, what am I doing here?" She says, "You should be home taking care of your children. You have no business being here." What kind of a remark is that to make! She was distinguishing between me and the person I'd come with. We're both Puerto Rican, but I guess the other person didn't look Puerto Rican. It was as simple as that. And I happened to be wearing an Afro, so that might have turned her on.

Puerto Ricans get caught up in this American definition of color which is so different from the definition given in Puerto Rico. It's not a concern to me in my personal life, not in relation to my husband or anybody else. You see, my husband is very light. My husband can go just about any place and say that he is a white American and they'll believe him. He speaks Spanish very poorly, but his English and his diction are not bad at all. He was born in Puerto Rico but came here when he was very young. If it weren't for his minimal education, he could change his name and no one would ever know. He won't talk about the blacks. He's a racist in the sense that he doesn't like people of color. I don't know why he married me. He can't stand the idea that I wear an Afro.

For instance, this morning we were coming to school and there was a big traffic jam on 2nd Avenue. There was a black traffic person directing the traffic. But just because there was a traffic jam, he said, "It had to be a black guy." I said, "What kind of crap is that to say? It could have been a white guy. I mean what difference does it make? The street is messed up. What's he supposed to do, fix the street so the cars can go by?" That kind of thing happens constantly between us. I constantly have to be saying that it's not fair for people to say that because I'm black or somebody else is black, we're stupid, or we're this, or we're that, or that you're better than anybody else. But what I say has no effect on him whatsoever, other than to get him angry. I tell him all kinds of things which challenge his attitude. But I have to do it. I can't let him go around doing that, especially while *I'm there.*

If anybody asks me my nationality I say Puerto Rican. I have no reason to say it otherwise, and I don't feel I should say it otherwise. It used to be the census taker would ask you, "Are you black or white?" There was no other category. A lot of Puerto Ricans don't like to be defined as black. But then again, for purposes of getting grants and monies, they can't be defined as white either. We should be defined as Puerto Ricans or coffee-colored or something like that. The truth is that the Puerto Rican population comes in all shades, colors, sizes. What difference does it make whether you are black, white, green, yellow? Of course, even within the Puerto Rican community it sometimes does make a difference. For instance, within a family the darkest child may have a rougher time than the others, but that isn't true in our family.

My emerging sense of career is not an absolutely clear-cut thing, but there are some specific influences aside from my own personality which account for this emerging sense of career, my willingness to put a lot of time in education. The kinds of things I see happening between groups of people have helped me decide what I want to do. It is the question of getting people together and getting them to unite on something. Some of my friends say that it must be discouraging to have to deal with so much conflict and antagonism, but it's not discouraging at all. It's frustrating because you can't get people to see the issues right away. We can't get them to understand the purpose behind what we are saying or what we are trying to accomplish in any given situation. But then again, you know, I am gaining confidence and feel that I can continue because certain things do make sense to me, no matter how much people refuse to understand and close themselves off. Eventually there will come a time when they will have no choice but to begin to understand.

I think you can do something for people by being a voice for a more decent community and society. If I had to clean their bathroom, I would do it. It doesn't make any difference to me. Whatever it is that I can do, even if it would be a great assault upon the way people now live and behave to each other, I would do it.

My religious experiences were haphazard. Some of the experiences that I had in the Catholic Church were often very traumatic. But others were completely the opposite. I have been literally hit by a priest and shaken by a nun teacher when I was a kid. And I was always being threatened with all kinds of things if I didn't follow certain rules and regulations.

I think that religion did offer some discipline in terms of my behavior and in terms of my character. If it weren't for my going to church and knowing certain rituals of the Catholic Church that require discipline, I probably wouldn't be where I am. So I have to take that into consideration and refocus my thoughts. I think that I will probably have to inculcate some religious beliefs in my kids.

Rosa Morales

I like working with kids but I like the business side of work also. There are two different things, but I don't have enough time to do both of them, so I do the one for a while and then I try the other one for a while. I work as a legal stenographer, and I do that well. It was exciting at first. I worked two years for a lawyer, until finally it become a routine and then it was boring. Being a secretary is nice, but if you're going to do that steadily, it becomes just a regular routine, once you know how to do it. While you're learning it's all right, but once you know it, there's nothing to it.

Working with children is different. It's a different experience with every child and especially with those in special education. You feel you can help the children more than in the public school system, where there are so many rules and regulations and everything is so laid out for you that you can't do things the way you want. There are so many restrictions on the teachers and the classrooms are so large that it's futile to attempt to do anything with kids. If you find that there's a slow child in the class, you know there's not much you can do for them.

I would rather not find myself in a position like that, because it's frustrating. For example, I worked as a tutor for a while and I had one bright child and I had one very slow child, but I was forced to divide the time equally between the two of them. I feel I would have preferred to work with the slow child. The other child was more capable of being tutored in a group, whereas this child needed individual attention. So I figured I could do better with special education where I could work in a private institution, or in the public school system where they have set up a nice system. Of course I don't want to have to contend with a couple of bad kids, bullshitting and hassling and stuff like that. I think I know how to get to a child. I keep trying different ways to get to a child, and I think I'm capable of doing it.

My parents wanted me to become a teacher. That's what they wanted because that's more or less what I wanted to do. Now that I've shifted, they're waiting to see what I intend to do. You really don't know unless you try. It would be better if you get a chance to work within a classroom, even if you're just an observer, before you go on and specialize, because you may find that it's not really for you. A lot of people prepare themselves for one thing and then find, once they get into it, it isn't for them.

I still have doubts about teaching. I'm not sure how I'm going to react to it, how it is going to affect me. Am I going to take it too seriously? Will I do the job to my own satisfaction? Will I be allowed to do it the way I want to do it as long as it's in a professional manner? But, then again, different schools have different ideas of what is acceptable. They may say, "No, not here. Try somewhere else where they're more liberal." Because of the job market it's hard to tell what's going on where. The opportunities for particular jobs rise and fall, depending on how many people decide to specialize at one time. No one can really say for sure, because in the time that you're going to college and you're finishing up in your senior year and you find out if you're in graduate school, already you may find out that the demand in that area is down and you're going to find yourself without a job. So then what can you do? Especially after specialization, what can you do?

That's why I'm afraid to specialize. I'd rather have something else to fall back on. Right now I'm going to take the psychology and go on for special education, but I'm not sure. For a time I got so frustrated here at college that I was going to just forget about this place and go work over at the law firm because the pay is good. But then I said to myself, "No, it falls too much into a pattern and I like things to be different. And I wouldn't want to be locked in by a job like that."

The frustration at the college was basically because of their lack of counseling facilities. Any time I wanted to know something or I needed someone to talk to, no one was available. I often felt, "I *think* I want to do this, but I'm not sure." I'm not asking for someone to make the decision for me, but I want someone who can tell from what I relate to them more or less where my interests lie, and where my strengths are. There's no one here that you can turn to for anything. It's just a matter of coming here, going to class, and leaving after class. They give you an advisor for your major, but he doesn't really care.

I had one and he just said, "You're taking the courses? Yeah, you're taking the courses. All right, I advised you." Then I would say to him, "I want to sit down and talk to you to see what I can do as a history major. I finished the major in history, I finished a major in social science, now I want psychology. That should show you I'm *not* sure what I want to do." So I can say I've accomplished a lot. I've gotten as much as I can out of here. But I still don't think it's been a satisfying experience. No one has any time for you. There should be people you can turn to, qualified, experienced people who you can talk to. When you go and say, "Well, I'd like to know about this," you should feel that they know about it and can refer you to someone. Instead they say, "Listen, I don't know. And you know you'll just have to check it out in this book or that book or go here or go to that agency." And you want the school to function as a placement agency for you, and they're not doing that.

The counseling problem isn't limited to this college. It's in all the schools. But I'm not familiar with many other schools because I've kept a very tight working and school schedule, and I don't visit any of the colleges. From what I've seen and heard, though, I would say it's more or less the same thing. They don't have the information, not even basic information. There should be a place where you could walk into a room and there would be shelves and shelves of books on opportunities and people qualified to talk to you.

They have conferences once every year, you know, for jobs, but that isn't enough. I've been to one and everybody was so formal. It's hard to approach someone you don't know and try to establish contact. Before you can tell them that you'd like to do this, you want to ask them, "Do you think I could do it?" And it has to be somebody who knows you. It has to be someone you see on a weekly basis, at least once a week, whom you see for half an hour or so. And that's real counseling. They see you all the time and they know all about you, what you are doing this week, what your problems are, so you can go in and say, "Well, I don't feel like doing this paper," and they can say, "Well, why—doesn't it interest you? Why don't you take another subject? Is it the teacher? Or is it some personal problem?" So you can say, "I'm not sure about my major," and they say, "Why don't you take a course in this area so this way you get an overview of the other areas of the school?" But that's not offered here, so you're left to decide for yourself.

My husband has a positive attitude toward my career, my intention to go to graduate school. He's the one who's been pushing me. I've known him for five years. But I didn't get much assistance at home. There are four of us, and all of us are in college at the same time. But my parents couldn't really tell us what we wanted to know because they don't know. My father didn't complete high school and neither did my mother. It's not that they're ignorant, but they're not on the same educational level as we are, and they don't know what problems we face. My sister is a pre-med student, so how could she give me advice? We don't relate to the same thing. My other sister's in the same state of mind as I am. She's not sure what she wants, so I couldn't get any help from her either.

But my husband suggested to me that maybe I should try to become a teacher. He said, "You work well with kids. You want to teach but you don't want to work in the public school system, so why don't you try working as a special teacher working with handicapped children? At least you would get more out of it because when you do something for them, you can see it even if it is the slightest little thing, as much as you put in. The little bit of improvement that they make gives you some measure of satisfaction."

You can see that my husband doesn't conflict with my plans. He's got his own goals. He wants to become an electrical engineer. So it's really a matter of our understanding each other's needs. He understands that I have to study, and he has to study. There are certain things that I have to do and that he has to do. We would like to complete this first step. We would like to get a career first and be working, and then we're going to have a family. In the meantime we better just help each other.

A lot of girls who got married expected to leave school. They think that a wife doesn't have to be worried about getting a job because she's supposed to rely on her husband. My husband asked me if I would prefer to be at home. I said to him, "I would prefer not to be at home." And he said, "All right. I'm not going to make you stay at home." We both want to go very far. And that's really what it comes down to. He is always checking to see what I'm doing at school. Am I still going to go to graduate school? Have I just got a book on graduate schools? He has just as much enthusiasm as I do about it. And that helps.

Right now I would say it has been an advantage and a disadvantage that I am Puerto Rican. Unless you're an extremely bright person and receive a scholarship, you couldn't go to college if you can't pay all the tuition yourself. In those terms, yes, being Puerto Rican has helped. For instance, the government has given so many different opportunities for minorities, and that has opened the way for us.

And yet because our culture is different from a typical white-class student, our needs are different. And though they may supply the opportunity and the money and maybe a job, there are still real problems. Because you have that piece of paper to wave in someone's face, it doesn't mean that they really meet your personal needs, and they don't understand your conflicts. Even though you're getting the education, you don't feel safe and you doubt. For instance, I always wonder, "Will I or won't I get a good job just because of coming out of here? Does it mean anything?" There's always this matter of competition. And if you think about it too much it's enough to make you say to yourself, "Forget it. I don't think I stand a chance. The odds are against me."

But I would still say that, for a career in teaching, being a member of a minority group is an advantage now because they are hiring minority teachers. This is in all fields. It's because the minority students are going to relate more to the teacher. They have a similar background, and if the teacher can say "I know," it is a great advantage. You can sense what a child's going through if you've gone through it yourself. If a teacher comes from a suburb, she doesn't understand what the child is going through if the parents are fighting or if it's a broken home. What type of attention does he need and what type of pushing does he need? They wouldn't understand this, and in that sense it's an advantage for us because we would be better able to understand the child.

So though I worry about it, I would say that the odds are in my favor if they base job opportunities on that and not so much on who you are. It's not who you know but what you know. No only your education but your own life experiences have a lot to do with it. Too many of these people in the middle class live in their own little world. Everything else is not a part of them, and they don't even try to understand it. Many of my teachers were like that.

I would say this about my teachers from grade school through college: you can't approach them because you know they don't understand you; you feel embarrassed to discuss some things with them. And it goes all through life like that. I think that the problem lies more with the teachers than with us. It is not that we don't fit into their models but that they fail to understand our needs. I don't think we should be forced to become complete Americans. I'm totally against that, and I take a negative approach to some Puerto Ricans who try to be typically American.

Who are they trying to fool? They're not fooling the Americans and they're not fooling me and they're really only fooling themselves. The time will come when, if you put that in proper perspective, someone will give them the grand shock and tell them, "Well, you know, you're not really one of us." And they tried so hard. So I don't try to do it. I may dress the same way as Americans and I speak the language when I am with them, I behave in a manner acceptable to them, yet there are certain things that I do that they don't do. My personal life is different and that's what counts. At work and at school you conform and you follow a pattern instead of trying to be yourself, because you don't want to feel like people are staring at you because you are acting different. Perhaps you feel it's all right for you to speak in Spanish in front of other people. You say to yourself, "That's my language." But there are situations where you have to remember that you can't do things like that, and that's not always easy.

Whatever I do at home is my business. It's a different thing altogether. I enjoy it when other people want to know about our culture. I like to discuss the simplest little things, like cooking. It always fascinates Americans to see we cook differently from them and I think our food tastes way better than theirs because it has more flavor to it. And I found quite a few people who are delighted with our music, and they just love to go to the island itself. But they always go to San Juan, and they always feel that's all there is for them to see. They don't really see the people. San Juan is very American.

When they ask me where I come from, I don't say San Juan, I say some place they never heard of. I came from a small town. I get very angry when I find people who deny where they came from because it's an out-of-the-way place, and it's not that well developed, and the people who live there are poor and ignorant. But I grew out of a place like that; and I'm willing to tell people that my grandparents lived like this and they don't have a beautiful house, but still they have a house. And my grandfather still works his farm the same way his father worked it. A lot of Americans say that the people who come here from Puerto Rico are hicks. But to Americans they're hicks because they don't act the same way as Americans do. When Americans go to Puerto Rico, the Puerto Ricans can spot them out of a crowd because they're different. And over there the Americans are the hicks.

The American culture is so diverse. There are so many different people and different ways of behaving. I think you can learn more from other cultures, but that doesn't mean you have to do what everyone else says. It's a matter of conforming as much as you think is necessary, without feeling, "Oh, I'm doing something that I really don't want to do." It's a matter of setting priorities. My husband is Puerto Rican and I wouldn't marry a non-Puerto Rican man. I guess I'm a little prejudiced.

It is true that you can learn a lot from a person from a different culture. If you loved that person, there are so many different things you can do together that the difference in nationality doesn't bother you. I think marriage isn't that great a problem. I think the real problem is with the children. It can create problems for the child. He doesn't know who he is. Let's say she is very Puerto Rican and he's very white but still and all they manage to live together and they're happy. Then they have a child, and the child can't decide which one to be and it creates problems for him; he asks himself which class or which people he should be with. Should he hang around with Puerto Ricans or should he hang around with whites?

There are many problems involved and society still hasn't accepted it, which makes it even harder on the child. And that makes it hard on the couple. When you're an adult it's easier for you to stay away from people who don't accept you and find surroundings that are more congenial to you. It is not easy for a child. He's going to be trapped. I think eventually society will accept this kind of marriage. Some people have been raised and conditioned in such a way that they only think in a prescribed way. For example, marry this one and I'll marry that one and we'll stay just this way and we'll stay within our class. They'll say, "Remember they're below us." For those people the only thing is moving up, that and money. They find themselves so motivated towards money because money means moving up on the ladder. But then they have no real personality of their own. I think they are like machines.

Some people want cars and status. They think all the time about status symbols. People who waste their time like that really don't have anything to them. The only thing they talk about is, "Oh, I have this, I have that and I went to here and I've been to Europe," and it seems so senseless. They don't really look and see what *they've* done. I think it's better to concentrate on what you can do for other people than go around acquiring things for yourself. You can't take it with you.

The American way is materialistic, and Americans do not behave naturally. They run around like machines. They have me running around like a machine and I resent it. I find myself in a crowded subway hassling in school and hassling in a job and living so crowded together that I just can't stand it at times. Sometimes I feel I have no privacy. It's hard to get away from all this, especially when you find yourself trapped in it and you can't get on a plane and leave it at all. If you could take what you have, it would be fine. For example, I have a nice job. I wish I could find a job like that some place else, or finish my school somewhere else, or make more or less the same friends, but in a nicer atmosphere. New York City is an absolute wreck. We all know it is. I love it but it's not a great place to live. It is so impersonal, and no one cares for anyone else.

I would prefer to live on the island and I intend to go back. We both intend to. What we're going to do is just work here long enough and then go over there. I think I could do more than I could do here. The island itself needs people like us who are trained in specific occupations to help it develop on its own. They're all so dependent on the United States.

My husband and I, we're for independence. We don't feel that we should knock off the Americans and all of a sudden not appreciate what they have done for us, because they've done a lot for us. Still, I think they should give us a little freedom. They wanted the same thing for themselves, and how can they not understand us wanting more or less the same thing? How can they force us to do things their way? We're so dependent on them that, if a crisis hits here, we feel it more over there. I resent that. Why shouldn't we be able to function independently and develop our own government and economy and everything else? We have people capable of doing it.

I don't think that speaking Spanish interferes with your ability to be versed in English. My Spanish isn't all that good. But I should study my Spanish and forget about the English. I think I know it so well that I wouldn't forget it anyway. But I think that it's an advantage to know more than one language. And for what I want to do I need Spanish. If I want to work with bilingual children I'm going to need it. I don't think they should try to eliminate our language.

People should learn more than one language. Just in the area of literature there is so much that you can read in different languages and profit from. When something is translated, a lot of people say it loses its meaning, and it does. That's because it was written in that language, and the person who wrote it had a certain feeling for the language, and the person who is translating it does not feel the same way. He puts it in his own terms and he has his own biases. There are so many things you can't translate that you sometimes ask, "Why try to?" As a means of communication, you need to translate, but aside from that I think we should learn other people's language and literature and culture.

I have occasionally encountered discrimination. I have a couple of teachers this year that are prejudiced about blacks and Puerto Ricans. I was told that one of these teachers was prejudiced about Puerto Ricans, but I got along very well with her. I just put it out of my mind because I don't believe in walking into a classroom with a negative attitude about a teacher, because then you may feel the teacher's against you anyway so why bother? I like to establish certain relationships with a teacher. I don't like to remain anonymous sitting in the back. I like to sit in the front and express myself. I am very seldom critical because I am leery about teachers. I may feel I have enough confidence to talk to a teacher, but you don't know how a teacher is going to react once you criticize them. You know, criticism may change the whole relationship you have with them.

I don't want to pass a judgment on everyone, you know. The majority of my experiences with people have been favorable. Of course there's always one person who gives you a bad experience. But that doesn't mean you should pass judgment on everyone. My parents never taught us to be prejudiced towards anyone. They never said, "I don't want you hanging around with blacks, and you can't trust whites," or things like that. They had their share of bad experiences too, but if my father was laid off from a job, he didn't say it was because the person who kept his job was white and he was Puerto Rican, you know, or if a promotion was given to someone else, he didn't come home and say, "Well, they gave it to him because he was white and I was Puerto Rican."

My parents felt it was up to you as an individual, and if you were qualified, you were qualified. It was a matter of just having confidence in people and hoping that they would judge you the same way you judge them. I know a lot of people who want to be a teacher's pet or want to be the favorite of the boss. I figure if I do my job and the boss knows it, I'll get what I want and I'll get what I deserve. When the time comes to ask for something, then I'm right and he'll have to take it into consideration. So I don't think the world should be divided between white, black and Puerto Rican.

I would like to know as much about different people as possible. That broadens my scope, and then I could pick the good things from each group, certain things from different cultures. For instance, take something from the white culture. I've taken working. I have to work. I have to get ahead, you know, and this is why I'm here. And from my culture I've taken emotions. And I sympathize with the black culture. And though sometimes I feel the blacks go about getting things in the wrong way, they're ahead of the Puerto Ricans in getting things.

I think they're motivated and that they are more able to voice their opinions. They aren't as scared as the Puerto Ricans are to face the opposition, regardless of riots and stuff like that. They feel enough about a matter to go through with it. I think that's what the Puerto Rican is lacking. I think that's why we haven't been able to get our independence. If everyone was motivated enough or felt strongly enough or wasn't *scared* , they could get it through. There are so many different ways of achieving things in spite of obstacles. I'm sure that, just as there is the way the

Americans manipulate the Puerto Ricans, there is a way we can manipulate them. There has to be some way. That's why I'd like to go live in Puerto Rico for a while and experience it.

A lot of people say that at the University of Puerto Rico there's a great deal of tension. They are very watchful for signs of militance and at the first signs of militance they arrest people. I'd like to be there to experience it. When people talk about Puerto Rican independence I don't feel it because I don't know exactly what's going on. I've never taken a course yet which shows you the impact of the American occupation, the political, economic and cultural impact. I haven't been to Puerto Rico since I was seven years old, so you can imagine how interested I am in knowing what's going on over there. Just going over there could change my whole outlook on life here.

Puerto Ricans are somewhat afraid to face the opposition because it's a matter of power and they're not sure that they can win. Americans hold the reins to practically everything, not only in Puerto Rico, but in quite a few other countries also. As I said before, Puerto Ricans are manipulated. They have to be careful because there are people in America who want to cut off everything. In that case, you know, Puerto Rico would be in a lot of trouble, and that's a reality they have to face. The process is very slow but I still think it can be done. I'm not sure how because I don't know the possibilities and potentials. I don't know whether getting actively involved in politics would work to our advantage. I have my own biases about it. That's the problem with politicians, they're all bought.

Most politicians seem to start with the intention of helping people. There are some, of course, who are going just for the money, the job, and prestige. But there are some who go into politics really wanting to help. But you become part of a political machine, and you manipulate people, if you are part of a political machine, whether you like it or not. You do as you're told because they're the ones who put you in the position. You may get the Puerto Rican vote or you may not.

It has a lot to do with what the political machine wants. They run the press and they work together, and they could turn so many things against a Puerto Rican candidate that not even the Puerto Ricans will vote for him. All they have to do is say, "Well, he's against this and I'll give you that, and I'll extend welfare and he intends to cut welfare." He even may have a good reason-because he wants to put things in order and help people on welfare to become productive members of society. But so many people would be scared to take that chance because that's a threat to the only source of income they have. And he's trying to push the welfare department to do something to make them productive members of society. That's a radical move. I'm in favor of it. But there's not enough support for it. There's not enough political clout in the Puerto Rican community for them to be able to attain any of their goals.

The media—television, the press—they aren't really against us. I think they tend to forget us, which is even worse. You know they concentrate on blacks. And though there are studies done on Puerto Ricans, not much is done specifically for us because people really don't understand us. They don't care to understand us because we're all here to function with the society and that means to function economically, you know. So many people work and work and work but they never become an integral part of society. They just go to work and they come home and that's it. They never assimilate into the American culture, the American culture doesn't even recognize them, except for their being part of the labor force.

It is rather frustrating for the blacks and the Puerto Ricans. We've both been here for quite a while, right, and you find that white immigrants from Paris, immigrants coming from European countries, particularly from countries in the Communist block, whatever their reasons for immigrating may be, are quickly assimilated and progress. They're starting off like everyone else does, like the Irish, or like the English started off, but they're moving up much quicker than we are. You find more of them in higher paying jobs than we have, and we have been here longer. So you ask, "What's the sense of doing all this when you know someone else is going to come along and get the dollar you feel you deserve?"

Discrimination will work against us if we use it as an excuse for not trying. But when you see other minorities, even the Orientals, moving up much quicker than we are, I don't think it's fair. These groups are all moving up quicker because they are more easily assimilated into the American culture, and this is because they are white. Their values are more or less the same, and they're willing to accept American culture and the demands which American society puts on them.

We Puerto Ricans are not so easily assimilated. We'd like America to accept some of our culture, to preserve the subcultures, instead of repressing them. There's an American culture but there are subcultures. Ideally then, we should conform enough for our own betterment without losing our culture. That's the most that we could do. We can't force our culture on America. And we can't live entirely in the American culture. We do have a subculture but we can't survive like that. We have to function within the society and that means adopting American culture as far as necessary. Sometimes it's selfish, but I don't think we should have to constantly give in to them.

We have a lot of South Americans and other Caribbean people here. Perhaps it is easier for them. I don't know too much about the Cubans, but I hear they are doing rather well. I think they are willing to assimilate a little bit more than the Puerto Ricans, but the experiences in Cuba are different from the experiences that Puerto Ricans bring out from Puerto Rico. Cubans are willing to forget their way of life and adopt the American way because of that. It may be a case of their not having much choice.

I think this is true for all groups. And once you start assimilating too much you go white, white! I don't know about the South Americans that much. I think some of them are here to get an education and go back because their countries are so underdeveloped. And I don't blame them for doing that. You know the opportunities are here, and they should be allowed to use them and let them go back to develop their countries. I don't think the United States should worry about their being a threat to the United States. I've come across a lot of immigrants from South and Central America, and they work and work and their main objective is to bring the rest of their family over here. They have no plans of going back. I think they and the Cubans are more or less in the same predicament. They want to stay here.

A lot of Puerto Ricans do not want to stay here. They would like to go back. It depends on your own experiences and has a lot to do with how you feel without having someone to tell you. Personally I would rather be over there. I'm going to take what I can get here and go over there and use it. It may be a dirty trick, but if it's here for the taking, it's here for the taking.

Whatever Puerto Ricans want to stay here should be allowed to. But they should be more unified here than they are, and that's why they're not doing as well. Puerto Ricans have been here quite a while, and they're not doing as well as they should. A lot of them still don't speak English. A lot of them aren't working. They're scared to join together, and they're afraid of people who come to them and say, "Well, you ought to get together. We can all get what we want if we join and become one." A lot of people are scared of that because that to them is being rebellious. A lot of older Puerto Ricans won't be involved in something like that. Speaking to a lot of them about the independence of Puerto Rico is like speaking to a blank wall. Some people think that independence is basically an ideal of the younger people, but it isn't. We've had a lot of people who have stood for independence for the longest time, but you also find a lot of people who don't want to be involved, and that's the problem.

I do notice a difference in the rate of assimilation and the rate of adaptability to the so-called American way of life between Puerto Rican women and Puerto Rican men. I think the women have done it more easily than the men. I think I've adapted a little bit more easily than my husband has. He refuses to adapt. He's not exactly fascinated with white America anyway, so he doesn't want to conform to their way of doing things. I feel I function a little bit more easily than he does in American society. That means I don't let it interfere with what I want to do. It's just a fact of life that you've got to do such and such to get such and such. And if you build up a wall saying, "No, I'm not going to do this!," then you're not going to get what you want.

The fact that a number of Puerto Rican women adapt faster than the men creates a certain amount of friction. Your husband might tell you that you're liberated, but as soon as a Puerto Rican woman wants to go out-of-doors, that's not part of the tradition. It creates problems and friction. The woman is supposed to be home, taking care of the kids. If the woman wants to work, to develop her own potential, it can create a lot of problems. And sometimes she has to sacrifice her own desires at home because of that.

The fact that we women adapt faster means that there's less stress in some parts of life for us, but we feel the stress when we attach ourself to a male, when we are trying to relate ourselves to a male. You find yourself playing roles. You play one role as a Puerto Rican wife or just a female, and then another role when you're dealing within a group of Puerto Ricans. When you're dealing with people outside of that you have to adopt a different role. And you have to remember to switch roles so there won't be any conflict. Like a lot of times you may feel this and that way about something. You may say to yourself, "Oh, well, I'd like to go to the opera or I'd like to go skiing," but you know this is out of place. So you can't always express yourself the way you want to, and you may never get around to doing things like that because your partner may not have an interest like that. In fact, he may have it, but you don't mention it because you are uncertain what the consequences might be if you say it.

I can't say that Puerto Rican men are usually consistently Puerto Rican throughout. A lot of them adapt rather easily, but we all play roles. We have one personality in school, another personality at home, and a different personality where we're working. It all depends who you're with. If you're with the people you work with or with your friends or family, it's all different. People say that you should be the same way all the time, but you can't. You may want to be, but you feel the pressure and you can't always be yourself. So to relieve the pressure, you do what the work requires and what reduces the stress of whatever role you have to adopt.

I went out with a guy for a while, and he thought that I was liberated. I was totally for Women's Lib because I felt this, and this I wanted to do for myself. I said I want to develop myself and have some satisfaction out of life for myself. It may seem selfish but then again it's not. If I pair myself with someone, unless we stand for the same things, we cannot function together, we can't be happy together. So that ended that. You know, people have different ways of thinking. And I wasn't about to subject myself to his. I wouldn't have been happy. Sooner or later I would have exploded.

There are quite a lot of Puerto Ricans on welfare, but that's because so many people have trouble getting a job or earning enough to live on. There are a lot of good jobs and some Puerto Ricans have good jobs, but the rest of them are left out because they don't qualify for the highly skilled jobs. I think a lot of the training programs have done quite well. I think their objectives were good. They *mean* well, but it doesn't always turn out that way. When you put somebody in a training program, their expectation is that you're going to get them a job because they know they may not be able to get it on their own. A training agency should also function as a job agency, as a placement agency, so that the cycle is completed. It should not include only training and preparing people, but also placing them.

A lot of people are on welfare because of lack of skills. People ask, why don't they take training? I don't know. A lot of them, I think, don't want to. I've seen too many who are content not having to work, and living off of welfare, and just reaping benefits from the rest of us. I resent those who do that. I'm not going to work for someone else. Every time there is an increase in taxes, you feel it is because the welfare rolls keep on rising and the government doesn't do anything for those of us who pay the taxes. It may seem unfair to say this, but some of these do ruin neighborhoods because they have no sense of property, so they don't care what they do to an area. Too many times they don't care about their kids either, they're too interested in themselves. And they keep on reproducing children who are the same way, because the kids are going to pick up attitudes from their parents. And they say, "Well, if I can live this way without having to work, why bother going to school? I don't have to go to school if I'm not going to work." So when you see one of these cases where you know the mother could work if she wanted to, you know there is no stable family life and the child isn't going to be interested in going to school. There is no discipline. There is no incentive. The parents aren't aware that you can do this and you can do that. They're really not out to do anything, so how can they impress it on the child to want to do anything? How can they give a child an incentive to go to school? They don't try to see what the child should do.

They have all these agencies like Aspira and Manpower to help Puerto Ricans especially. The Aspira organization is well known but I don't think it does all it should do. It is true that they have gotten a lot of kids into college. They're aware of a lot of opportunities that are primarily for Puerto Ricans, like scholarships and different schools, fellowships and jobs. In that sense I think it is great, but they only function in that capacity. You can't expect Aspira to solve all our problems.

Carmen Hernandez

The first job I can recall was when I was in high school—I must have been about 15, and it was a candy-striper job in a hospital. In those days I remember all the girls wanted to be candy stripers. You work at a hospital. It's volunteer work. You feed patients that are too elderly to feed themselves. Sometimes they teach you how to take a blood pressure, a pulse, and temperatures. It's general work. Usually girls who want to become nurses do it.

I wasn't sure whether I wanted to be a nurse. That's part of the reason why I did it, to see. Maybe I could make up my mind as to what I wanted to do. I really enjoyed it and I worked there for about five months. I don't think I needed working papers because we didn't get paid. Of course it was part-time, only a few hours. And it was nice because it was within walking distance from where I lived and I could work immediately after school and then go home.

A lot of girls were doing this at my school. I remember that for some reason nursing was very popular then. I guess it was because in high school they push the Florence Nightingale image. I worked in the various departments, physical therapy, the maternity ward. The Director of Nursing supervised us. She was the one who decided which department I would work in. Since I was a volunteer I would go wherever they needed me at the moment. They did ask you, "Which do you prefer the most?" and they would try to give it to you.

I had a friend who worked there, and for some strange reason she liked the maternity ward. She liked the idea of new life, and she worked there a lot. One of the nurses I remember the most—she was Greek and she was from Pennsylvania—she was extremely nice. She urged me to become a nurse and talked about it with me.

She enjoyed her work immensely. She was a very nice person. She always had a smile. She loved young people. People tell me I should have been a nurse, but this is related to another work experience which came a few years later. This later job was out of necessity. I was a military wife and had to work. The only job I could find was in a hospital affiliated with the Air Force base. They used to give preference to military wives, simply because they could hire them cheaper. I worked there as a nurse's aide. I was trained on the job. And that definitely encouraged me. I didn't like the work. Maybe it was because I was older. Maybe it was because when I was a candy striper I was protected from seeing certain things.

But when I was a nurse's aide for the first time I was exposed to death. I remember one night when I had to go through an overnight vigil. I had to wait for the person to expire. I saw more death than life. But what I didn't like most of all was the doctors lying to people. One day I was to give a lady a bed bath. The doctor walked in with me and said, "You can come because after I leave I'll give you the report and then you can give her the bed bath." The lady had cancer and he said, "Oh, hello, Mrs. so-and-so. You're looking great. You should be out of here any day now and dancing." And then after he was through examining her he walked out and said to me, "I give her three days." I didn't like that. This is an American thing, the inability to face death. I hated him at the moment because she was staring, she was semi-conscious, but when he said that she was getting much better, a smile came to her face. It was wrong to give her false hope.

After the candy-striper job I took a job for pay. It was at a company that made staples, and the job was putting them in boxes. That was the whole job. They contacted the high school and they said, "We need a number of girls." It was across the street from the high school, and I was one of the ones that raised her hand for the job. I did that just for a year because it was just an assignment. I don't remember how much I was paid at the time. I think $2, which was not bad. It was three hours after school for every day except Friday.

That seemed like a lot of money to me. I remember the first pay check. We went out and started splurging.And I enjoyed it because I was with girls who were my own classmates. Those were the only two jobs I ever had in high school that I can recall.

My mother was working steadily at the time. I used to hate going home after school because my mother used to work, and to me the thought of going home to an empty apartment was hateful. So I used to do anything to not have to go home until she arrived. I didn't resent her working because I knew she had to. She had no choice. She was and still is a seamstress—sewing machine operator. But I do resent the fact that she is so talented and she is so underpaid. She belongs to a union, but she doesn't have any benefits. She misses a day of work, they call her up, they threaten her. If she doesn't attend a meeting, they deduct so much pay.

The boss was always calling her up. I used to tell my mother, "Mom, he calls you because he knows you are good. You think that you need him, but he needs you too." I was very young and I used to tease him and say, "When are you going to give my mother a raise?" I used to go up to the place where she worked. There was a rule that no children were allowed to go up. I told my mother, "Well, that's a rule that you're not going to have to listen to because I can go up there any time, because you don't know when there is an emergency. They don't know why I'm going up there."

The place was the seventeenth floor on 34th Street. Usually my mother made skirts, woolen pleated skirts, but sometimes she made dresses. Everything was mass-produced; they were clothes that were not really high quality. My mother came from a very large family, and her mother was very talented. Her mother used to sew. And all the girls in my mother's family—she came from a family of 13 and seven of them were girls—they all knew how to sew. And they used to experiment with clothes. That's how they developed their talent. They used to design their own clothes, so my mother really could design clothes.

She tried to set up her own business. She had a small place. There were seven sewing machines and she hired women. She did subcontracting work for a larger firm. That was fifteen to twenty years ago. I don't remember the details of what went wrong, but I know it didn't last very long.

I wanted her to do designing on her own, but she is very self-conscious about her limited English. She is a shy woman, a woman of few words. She learned English when she came to the United States. She was in her twenties. But she has a strong accent. Sometimes I tell her, "Okay, Mom, we have got to speak English now. You have to practice." Then she speaks it very well. But when she speaks to someone who is American she gets nervous, the way I do when I'm speaking Spanish with someone.

I think my mother went through the fifth grade in school. And that is also a pity because she is a very intelligent woman. All the children in her family had to leave school. That is such a common story. It had nothing to do with personal ability. People who knew her when she was young say that she was so advanced. She was two levels ahead in mathematics. She could read and write when she was extremely young. She had already started working on the island before she came here. She did sewing work. That's the only thing she has ever done, except that at home she would work part-time making costume jewelry for firms.

She is very creative. I used to help her so she could make more money because it was piece work. From what my mother tells me about my grandparents I think that her parents were protective of their daughters. They wanted them in the house. They used to get them interested in things that would keep them in the house. They were encouraged to paint. They would paint any little thing and the parents would boast and rave. Anything to keep them at home.

My mother taught me a little bit about sewing when I was very young. I remember when I was nine years old I made a skirt. We were very proud of it. But I don't sew. I think my mother would have been upset if I had done the kind of work she does. In her work she has encountered a lot of hardship. And she encouraged us—my sister and myself—to develop our mental rather than our manual abilities. She would say, "You don't know what is going to happen in the future and you should be prepared to deal with any situation."

This is something that is often passed on to children. The less schooling and more hardship that parents went through, the more they are apt to encourage the children to get a good education. It is almost like protecting them from their own experiences. My mother expressed a lot of regret that she never finished school. She has taught herself a great many things, even if she only went to fifth grade. She can do algebra and trigonometry that she taught herself to do. She once thought of going to school in the evening, and she started going part-time in the evening, but because of the pressure of family duties she had to quit.

She always used to say, "Get all your schooling before you get married because your husband might just not want you to afterwards." My mother is a very extraordinary person. She is amazingly talented. Her life seems to me to be one of great hardship and such a waste of her abilities. That's part of the reason why I decided to go to college. The thing that always gets me is that my mother's parents weren't rich, but they were well-to-do. They owned land, they had hired hands, and she has gone from all that to now. She works so hard and she has to live in such an inadequate apartment. It shows how much can be lost in a generation.

What has happened to mother seems in part to be related to fundamental characteristics of Puerto Rican society, the moral code, the extremely submissive role of women, the man as authoritarian, unquestioned decision maker. A lot of it was inevitable. It is true that once-prosperous farms were collapsing all over Puerto Rico. But there was also the fact that the values that her parents instilled in her are values which I would never instill in my daughters. They emphasized submissiveness, quietness. These are pretty much in her to this day—you know, speak when spoken to.

Now I don't believe in that. I feel that if you have the the ability, you should do what you wish. I don't think most people care that much about you. I think it is each man for himself. And my mother is too kind. It is interesting that she did not try to instill these values that she received from her parents in me. Quite the opposite. She used to teach me not to trust people and keep an open eye, be firm. She knows the way she is. Not too long ago we had to attend a dinner and she was very upset about it—"Oh, what will I say? What will I do?" And I said, "Well, you say whatever is on your mind. And if they don't like it, that's their problem."

She's had to go through a great cultural shift—from a productive, stable farm existence to urban life. She is kind of heroic. I imagine that it is not easy to raise three children alone in a country where you have to learn the language and cope with all the things that she was faced with, all the problems of urban life.

My mother had very ambiguous attitudes. She wanted me to be half American and half Puerto Rican. She took the best from both cultures and that is what she wanted me to do. From the Puerto Rican side she wanted me to be a mother when I did get married. That's a very Latin value. In America this business of mothers working has been going on for a while. Nobody thinks anything of it. But as prevalent as it is now in New York City, it is frowned upon by Puerto Ricans in Puerto Rico. She felt when you have children you should not have to work, and you should stay home.

From the American side, she wanted me to be independent, not to have to rely on a man, to know that the decisions weren't his wholly, that it was a meeting of two minds. And there were a lot of cultural things. For example, she wanted me to like Spanish music, and not American music. Ideally, it would be nice if you could fuse two cultures—a little from one culture and a little from another—and integrate them in a unifying way. But it doesn't work that way. I have problems even now because of it.

As a matter of fact, most of the Puerto Ricans that I meet say that I'm not very Puerto Rican, and they're offended by it. I don't like Latin music. I don't know how to dance to Latin music. I never developed a taste for it. My ways are considered American by Puerto Rican young people I meet. On the other hand, when I encounter American people, they do not treat me as an American. I'm Puerto Rican. My surname is Puerto Rican and that's what they look at. In a sense, neither side allows you to be what you want to be yourself.

I have come across a number of people that have found themselves in that situation. People overlook the fact that taste can also be individual. I don't know why I like some of the things I like. But some of my values, some of my ideas are Puerto Rican, some are American. I guess that is because I am a Puerto Rican living in New York, and my contact has been with both groups.

I have one aunt in Puerto Rico. She has seven daughters, and four of them married men who are not Puerto Rican. Now these girls have never left the island in their lives. Maybe it is possible for a young person living in Puerto Rico to be somewhat freer in terms of the pressures of culture than in New York City. Here in New York City there's the awareness of different cultures, so immediately when your behavior doesn't fit into your culture, people start analyzing your behavior. They ask, "Well, what culture does it fit into?" In Puerto Rico they just shrug it off as an individual thing.

I think my mother would have liked to be able to stay home. She was very protective when we were very little. She expresses displeasure with the fact that work hasn't really paid off, not in any way, not in any form, not financially, not from the point of view of benefits, security or anything. It has just kept her alive, a matter of survival, existence. I don't think my mother ever even considered getting something like Aid for Dependent Children. She has a friend who's on public assistance, and my mother frowns on that because she believes the woman could work if she wanted to.

My mother accepts the stereotype—you know, people on public assistance driving Cadillacs. She says, "So-and-so just married his daughter. They had six limousines at the wedding and do you know that he's on welfare?" And she'll laugh. I think it would be hard for my mother to find any circumstances which would make welfare justifiable. She looks down upon welfare. She just calls it laziness. She has a notion which a lot of people have that a lot of those people on welfare are capable of working.

It's very bad to be lazy, yes. On the other hand, Puerto Ricans in New York are often thought to be lazy. For one thing, when people think of welfare, they think of blacks and Puerto Ricans. And some people think they get away with murder. They tell me about Puerto Ricans being on welfare. And they often say, "How come Puerto Ricans don't go for higher education? Don't they care to better themselves, to make a good life for themselves and their families?" And they say that it all amounts to laziness.

A lot of people I have worked with have these attitudes. I was asked by a southern man, "You're Puerto Rican?" He had thought I was Oriental. I was in the South and people there think that anyone with black hair is Oriental. He was from the backwoods. He asked if I had ever been involved in a felony or a crime. And that's the idea people get about Puerto Ricans in New York. A lot of people have actually said this to me.

My mother didn't consciously transfer to me her ideas about laziness. It was just in the atmosphere. She hasn't even told me, "You must work." It's just her criticism of people who don't.

I have mixed feelings about my high school. Basically they were good years. I enjoyed high school, all the activities, the social part of it. But I went to a high school where all the girls were Irish. It was an all-girl Catholic school. There were so few minorities. And there was favoritism— explicit favoritism on the part of the teachers, yes. The Irish kids could get away with murder. I noticed these things very early and I didn't like it. But it was a good school. And my mother was very proud of the fact that I got in because at the time it was a prestigious school. My mother didn't want me in public school. I wanted to go to that high school too. I wanted the discipline. We felt that the Catholic schools were better than the public schools, and it was a college prep and I wanted to go to college. But the favoritism in the high school—that was one of the things that I recall most vividly. There were also a lot of racial slurs. I can't quote them verbatim, but I recall them. They weren't aimed strictly at Puerto Ricans. I remember a Cuban girl once being a target.

I'm not a trouble maker. I know my faults and I know my good qualities. And I can be very patient and tolerant. But some girls would talk to you and keep their distance. It was expressed by their posture and just their glance. They would look at you as if you're a germ-carrying thing, just that. Prejudice manifests itself in many ways. It is not only verbal abuse. It is often just a glance.

There was only one teacher I liked. She spoke Spanish. She used to seek out Spanish kids. And I thought, "Oh, of course. She speaks Spanish. She wants to practice." At the time it seemed ironic to me that the only one who sought Spanish people was one who spoke Spanish. And every time she spoke to a Spanish person it would be in Spanish.

Now with Father Tom, one of the teachers at the college, his speaking Spanish is sincere. I mean he travels to the island a lot, and he is honest and jokes. He is Irish and he is enough aware of the experience of the Irish to feel very real parallels between them and Puerto Ricans. We have spoken about this, about what they went through. Now it is spics; it used to be micks.

I've found that you can see those parallels, but it doesn't help you when you sit on a bus and somebody makes a vicious remark about Puerto Ricans. I think that when the larger society treats you in a certain way, when you're exposed to prejudice more or less constantly, it's bound to affect your behavior and your image of yourself. You start wondering if it is justified. It fills most people with self-doubt.

For example, take two people—white Anglo-Saxon and a Puerto Rican who have more or less the same intelligence and more or less the same attributes, the same qualities. The society would appreciate the white person more. But, like Avis, that makes some Puerto Ricans try harder. That is what it did to me. I would try harder. I can give you a concrete example. I used to wonder if men were approaching me because of my own qualities or because I'm Puerto Rican and they have these notions about the facility with which they can become intimate with them. And so I would work at being aloof on purpose. I used to say, "Well, if he has to ask a white girl out twice for a date, I'll make him ask me four times."

When you are Puerto Rican you can never get outside of that, really. Your potential is limited because people are responding to you first and foremost as a Puerto Rican. I shouldn't have said that the potential is limited. What I meant is that the potential is there; the opportunities are limited. I think perhaps in the labor force you are most limited. There are certain kinds of jobs where you just don't fit the mold.

I read an article not too long ago that made some flat statements, for example, that Puerto Ricans and blacks were capable and competent in manual skills but not in mental skills. I think that there is a stereotype about us, but I think things are changing. There is a larger enrollment of Puerto Ricans in higher education now. And they are going for jobs as lawyers. Puerto Rican girls are going in for jobs as airline stewardesses. They're not afraid to reveal their sexuality. I think it is changing gradually. The rest of society is too. There is more freedom, more openness.

The problem of being stereotyped is more serious for a Puerto Rican woman. To me it sounds trivial and ridiculous to hear about the problem of emotionality, but people have stereotyped Puerto Ricans as being high-strung, as unable to deal with pressure, as apt to crack under pressure, unable to deal with serious decisions. I've had people comment on my calmness during situations in which they expected me to cry or scream or faint. And I'd say, "Why? Why should I?" And they'd reply something about my being Latin, or Puerto Rican.

There are some other things that interfere with our being accepted for what we are. For example, if I wanted to be a lawyer, there might be some barriers to my becoming a successful, influential lawyer. Besides the general difficulties that people face, I think most of my clients would be Puerto Rican. I think people get threatened when they see a Puerto Rican who has backbone, who can stand on his or her own two feet. I think that Puerto Ricans have been exploited so much. It has happened to me.

All that I'm saying is based on my own experience and on what my friends tell me. I look much younger than I am. People think that I'm a teenager. But when I start speaking, it is not a teenager's mind that is speaking. I don't know whether it is that I appear mild and I appear as if I'll break at the seams, but I notice that with employers the minute I say, "Okay, Mr. so-and-so, I would like to see you now," and I state in no uncertain terms what I want and I want to know their answer, they become shocked. I don't know if it's because I look so mild, or because I am Puerto Rican and it is not expected.

Part of my high school life was a good experience and part of it was a bad experience. I liked the social life, and it was a good academic program. In your senior year you had your choice of college. I was encouraged to go to college. Even then I knew I was going to go to college, but I decided I would work a year and then go to college. I wanted to work hard for a year, have maybe one full-time job and one part-time job, because I wanted to save money, to help myself through college. I didn't want my mother to have to put out the money. My mother would have wanted to pay for my education because she wanted me to go, very much so. I got a job right after I graduated from high school. I worked as a dental assistant. It was in a Medicaid office. About 99 percent of the patients were Puerto Rican. And that's why I was hired—because I spoke Spanish. I had no experience to speak of. I was trained on the job in dental assisting. I handled the tools, and prepared chemicals and things.

I liked the work but I didn't like my boss. Dentists are hard to work for. They are nervous and demanding. I liked the coworkers—the other girls. But I didn't like the man in charge. He was domineering. If he called you, you had to be there before he called you the second time. And I walk slowly on purpose. But I will say that he was a very good dentist.

All the dentists were Jewish, with the exception of one dentist who was from Peru and another dentist who was Chinese. The dental assistants were all Puerto Rican, all of them. The patients were primarily Puerto Rican. The dentists used to make a fortune. One day two of us sat down to figure out how much one of the doctors made, and we arrived at some atrocious sum. We decided that maybe we should ask for pay raises. We spoke with the other girls and said, "Hey, we're being exploited." And we all went into his office. This is one of the things that I resented. He tried to appease us with a smile, and he flattered us. One of us told him, "Doctor, we're not here for compliments." She was very outspoken. I loved her for it. But we didn't get our pay raises. Eventually he fired me, because if I didn't like something I wouldn't put up with it. But I was young and I thought that jobs were a dime a dozen in those days. This was only one job, and I figured if I found this one so fast, I could find another one just as quick.

In this first job I started out at $95, which wasn't too bad for 1968. I could have become a dental assistant, but I didn't like it and I would never have thought of it as a career. When you're a dental assistant, you're in too close contact with dentists. You're there with him for eight hours. You're handing him tools and preparing solutions for him and taking X-rays. It's okay, perhaps, if you have temperaments that do not clash. But again, I used to hear racial remarks.

There was one dentist who expressed these attitudes about the patients, mostly to us dental assistants. The dentists used to overcharge the patients. They would lie. "Well, that work cannot be done because there isn't a root there." But I would go to another dentist, and not tell him what was going on. I'd just ask, "Is this a root?" And he'd say, "Sure it is. Don't you know?" Meanwhile the other dentist was saying to the patient that he didn't have a root so that they would have to do a different kind of job, which cost three times as much money.

After a while I got so discouraged that I would tell the patients in Spanish that it was a lie. I would tell them that they could do as they wish, but that I could not just sit back and see somebody's money taken like that. And this dentist, he knew what I was saying. He could understand Spanish. And I didn't know this until one day he called me aside and he told me, "I would appreciate it if you left the dentistry to me." And I said, "And also the stealing to you, right, doctor?" So he fired me.

After that, I got married to someone in the military and we went to Georgia first. That is where I got a job as a nurse's aide in the hospital. Then we went up to Alaska. I had a nice job there, but the people weren't nice. When I got married, I thought I was going to be able to go to college. I thought the army made provisions for wives to go. My husband approved of that before we were married. But in Georgia we were in a very small town, and there was no college there. I would have had to go to the next town, Macon, which is a dangerous town. Since we knew we were going to Alaska, I thought I would go to Alaska University or Fairbanks University. But when I could finally go to college, my husband decided he didn't want me to go, because he wanted me to be dependent on him. I went to a business college in Alaska instead. That he approved of because that would make me a secretary. I didn't want to become a secretary, but it was another skill. I figured I might as well do the most I could do for the moment. I knew I was eventually going to go to college, because I really wanted to go. I didn't have a career choice in mind. I didn't want to be a scientist or anything like that, I just wanted to go to college.

When I went to the business college in Alaska, I was just going to have one more skill that would add to that college degree when I did get it, and to the fact that I spoke Spanish. I took speedwriting because secretaries can make pretty handsome salaries if their speedwriting skills are very polished. And I became very good at it, which made me angry because I didn't want to be good at it. I didn't want to be tagged as a secretary. This may sound unfeminine, but I wanted a job that was not strictly female.

When I started getting out into the world and I saw the business world and people, I noticed that everyone would respond to me as a woman first and foremost, which is nice. A lot of girls envy that and would like to be in that position, but I wanted people to respond to me as a person too. I think that if you're in a job which is primarily a woman's job, you are more likely to be exploited. I think that if you're holding an administrative position or a managerial position, there is less probability of being exploited. I also think that there are more chances for promotion in that type of a job. I know that administrative jobs or managerial positions would generally be in a large firm, because only large firms have such jobs.

I know that many young Puerto Rican men don't want to work for a large firm. They hate the idea of large corporations and bureaucracies. But the situation is different for Puerto Rican young women. Maybe because they are women they like the glamor of a large firm, the idea of being surrounded by so many people, or perhaps it's because young Puerto Rican men facing a large corporation have a sense that they're never going to go up in those ranks. And so they just keep away from something where they feel that they would fail.

I don't know whether I could really succeed within a corporation, but this doesn't disturb me. I spoke recently with the college placement officer because this is the month when the large firms contact him and they request students. I wanted to be hired in an assistant manager position and I didn't qualify. But I'm not frightened by it. I think Puerto Rican men are more frightened than the women. They feel that they can never get to the top, not necessarily the top, but towards the top. I think women feel, "Well, what difference does it make? I'm only going to be doing it for five years and then I'm gonna get married." A lot of the girls I have spoken with don't have really big career aspirations.

I would like to do some sort of managerial job, because I like decisionmaking. I don't like sitting down and typing all day or a job where at the end of the day you have not used your mind at all. My friends don't think like this. There is a lot of business that I don't like. But, given the choice of a secretarial position or a managerial one, I'd prefer the managerial.

It's like being an assistant buyer in a store. There's more to it than meets the eye, much more. You have to be avant-garde. You have to know what's going to come into vogue. You have to keep abreast. You have to be susceptible to cues. A motion picture can determine the latest fashion, and that's complicated. You have to be well rounded, well read.

When I left Alaska I came to New York. I needed to get work immediately. I got a job with a Spanish television channel. I was hired because I spoke Spanish. After awhile that deflates your ego, much as I enjoy the language. But there are plenty of Spanish-speaking people around. I don't like the possibility that the only reason I got the job is because I speak Spanish. I was a receptionist. I had a lot of odd jobs— typing up show schedules, some translating. It really is a good television channel.

But then the idea hit me that if I apply for work at a university I get tuition remission. I can work and attend college too. So I applied at N.Y.U. and got a job there—also because of my Spanish. That really does irritate you after awhile, because the first job when I graduated high school was the same thing—the dental assistant job. But anyway I took the N.Y.U. job. I wanted to go to college but I never got to attend. I started when the semester was already in session. The work was very pleasant. It was translating at the dental college. It was more or less like the first job I ever had except no dental assisting—just translating.

It was a very unusual job. I enjoyed it because again I wasn't told what to do. I had to use my own discretion, and if anything went wrong I was held responsible for it. I liked the challenge, the risk involved. I was allocating work to the students. For example, I would tell a student, "You take care of so and so because you have done too much periodontal and now you have to do some surgery." I even made sure that they had the proper academic credit. I enjoyed the work but it was on 25th Street, from nine to five, and then I had to go to N.Y.U., all the way down to Washington Square, so that I really could not get there until six o'clock.

Since I was usually moving around all day, at the end of the day I was exhausted. I wasn't standing up on one spot or sitting down in one spot. I was walking all day throughout the whole college. By this time I had money saved. I used to save every penny. I was living with my mother and saving for education. I would give her money weekly, but for one year I don't think I made one purchase, one dress or anything. Not to spend money for a whole year is a pretty hard thing for a young person. There are so many temptations. You turn on the television and there are all these advertisements. My entertainment was all free—you know, city events and things like that. I wanted an urban college. I didn't want to be around the sons and daughters of doctors and lawyers exclusively. I didn't want to be surrounded by children who are 18 years and have been spoonfed all their lives and don't know anything about hardship. And I figured that, in an urban college, I would be with both groups, those who have been through the mill and the ones that were born with a silver spoon. I like the college very much because there are diverse groups here, people of all ages, everything from 18 years old to "College at 60." I think that there's a lot to be gained from being exposed to different people.

So I've completed two years of college now. I didn't go to the evening school because I had money saved up and I was trying to accelerate. I thought I would do three years of college in two years. And in my final year I planned to go in the evening and work. And I knew about life-experience credit which I am eligible for. I hope to get 12 credits. I would get it for Spanish and some of the other things I have done. Even theatre and dance departments give them to you if you've taken dancing lessons. While I have been going to college I worked at the university in the work-study programs. So I've had to dip into my savings, but I thought it would pay off cause once I got the bachelor's degree I could work full-time. I had it figured out pretty neatly.

I got a National Defense student loan. But I don't want to accumulate loans because it is only postponing payment. I also thought of joining the Peace Corps. If you're a volunteer they incur part of the expenses, if you work with mentally retarded children.

I have to take it one step at a time. I can stand back and think, "Now let me see what I'll do next." Right now I'm on leave of absence for one semester. I'm looking for a full-time job. Then I would go part time in the evening. It is disconcerting to have to postpone getting my degree.

After the work at the college, during the summer the first job I had was at a perfume company. I was a girl Friday. At first it looked very promising and I was very happy about it. I thought this was it. I didn't think it would be a career, but I thought I would stay for a while and I could attend college. It was conveniently located for going to college in the evening. It was really a nice job. It had a certain amount of glamor. But then I lost the job. It was a typical story of a boss trying to take advantage of a girl, not a rare occurrence in New York. I only had the job about three weeks.

So then I had to look for another job. I got this first job through an advertisement in *The New York Times*. I wish I hadn't. After that I got another job with a chiropractor as his receptionist. But I'm really tired of being a receptionist. Once you get into a certain kind of job, it's like a circle. Now I've been applying for jobs, and employers have stated that I have a lot of receptionist experience and they want to offer me that kind of job. They're categorizing me. I try to explain to them that I'm willing to learn, that I'm a self-starter, and all these things, but it doesn't seem to matter. They still think of me as a receptionist.

It's difficult to argue when employers say to you that most of your jobs have been temporary. They sort of expect you not to stay with them. They'll say that I don't have too much work experience. And I made the mistake of putting on my resume that I worked at the university and at the college. So they think that I'm very much into academia. One lady who interviewed me stated that. She said that most of the places where I've worked have been educational institutions and "You know, honey, the business world is quite different" as if she were talking to a 13-year-old girl.

Recently I had a curious and disturbing experience. I called up in answer to an advertisement for a receptionist job. This kind of work is mostly what I've done, dealing with people, answering the phones. I do type more than is required for a receptionist. And that's all the qualifications that were needed for this job, good typing, able to handle the phone, and greet the public. The advertisement didn't say what kind of company it was. When I called up the company I told them I was calling in reference to the ad. The man who took my call asked me to tell him a little bit about myself. So I told him about my work experience and he was very pleased. When you apply for this kind of job you have to name everything you can do—even filing. Strange as it may seem there are people who cannot file.

So I stated all of these things, and he was pleased. So he decided to set up an interview. He asked me my name and I told him my name. When he heard the last name he asked me my nationality. I answered Puerto Rican. And he said, "Oh, I forgot to mention. An engineering background is required." And I said to him, "Is this a requirement solely for Puerto Ricans?" He got angry. He said, "As I said, I simply forgot to mention it. An engineering background is required." I don't see how that can be a requirement for a position as a receptionist. So I told him that.

I see all these things and I feel so helpless because there's nothing I can do. There is nothing really constructive that one individual can do about this kind of treatment. I saw an ad in the newspaper several days ago. They needed a girl. All it said was that she must be able to speak Spanish to Puerto Ricans—as if Puerto Ricans speak a brand of Spanish that is unique. I was offended by that. On the telephone the man was blunt about it.

Usually it is done more indirectly. Sometimes people who interview you don't make eye contact. Of course some people are just the type that are not as visual. They don't gesture with their hands, they are very bland in appearance, in manners. But sometimes I get the feeling that they're not making eye contact on purpose, as if they're working at it, telling you indirectly that you aren't going to be considered for the job. They're just going through the motions. This is something which can really be on your mind—that maybe this interview is going to suddenly turn into a fiasco.

But when I go for an interview I don't act like that. I act as if I anticipate the person's behavior towards me to be the way it would be towards anyone. I think that if you anticipate discriminatory treatment you can actually bring it on without being aware of it. I walk in with a cheerful attitude and ask questions, and answer all their questions.

I went to one employment agency. The lady who interviewed me was nice. It was an agency specializing in office jobs. But again something happened that made me angry. I called up the day before I went to make an appointment so they would know I was coming. And I asked them if it was worth my while to go down there, if they had positions available. And the lady said to me, "Oh yes, all types." She told me to come down first thing in the morning. So the first thing in the morning I got dressed in my business attire. That is, a conservative dress. I don't wear slacks, and I stay away from black stockings. And I went down there first thing in the morning, and the lady had me fill out an application. After she reviewed it she said to me, "Well, we don't have anything at the moment."

I said, "Well, since yesterday all those positions have been filled." And she said, "Well, you must've been misinformed." She said *she* didn't say it, and I told her, "Well, someone in this office told me to rush on down 'cause you had ample positions of all types." I told her, "I called here yesterday at four o'clock and there were plenty of positions. And now, at nine in the morning, they're all filled!" She laughed but in a nice manner, as if to recognize the error. Maybe they were just trying to get me down there, but I was so angry about it.

I don't know exactly what it is. It could have been that they do like to have you on file—for statistics reasons even. They have to have so many names and things. I don't think it was because I was Puerto Rican, but it is always a possibility, you never know. That's unpleasant—not knowing.

Things like this occur in the employment situation, but where I encounter this the most is sitting on the bus, minding my own business, going home, or walking down the street. But perhaps the situation is getting better. I think people either get tired or they adjust. I mean when a new people come to a land—for example, the Puerto Ricans—they stand out more because they are the new immigrants. Then they begin to fit in gradually. There are other issues besides them. I think the novelty of the new arrivals wears off.

But among Puerto Ricans there isn't solidarity as a group as there is with the Italians. I know there is solidarity there, and the Italians have been able to help each other so much. But then there are these new terms that are used now such as "culturally deprived." That's humiliating. I never felt culturally deprived. I felt culturally enriched, but I think that if you label a people in a certain way, you can actually produce the behavior. Culturally deprived! Deprivation in a culture.

When I went in to elementary school I already had an extensive English vocabulary. I was bilingual before I started school. None of these things have to do with intelligence. My mother saw to it that we learned English before we started school. Some American girl friends of my uncle used to baby-sit for us and they used to speak English. We were allowed to watch television as much as we wanted when we were preschool. My mother felt this would help us to learn English. And we did. We spoke both.

Then when I started school, knowing Spanish used to help me. My English vocabulary was no less than that of anybody else, but I knew words with Latin roots. I remember in the third grade the teacher asked, "Does anybody know what the word masticate means?" And I knew because of the Spanish *masticar,* the same word. The same thing happened when I was taking French. The teacher once said, "What does 'crepuscule' mean?" And I knew *crepusculo* in Spanish. And the teacher would say, "How'd you know that?"

Anyway, I never felt culturally deprived, not even in high school. But I have a nephew who's 11 years old and he knows these expressions—culturally deprived. He asks his mother, "Mom, how come I'm culturally deprived?" My sister sits him down, and there goes the lecture. "You are not culturally deprived and don't you let anybody tell you otherwise."

If someone says you live in a ghetto, it has a negative connotation, and I resent that expression very much. I resent the term, "the language barrier." I think that what they call a language barrier can actually be instrumental in helping you. Children love languages, and they pick them up so fast. I think a bilingual program can be very good. But I think that they're placing too much emphasis on this. I think this whole thing is overblown. I love languages, and I think a child can speak Spanish at home and English at home. I hate expressions such as Hispanic. It's just a term that was invented. It's not an English word. It didn't exist a few years ago. It's not a Spanish word, although it derives from a Spanish word. It is just a catch-all phrase.

Puerto Rico is called the Island of Enchantment. They call it the Pearl of the Caribbean. That means something to the people back home. It also means something to me. But the thing is that I've been raised here, and I'm not sure I can live there. So this sense of being Puerto Rican changes. I guess there are a number of factors. Most Puerto Ricans came from the island seeking economic opportunity. When they don't find it here, there is bitterness. They recall Puerto Rico with its fresh air and greenness. But most of them don't go back. It is difficult to make heads and tails out of all this, to put the pieces together, and come up with concrete answers—to answer questions like "Why?"

It's not that easy to pick up and leave New York City—from a financial point of view or any other. You know, Puerto Ricans are all mixed in together, but there are Nationalists and the other parties. In the American culture—Democratic and Republican—you don't think in those terms, except at election time or something. But the whole philosophy of life in Puerto Rico—not only the potential, but a lot of other things—is very different. The Puerto Ricans who stayed in Puerto Rico are very different even in the way they speak.

There are three major political groups. It's astonishing that the image that many people have of Puerto Ricans is not of Puerto Ricans, but of the Nationalists. The Nationalists want to speak English with an accent even when they don't naturally have an accent. Their purpose, their message is to show the negative effects of Yankee imperialism. They are saying, "We cannot speak Spanish perfectly, but we also cannot speak English because this mish-mash causes confusion." Most of the Puerto Ricans in New York who you hear speaking slang are Nationalists. They seem to be saying, we won't be bought, we won't bargain, we won't become a part of you.

I have noticed people who are brilliant who do not want to sound well versed, who do not want to be articulate. These people form theories about Spanish as spoken by the Puerto Rican. But on the island they don't speak like this. There are qualities that are stressed, like posture. It is emphasized that you must stand straight. But the Puerto Ricans in New York don't want that; they want to sway.

I knew before I enrolled at the college that it had a sizeable amount of Puerto Rican students. This may sound trivial, but it has deep meaning if you take it apart. I thought I would get to speak Spanish with Puerto Rican kids and we would have something in common. But I came here and a few Puerto Rican men asked me out. At the time I was not interested in going out with anybody. But then they found out that I was dating a non-Puerto Rican, and that was it. I'm an outcast in the Puerto Rican community at the college for going out with one person who is not Puerto Rican. This hits the very important question of the relation between young Puerto Rican men and women.

A girl would not get that upset if a Puerto Rican male dated an Irish-American or German or whatever girl. But the men seem to get upset, and they resent it even if they don't say it. In this case they said a lot of things. But anyway, because of that and also because of the fact that I do feel more comfortable speaking English than Spanish, they take it as a personal insult.

This is a very complicated thing. I get sneers from Puerto Rican men because I am slender. The Puerto Rican concept of beauty is not slender—it is plump. And they think I starve myself to death to be slender because I have whitey values so ingrained in me. Now these are things that do not readily meet the public eye. But you know, this preoccupation with plumpness is also typical of a poor society. For example, Puerto Ricans will say, "I saw Margo the other day. She must be doing pretty well for herself. She's fat." If you are fat it is because you eat a lot. And if you can afford to eat a lot it is because you are financially well off.

This is partly a class thing, of the poorer classes. In Puerto Rico in the city it is not like that. That's one of the problems, that people place these constraints on your behavior. Another problem is prejudice and it creates problems. People who are discriminated against start questioning. Then they start seeking, analyzing, and there is no end to it. It's like a circle. Life is simple. It is people that are complicated. Puerto Ricans are in a sad spot because there is discrimination from others and there isn't solidarity. The male-female problem is quite pervasive. They both feel threatened but I think the men feel this more. The older generation wants the younger generation to go to school, become educated and prosper, but not to change—not to renounce old values, not to give up the emphasis on transcendental things. And that is not always possible. You go to school, you are in the hustle and bustle of the business world, and you do change.

I would disagree with those who say there is a profound split between the older and the younger generations of Puerto Ricans in New York City. My own observation would not justify that. I think that, in fact, there is greater unity between younger and older generations among the Puerto Ricans than among the Americans. I think that this concept of a generation gap is primarily an American thing. I notice that in Puerto Rican homes the children leave home at a later age. There are 37-year-old men and girls living with their parents. This is common. In America when you become 18 you go off to college or otherwise leave home. After they are married, Puerto Ricans visit their parents more often. In America it is anything to get away from those "squares."

The Puerto Rican parent gives his child less freedom. If I asked "Why?" I was told by my mother, "Because I say so." That means she was the mother and that was it. It was unquestioned. In American homes, parents run to Dr. Spock. I think there is more communication between Puerto Rican parents and their children. Girls are taught to cook by their mothers. In American society, home economics class in high school does that for you. But perhaps there is not so much between father and son. Puerto Rican women—maybe not the younger group, but the older—tended to be very possessive mothers, and they interfered in the husband's role as father.

COMMENTARY

As with the life histories of the Puerto Rican men, the stories of the three young Puerto Rican women reflect a common experience and reaction as well as individualized responses. All three young women came from families with limited economic means and occupational status and a working mother. Since Carmen mentions neither her father nor any other man during her formative years, since Maria's father is a drunkard whose behavior demoralized the family, and since Rosa offers little information about her male parent beyond the statement that her parents could not help her clarify her career and life goals, we must see their mothers as the dominant influence on their development, at least until they married and the attitudes of their husbands began to play an important role.

The assumption that Puerto Rican men want their wives to stay at home and run their households may be valid in theory, but not in practice. As is so often the case, economic realities have a way of forcing major changes in a culture, even with respect to so central a value as the appropriate role for a married woman.

As we read the life histories of these three young Puerto Rican women, we soon learn that their mothers encouraged them to get an education so that they would have more control over their own lives. The mothers themselves had been trapped by husbands who were unable to support them, and their own inadequate education had limited them to the lowest rung of jobs in the society.

Maria Diaz's story is the most remarkable since she was forced out of school when she became pregnant at fourteen, and only reentered the educational channel many years later, first by completing her high school equivalency program and then by gaining admission to college. Her work there encouraged her to look forward to entering law school and to becoming a qualified professional who could later enter politics in a leadership role. By helping Maria back onto the educational track, her husband, despite his own limited schooling, played a constructive role by encouraging her to realize her more and more ambitious educational goals.

In Rosa's case, she and her husband reached an early understanding to support each other's effort to achieve desired educational and occupational goals. They even decided to postpone having children until they were approaching the realization of their goals.

Only in the case of Carmen do we encounter the remains of the machismo approach. She reports that, under pressure from her husband, she did not enter the university when he was stationed in Alaska but took a course in speed writing to add to her stenographic skills because, as she put it, "He wanted me to be dependent on him."

Developing educational and occupational goals and implementing their plans, with or without the help of their husbands, was only one part of the difficult road that these young women had to travel. The other was keeping in perspective the pulls and counterpulls exerted by Puerto Rico past and future, the attractive and repellent aspects of American culture, and such potent forces as discrimination, cultural diversity, and personal taste. Maria is deeply disturbed by the intensity of her husband's color prejudice. He constantly offers negative comments about "blacks" despite the fact that she is dark skinned and enjoys wearing an Afro hair style. Her fluency in English adds to the equivocation of many non-Puerto Ricans who cannot classify her or react to her as an individual, only as a racial or sex type. Most of these problems are experienced by others with whom she comes into contact who are surprised to find a competent, soft-spoken, but determined young woman who knows what she wants and is fairly experienced in getting her rights and those of her clients. But the fact that most of these contacts respond equivocally to her adds to her difficulties in sorting out the important from the unimportant values.

For Rosa, the uncertainties and tensions seem even more deeply rooted, because her occupational plans are not as firm as those of Maria, who has much more varied experience in and greater exposure to the ways of white America. Rosa complains at length about the inadequate counseling she received in high school and college. She believes that if she had been better advised, it would have been easier to decide among her several alternatives, none of which she felt competent to assess at the time. Attracted to teaching but uncertain about the future demand for teachers, she has recently begun to hedge by selecting psychology as her major with the intent of preparing herself for "special education." But she is worried that if she decides to specialize and guesses wrong, she will be even more restricted than if she had not specialized. People like Rosa are often prone to believe that experts have more skill than in fact they have. The problems which Rosa faced throughout her educational decisionmaking might have been helped through extended discussions with a wise counselor, but it is doubtful that they would have been solved. The risks that upwardly mobile young people face cannot be eliminated; at most they can be reduced and hedged.

Rosa is conscious of many conflicting pressures and roles. First, she shares with some of her peers the fear of being locked into a routine position which will rob her of excitement and the opportunity to make a uniquely personal contribution. Next, she notes that there are challenges that stem from her being a woman in a male-dominated economy. Furthermore, during the work day her responses must be in terms of conventional American attitudes, expectations, and behavior patterns, but since she is married to a Puerto Rican and lives among Puerto Ricans, she must be sensitive to a wholly different set of attitudes after work.

All three of the young women invest considerable emotional and intellectual energy in sorting out their roots in the American and Puerto Rican cultures. Carmen mocks those who call the Puerto Ricans "culturally deprived" by pointing out that a knowledge of two languages, two cultures, two histories, and two environments is surely better than one. She considers it senseless to label as culturally deprived a group with a wider, a broader, and a deeper reach.

As did their male peers, all three young women refer to going "white": the difficulties they face in the aggressive pursuit of some dominant goals of high educational and occupational achievement in their American environment. The pursuit of difficult goals always involves the individual's breaking loose from established ways of life and thought. This breaking loose is often resented by others who are unable or unwilling to make the effort. Carmen believes that able women are more willing to compete for better jobs within a large corporation than are her male associates who, conscious of past discrimination, are too unsure and uncertain of themselves to make the effort.

In the background, the territorial homeland, the gem of the Caribbean, is always the migrant's idealized picture of a wholesome easy-going life. This stands in sharp contrast to the high unemployment and low income that are omnipresent aspects of the current reality. Additional confusion is introduced by the knowledge that Americans have controlled the island and manipulated its people for many years. This fact makes the push for independence attractive, but there is no assurance of solutions to the present and future problems.

AFTERWORD

The 18 life histories of older blacks and younger Puerto Rican workers provide an insight into the preparation for, adjustment to, and withdrawal from work that is rarely encountered in social science literature. Minority workers are seldom the center of attention, and seldom have the opportunity to recount their stories at such length. Moreover, the accounts of the black men and women span a long period, roughly three-quarters of a century, beginning prior to World War I and ending in the post-Vietnam era.

The purpose of this Afterword is to broaden and deepen the insights that can be gained from this rich collection, insights which go beyond the generalizations formulated in the preceding commentaries. There are several ways to proceed. One is to formulate a set of propositions about the lives of the two minority groups. Another, to consider how the materials presented here could illuminate aspects of our national development that previously have been ignored or minimized. A third is to single out a limited number of sociological theories which can be strengthened by using the evidence in these case histories. There is no reason why each of the three approaches cannot be followed.

From the beginning of our country's colonial experience to the present, the white majority has been at odds about how to cope with the black minority in its midst. The dominant view has been that black people are different from white people by reason of color, blood, history, and experience. The Constitution strengthened this viewpoint by stipulating that a slave, for purposes of representation, counted as three-fifths of a man.

The contemporary version of the unresolved conflict takes a more sophisticated form. There are a number of distinguished academicians who emphasize that the assimilation of blacks in the northern cities differs in important ways from the earlier assimilation of Germans, Irishmen, Jews, and Italians. These scholars make a sharp differentiation between the absorption of the earlier white and later black groups. They are also quick to offer explanations for these fundamental differences by emphasizing the weakness of the black family, the lessened capacity of black children to profit from public education, the unwillingness of better-positioned blacks to assist their brothers and sisters, and the preference for immediate consumption and gratification which works against a strategy of saving and planning and a desire for upward mobility. These social critics are in the main line of the American tradition which sees the black person and the black group as inherently different, and flawed to an extent that they are unlikely, in the near and intermediate term, to become fully integrated into the economy and society.

But this doctrine of "inherent inferiority" has never commanded the allegiance of the entire population. In the beginning of our nation's history there was a small minority—and with the passage of time the proportion has become much larger—that believed that the oppressive and handicapping conditions under which blacks lived were more than sufficient to explain the demonstrated differences in performance between the two groups. This growing proportion of the United States population views as a challenge primarily the removal of multiple environmental evils—discrimination, poverty, poor schooling, and powerlessness—which influence the black community. As these barriers are lowered and removed, they believe that the performance level of blacks will no longer be below that of whites.

It may be useful to recall some of the horrendous forces of oppression that dominated the lives of our black population in their formative and adult years, creating a condition of powerlessness that resulted in responses by blacks as varied as murder, draft evasion and permanent relocation. In terms of economic exploitation, blacks suffered from inferior schooling and training that forced them into the most menial types of blue-collar and service jobs; trade union intransigence blocked a black man from membership even in the North; and governmental and employer practices kept ambitious blacks "in their place" by putting major hurdles in their paths as they sought to expand their business or improve their skills.

American society marked the cards to assure that even if blacks won an occasional small pot, it would be impossible for them to walk away with a larger prize. With the whites dealing the cards, there were few slip-ups. Blacks were relegated to the lowest rungs of the ladder in the agricultural South as well as in the industrial North.

Once the evidence of pervasive powerlessness, poverty and prejudice is recalled, there is little need for speculation whether the black person is genetically different from the white. Inferior performance no longer requires explanation. The miracle that defies understanding is the ability of blacks to surmount their oppressive environment and to become self-supporting and self-respecting citizens.

Let us now shift attention from the onerous conditions that long dominated the lives of the black minority to the larger forces that have altered the American economy and society and, in the process, opened new opportunities to minorities.

The first phenomenon is war. World War I, under the slogan of "Make the world safe for democracy," weakened the oppressive segregation that was so firmly ensconced when Woodrow Wilson entered the presidency in 1913. The same war served as prelude to the restrictive 1924 immigration legislation which, by the time of World War II, had created a tight labor market that gave black workers their first real opportunity to move ahead.

World War II and the Korean conflict accelerated the forces operating to reduce racial bias, not only within the military but in all American life. The first large-scale governmental action against racial discrimination in employment dates from President Roosevelt's executive order of 1942. General Ridgeway's action to integrate infantry battalions in Korea reflected both a response to manpower needs and an effort to speed the desegregation goals established by President Truman.

In the aftermath of World War II, the establishment of the United Nations, the creation of a large number of new independent nations in Asia and Africa, and the United States' assumption of the role of the leader of the free world all created a backdrop for democratic reforms on the racial front. But it was incongruous for the United States to press for reforms overseas while tolerating overt discrimination at home.

Wars and their aftermaths, however, were not the only factors concerned. Two other forces must be identified; the ebb and flow of the economy and the vast increase in social welfare programs. Two periods of major economic growth occurred: the expansion of the early 1920s, and the much larger sustained expansion that began in the 1940s and continued for three decades, creating a large number of jobs for minority workers in and outside the South. Although neo-conservatives claim that blacks and Puerto Ricans came to the northern cities because of the ease with which they could get on the relief rolls and the relatively high benefits they would receive, the facts are clearly different. Most immigrants came in search of jobs, and most of them found jobs which enabled them to become self-supporting. The tremendous growth of the welfare rolls dates from the late 1960s, the reasons for which are still only partly understood. (See *Work and Welfare in New York City*, by M. Ostow and A. Dutka, Baltimore: Johns Hopkins Press, 1975.)

The changing American economy, especially the revolutions in the automotive and air transportation industries, played a major role in the large-scale migrations from the South and Puerto Rico to New York and other northern cities. It was much easier for younger and older people to break out of their surroundings to sample new environments without having to make a definite break with their past before they had satisfied themselves that the new was what they wanted.

The expanding economy of the early post-World War II years, however, was not completely favorable to the new minorities who had crowded into the northern cities. Manufacturing plants began to leave the city centers and relocate in the outlying areas, beyond the reach of easy commuting and where housing was not available for low-income persons, particularly blacks and Puerto Ricans.

Another unfavorable event was the continuing rapid growth of white-collar jobs in the cities as the urban service sector continued to expand. Only persons with adequate communication skills were hired for these positions, and many newcomers and their children were unable to meet these requirements. When the economy encountered periods of high unemployment in the 1970s, minority workers became even more vulnerable. They found themselves at the end of the job queue behind the ever larger numbers of educated white women who had entered or reentered the labor market and who were competing successfully for the available openings.

If one were to summarize the consequences of these multiple developments in the employment and income of minority workers, one would have to acknowledge that the 50 percent increase in total jobs between 1950 and 1975 and the more rapid gains in real income enabled many to improve their positions. But the sluggish and inflation-prone economy of the 1970s and the shift of investment from the North to the South have worsened the condition of the vulnerable minority population.

During the past forty years, government, particularly the federal government, has vastly expanded its efforts on behalf of those at the lower end of the income distribution—older persons, the disabled, the unemployed, families with only one parent, and still others bereft of income and in need of special assistance. In the present backlash to the programs of The Great Society, only the expert is aware that President Johnson's promise to eliminate poverty, defined in terms of income, has almost been fulfilled. Restated, this means that when not only the money that the poor receive from the government and the benefits in kind (such as food stamps, Medicare or Medicaid, housing allowances and still other transfers) are taken into account, only a small number of families are below the poverty line. To raise these families, too, above the poverty line would require only an additional $10 billion of transfers to them.

The scale of these transfer payments, a high proportion of which goes to members of minority groups, has helped to moderate some of the worst problems that minorities confront. Few people go hungry; rarely does someone fail to be admitted to a hospital when in need of treatment. But welfare is always a second-best approach to obtaining income and patterning a way of life. The welfare recipient recognizes that he is out of the mainstream and is looked upon as a social aberration. Only the most despondent among the recipients find welfare a satisfactory condition.

American society still expects everyone who is not physically or mentally incapacitated to support himself. The extent to which people are able to meet this expectation depends primarily on their preparation for work, that is, their basic skills, acquired at home, in school and in the community. Many minority group members are poor and therefore are forced to live in deteriorating neighborhoods. Because of poverty and other dysfunctional aspects in their lives, many families are disorganized. Finally, many young people attend schools where their opportunities to learn are, at best, limited. The consequences of these circumstances leave them ill-prepared for work and life, and many fail to perform effectively as adults.

This is only one part of the complex situation. The last quarter-century has seen large societal investments in post-secondary education and training that have vastly expanded the opportunities for young people from low-income families. The financial barrier has been largely removed from their paths. While many are unable to avail themselves of these greater opportunities because they lack the prerequisites for further education and training, many others are surmounting the barriers in their restrictive environments and are able to forge ahead. The pessimists point to the large numbers who remain trapped; the optimists call attention to the considerable numbers who successfully extricate themselves. Each holds part of the truth.

One further area must be explored—how the life histories considered in conjunction with these large societal patterns can help to illuminate the variations in outcome of black and Puerto Rican workers. (Variation among minority group members is a key theme of this book.) Can one pinpoint the critical elements in the lives of these older blacks and younger Puerto Ricans that differentiate the more from the less successful?

What happens to a person, even one handicapped by minority status, depends in considerable measure on his ability and goals. Several of the black men were able to find niches for themselves in small business or management that enabled them to earn a decent livelihood and accumulate some property. In several instances, they acknowledged that their wives, who possessed a flair for money-making and domestic management, were full-fledged partners.

Steady employment, even at a modest wage with pension benefits, provided a secure foundation for several black men and· women. Social Security benefits, in addition to a family's small savings and an occasional bequest from a relative, provided a safety margin for several older blacks who were no longer able to work.

Milton Friedman used to argue and probably still does that the poor are poor because they have too many children. What is conspicuous about the black men and women whose life histories are recorded here is that many were childless and others had only a single child. Two points are worth noting: it is easier to save something, even from a small wage or salary, if a family has no children to support; and it is easier for a woman to work intermittently or regularly if she has no child-raising responsibilities.

There is a third factor operating in the case of the more successful blacks that is easier to identify than analyze. Faced with repeated rebuffs from the white community—from trade union obstruction to the antagonism of a civil servant—some minority group members are better able than others to ignore hostility. They do not permit the adverse environment to get or keep them down. Hence they are able to try and try again to achieve their goals, which for the most part are shaped to the reality of a discriminatory society.

What about the minority members who fail to make a satisfactory life for themselves or who, after having done so, fall into serious difficulties? In the case of some, their health gave way, and reduced their capacity to keep on the path along which they had been moving. One of the risks facing the minority members of the labor force is that the often unfavorable working environments will eventually lead to ill health or disablement.

One final point: many of the blacks were disheartened as they spoke about their later years, not only because of their personal circumstances— inability to continue working or loss of a spouse—but because of the erosion of the neighborhood where they lived and from which they could not escape. People derive much satisfaction in life from interactions with their friends and neighbors. When they are too frightened to go to the store and even feel insecure in their own apartments, they are stripped of the minimum security and freedom that each individual requires. One of the problems faced by minorities in a color-conscious society is that their narrow confinement is compounded by a combination of limited income and housing discrimination.

Is there any way to summarize the variations that have just been reviewed? In this way perhaps: despite the overwhelming and ever-present reality of discrimination and all that it connotes, the majority of black men and women were able to shape lives for themselves that were superior to those of their parents, although inferior to those of white people. If they were able to keep their health, they could cope with the difficulties they encountered in a world that gave them a few breaks.

The easiest and perhaps best way to consider the young Puerto Ricans is to highlight the extent to which their difficulties and opportunities paralleled and differed from those of the older blacks. One must first emphasize that racial discrimination, although it may affect the 10 percent of the Puerto Rican community who are overwhelmingly of Afro-American background, is not the crux of the problem facing Puerto Ricans. The white community may be restive about the "color" of Puerto Ricans, but it does not equate them with black people.

While color is one negative factor with which Puerto Ricans must contend, they also face such additional problems as language, and a heritage with different cultural values—from the established relations between men and women to the importance of the extended family. Above and beyond all these differences, they face in theory and in fact an alternative: they need not remain on the mainland and can locate or relocate in Puerto Rico. Blacks have no comparable alternative.

Especially for persons born and brought up in a nonindustrialized environment, seeking roots in New York is a difficult undertaking. Those in the first generation are likely to obtain the least desirable jobs with the lowest pay and the dimmest prospects of promotion. They lack the political clout to get even a small proportion of the "public" jobs to which they are entitled in terms of their percentage of the voting population. Since housing is generally tight, and housing for low-income families is even tighter, most Puerto Rican families have been crowded into a limited number of barrios in Manhattan, the Bronx, and Brooklyn.

The life histories of these few young Puerto Ricans help to underscore that, even within the first quarter-century following the mass inflow, some of the newcomers have been able to extricate themselves from poverty and place their children in a position from which they can make further advances. If a wife is able to work as well as her husband and the number of her children is not excessive, the combined incomes often enable some families to escape from the barrio to a neighborhood where children have a better opportunity to grow up, protected from the negative influences of slum life.

More remarkable is the fact that certain female-parent-only households with very little income—welfare and marginal earnings—are headed by women so strong that they have been able to stimulate and encourage their daughters to strive for an education which they believe to be the pass to freedom and prosperity. Another ingredient of success is the availability of conventional and unconventional opportunities for several of these young women to obtain a high school diploma, a college degree, and a professional education (i.e. advanced skills and competences).

A careful reading of the life histories of both the young men and women is a reinforcement for the belief that education is an important mechanism for upward mobility for many of the newcomers. These young people like school, enjoy reading and have good relationships with their teachers. They call to mind the idealized picture of the bright Jewish immigrant child of the turn of the century.

There is another respect in which these Puerto Rican stories parallel the experiences of earlier immigrant groups. Here, again, considerable tension exists between the generations as the young people struggle to find their identities in a culture that looks upon them as second-class citizens. If one accepts Thorstein Veblen's view that there are gains—as well as some losses—growing out of such a cultural confrontation, then one finds here a potent force for progress, particularly for the individuals who are capable of achieving a synthesis.

One final point for the white majority. I defy any white reader to conclude his reading of this book without a feeling of shame or anguish that the society for which he shares responsibility has inflicted so much injustice and misery on innocent people. It is true that one may find consolation in the fact that society has at long last acted to remove some of the most oppressive of the rules and regulations that have embittered the lives of so many generations of black people. But consolation is not enough.

A dominant white society that does not want to jeopardize its future has no choice but to act now to remove as quickly as possible the effects of discrimination that have accumulated for generations and centuries. Justice alone can be grounds for action, but in this instance the claims of justice are reinforced by the concern for self-preservation. As the *New York Times* once entitled an article I wrote: "The Negro's Problem is the White's."

ABOUT THE AUTHOR

Dean W. Morse is Senior Research Associate, Conservation of Human Resources, Columbia University. He is the author of *The Peripheral Worker*, and coauthor of *The Labor Market: An Information System*, *Comparative Metropolitan Employment Complexes: New York, Chicago, Los Angeles, Houston and Atlanta*, and *Early Retirement: Boon or Bane?*

3 1542 00053 4143

WITHDRAWN

331.6
P947   811858

331.6
P947   811858

Pride against
prejudice

Haas Library
Muhlenberg College
Allentown, Pennsylvania